Literary Afrofuturism in
the Twenty-First Century

NEW SUNS:

RACE, GENDER, AND SEXUALITY IN THE

SPECULATIVE

Susana M. Morris and Kinitra D. Brooks, Series Editors

Literary Afrofuturism in the Twenty-First Century

Edited by Isiah Lavender III and Lisa Yaszek

THE OHIO STATE UNIVERSITY PRESS
COLUMBUS

Copyright © 2020 by The Ohio State University.
All rights reserved.

Library of Congress Cataloging-in-Publication Data
Names: Lavender, Isiah, III, editor. | Yaszek, Lisa, 1969– editor.
Title: Literary Afrofuturism in the twenty-first century / edited by Isiah Lavender III and Lisa Yaszek.
Other titles: New suns: race, gender, and sexuality in the speculative.
Description: Columbus : The Ohio State University Press, [2020] | Series: New suns: race, gender, and sexuality in the speculative | Includes bibliographical references and index. | Summary: "Explores the cultural valence of Afrofuturism. It examines works by a wide range of authors, including Phyllis Wheatley, Samuel R. Delany, Octavia E. Butler, and N. K. Jemisin"—Provided by publisher.
Identifiers: LCCN 2020004433 | ISBN 9780814214459 (cloth) | ISBN 0814214452 (cloth) | ISBN 9780814278154 (ebook) | ISBN 0814278159 (ebook)
Subjects: LCSH: Afrofuturism. | American literature—African American authors—History and criticism. | American literature—History and criticism. | Science fiction—History and criticism.
Classification: LCC PS153.N5 L476 2020 | DDC 810.9/896073—dc23
LC record available at https://lccn.loc.gov/2020004433

Cover design by Black Kirby
Text design by Juliet Williams
Type set in Adobe Palatino

CONTENTS

Acknowledgments vii

Introduction Imagining Futures in Full Color
 ISIAH LAVENDER III AND LISA YASZEK 1

PART ONE • AFROFUTURISM NOW

Chapter 1 Author Roundtable on Afrofuturism
 ISIAH LAVENDER III AND LISA YASZEK 23

Chapter 2 Dangerous Muses: Black Women Writers Creating at the Forefront of Afrofuturism
 SHEREE R. THOMAS 37

PART TWO • AFROFUTURISM IN LITERARY HISTORY

Chapter 3 This Time for Africa! Afrofuturism as Alternate (American) History
 DE WITT DOUGLAS KILGORE 59

Chapter 4 Middle Age, Mer People, and the Middle Passage: Nalo Hopkinson's Afrofuturist Journeying in *The New Moon's Arms*
 GINA WISKER 73

Chapter 5 Young Adult Afrofuturism
 REBECCA HOLDEN 87

PART THREE • AFROFUTURISM IN CULTURAL HISTORY

Chapter 6 Space/Race: Recovering John M. Faucette
MARK BOULD   109

Chapter 7 Runoff: Afroaquanauts in Landscapes of Sacrifice
ELIZABETH A. WHEELER   128

Chapter 8 Black Futures Matter: Afrofuturism and Geontology in N. K. Jemisin's Broken Earth Trilogy
LISA DOWDALL   149

PART FOUR • AFROFUTURISM AND AFRICA

Chapter 9 We Are Terror Itself: Wakanda as Nation
GERRY CANAVAN   171

Chapter 10 Global Afrofuturist Ecologies
JEROME WINTER   189

Chapter 11 "You Can't Go Home Again": Deji Bryce Olukotun's *Nigerians in Space*, Science Fiction, and Global Interdependence
MARLEEN S. BARR   203

Chapter 12 Faster than Before: Science Fiction in Amos Tutuola's *The Palm-Wine Drinkard*
NEDINE MOONSAMY   216

Coda Wokeness and Afrofuturism
ISIAH LAVENDER III AND LISA YASZEK   231

List of Contributors   235

Index   241

ACKNOWLEDGMENTS

First and foremost, I thank God for guiding my steps in all that I do. Second, I thank Heather for giving me the time, space, and distance required in performing intellectual labor. Likewise, she kept the boys out of my hair when I needed it most. In this respect, I thank my sons, Kingsley and Frazier, as my junior movie buddies for all of the necessary breaks in my work. My sister and brother also aided in my downtime. There are so many people in the academic community to thank, including the International Association for the Fantastic in the Arts (IAFA) and the Science Fiction Research Association (SFRA), organizations near my heart, but Sharon Weltman, Carl Freedman, and Brooks Landon stand out because of their unwavering support and advice. Outside the academic world, the Baton Rouge Soccer Club 06 Boys Black team and its parents have become a wonderful family to us as we traipsed all across the country together. My neighbors, the Teeples, have been grandparents to my children, and I cannot thank them enough. Importantly, I want to give a shout-out to my coeditor Lisa Yaszek, who made this project a joy to complete, and I look forward to working on other projects with her in the future. If you are in the science fiction community and don't know Lisa, you need to introduce yourself.

—Isiah Lavender III

As always, I am profoundly grateful to Doug and Case Davis for their love, support, and unwavering enthusiasm for all things speculative in all media. I'm also profoundly grateful to my friend and colleague Isiah Lavender III for suggesting that we collaborate on what eventually became this volume. With Isiah, it's not a cliché but stone-cold truth: teamwork really does make the dream work. Watch out for more from us in the future! Afrofuturism has always encompassed both art and criticism; accordingly, I want to give thanks to those authors and scholars who have influenced my own thinking about black speculative fiction. I'm especially indebted to Milton Davis, Bolgun Ojetade, and Ed Hall for introducing me to the State of Black Science Fiction Society in Atlanta and inspiring me to explore the connections between local and global black speculative practices. I also want to give a shout-out to Bill Campbell and Minister Faust for challenging me to think and then rethink my ideas about such practices—they never let me rest on my assumptions, but they always seem to have my back. Finally, special thanks to Sherryl Vint, Patrick Sharp, Lars Schmeink, Bob Markley, Ariel Saiber, and Stephanie Evans for inviting me to speak about Afrofuturism at their respective universities. The production of knowledge is always a communal effort, and you all have made it a generous and joyful one as well.

—Lisa Yaszek

INTRODUCTION

Imagining Futures in Full Color

Isiah Lavender III and Lisa Yaszek

"*Brrrrrriiiiiiiiiiiiinng!*" The alarm clock sounds off in 1940 (R. Wright 3). The reality-check for America for which Richard Wright called with the opening word of his blistering masterpiece *Native Son* (1940) is happening right now, and it is called Afrofuturism. Amiri Baraka's urgent "SOS" in 1969—"Calling all black people, man woman child"—has finally been answered by Afrofuturism (line 2). That is to say, "reality rolled over" with these calls to action, as N. K. Jemisin imagines in 2004's "Too Many Yesterdays, Not Enough Tomorrows," when she implores readers to wake up (12)! And we have! Black people have finally wrested control of their own future images, using the speculative art form known as Afrofuturism to reboot black identity, challenge white supremacy, and imagine a range of futures in full color.

Such changes have not gone unnoticed. In his 1999 essay "Racism in Science Fiction," author Samuel R. Delany predicted that the largely white science fiction (SF) community would pay attention when "black writers start to number thirteen, fifteen, twenty percent of the total . . . [and when] the competition might be perceived as having some economic heft" (386). It turns out that Delany was correct. As authors of color from around the world have become increasingly central to the production of speculative fiction, hate bubbles have risen to the surface in events like the RaceFail '09 flame war, the Gamergate controversy of 2014, and the block-voting controversies of Puppygate 2015 and 2016, which unfolded at the heart of one of SF's oldest and most revered traditions: the Hugo award ceremonies.[1] In each case, a relatively small group of American-born white men loudly (and in some cases, violently) proclaimed that artists of color were out to ruin the fun of popular culture for everyone with their insistence on exploring issues of diversity and social justice.

What Delany didn't predict was that even larger segments of arts and entertainment community would actively support Afrofuturist visions of tomorrow. Consider, for instance, Netflix's adaptation of the Marvel Comic *Luke Cage* (2016), which was so wildly popular that it supposedly broke Netflix's servers the day after the first season was released; Ryan Coogler's international blockbuster *Black Panther* (2018), which made a record-shattering $427 million worldwide in its opening weekend, while garnering a 97% Rotten Tomatoes ranking from more than 284 film critics; and web series such as *Send Me* (2016), which earned an Emmy nomination for its depiction of black volunteers who travel back in time to the Antebellum Era (Nickalls; Desta; Mills). In music, Janelle Monáe has earned accolades from Billboard, the NAACP, and *Glamour* magazine for successfully repurposing the figure of the female android as a symbol of discrimination against all minorities, and the experimental hip-hop group clipping has earned a 2017 Hugo nomination for their 2016 album *Splendor & Misery,* which revolves around a mutineering starship slave and the computer that loves him (Heller). Meanwhile, corporate titan Intel has responded to Gamergate by channeling $300 million into a brand new "Diversity in Technology" initiative, and the SF community has sent an equally firm message to the architects of Puppygate by giving the Hugo Award for best novel of 2016, 2017, and 2018 to African American author N. K. Jemisin's Broken Earth trilogy, thereby making her the first author of any race or gender to win SF's most prestigious award three times in a row (Wingfield; Schaub). Clearly, people of all colors do indeed want to see black heroes remaking the world in their own image.

This anthology is designed to introduce readers to Afrofuturism as an aesthetic practice that enables artists to communicate the experience of science, technology, and race across centuries, continents, and cultures. As the accomplishments of directors such as Ryan Coogler and musicians such as Janelle Monáe illustrate, the visual and aural aspects of Afrofuturism impress fans and critics alike and are important aspects of this multigenera-

---

1. For further details about RaceFail '09, see "RaceFail '09" on Fanlore.org; for more information about Gamergate see Jay Hathaway's "What Is Gamergate, and Why? An Explainer for Non-Geeks"; and for more details about Puppygate, see the eponymous entry on Fanlore.org.

tional, multimedia artistic experiment. But such powerful artistic statements derive from a much older entertainment medium: the printed word. Indeed, as scholars and artists including both of us have argued, Afrofuturist literary experiments extend back to the writing of eighteenth-century poet Phyllis Wheatley and nineteenth-century abolitionist, soldier, and journalist Martin Delany and continue today with the award-winning SF of Delany, Jemisin, and a host of other authors.[2] This book demonstrates the dynamic nature of literary Afrofuturism with essays that explore representations of science, technology, and race as both an historical and global phenomenon.

Defining Afrofuturism

Although black people have produced science fiction, fantasy, and horror as long as those popular genres have existed, it is only in recent decades that scholars and artists have begun discussing this generic production as part of cohesive aesthetic and social movement. White US cultural critic Mark Dery coined the term "Afrofuturism" in 1993 in a series of interviews with African American writer Samuel Delany, cultural critic Tricia Rose, and writer and musician Greg Tate. As Dery puts it, Afrofuturism is a process of "signification that appropriates images of technology and a prosthetically-enhanced future" to address the concerns that people of color face in contemporary culture ("Black to the Future" 180). In its initial conception, Afrofuturism was an extension of the historical recovery projects that black Atlantic intellectuals have engaged in for well over two hundred years. Toni Morrison explains that such projects demonstrate how the conditions of homelessness and alienation experienced by African slaves and their descendants anticipate what Nietzsche claimed were the founding conditions of modernity (in Gilroy 78). For British-Ghanaian music critic Kodwo Eshun, stories about

---

2. In her 2000 anthology *Dark Matter*, Sheree R. Thomas claimed nineteenth-century author Charles W. Chesnutt, turn-of-the-century sociologist W. E. B. Du Bois, and early twentieth-century journalist George Schuyler as pioneering Afrofuturists; more recently, in her "Crash Course in the History of Black Science Fiction," Nisi Shawl added nineteenth- and early twentieth-century authors Martin R. Delany and Pauline Hopkins to this list. In a similar vein, a number of scholars have also looked backward to map a history of Afrofuturism that is as old as SF itself. Key works in this tradition include Mark Bould's "Revolutionary African American SF before Black Power SF"; Isiah Lavender's *Afrofuturism Rising: The Literary Prehistory of a Movement*; Adrienne Brown and Britt Rusert's "Introduction to 'The Princess Steel'"; and Lisa Yaszek's "An Afrofuturist Reading of Ralph Ellison's *Invisible Man*," "Afrofuturism, Science Fiction, and the History of the Future," and "The Bannekerade: Genius, Madness, and Magic in Black Science Fiction."

"travel through time and space" and "encounters with the alien other" are an ideal way to bring Afrodiasporic historical experiences to life for new audiences. Indeed, riffing on the great sociologist—and SF author—W. E. B. Du Bois, Eshun proposes that SF is a way to double, triple, and even quadruple our collective consciousness about the range of race relations that might exist in the future—and the range of futures those relations might engender (298).

African American sociologist Alondra Nelson made Afrofuturism increasingly central to both aesthetic and critical thinking with the creation of the first Afrofuturist online community in 1998 and the publication of the first scholarly collection on the subject in a 2002 issue of the journal *Social Text*. Much like Dery, Nelson treated Afrofuturism as a primarily literary and artistic movement characterized by "African American voices" with "other stories to tell about culture, technology, and things to come" grounded in the historic experiences of black individuals and communities (9). For Nelson, this project is especially important for African Americans whose stories have long been marginalized and erased in dominant histories of science, technology, and culture. But this erasure was particularly so at the turn of the millennium when new information and communication technologies such as computers and the development of the World Wide Web prompted cybertheorists and advertisers alike to develop a rhetoric of "the digital divide." Such rhetoric posited that new cybertechnologies would either utopically liberate humans from racially marked physical bodies or dystopically exacerbate inequality between white and black people. With its emphasis on extrapolating from past and present Afrodiasporic engagements with science and technology, Afrofuturism provided a strong antidote to prevailing assumptions that "racial identity, and blackness in particular, is the anti-avatar of digital life" (Nelson 1).

Today, the concept of Afrofuturism is very much a part of everyday culture, as illustrated by the commercial success of Ytasha L. Womack's 2013 *Afrofuturism: The World of Black Sci- Fi and Fantasy Culture* (which ranks #22 on Amazon.com's Kindle list of most popular SF criticism) and the 1.3 million results that come up in Google searches of the term. But the rise of social media and Web 2.0, coupled with an explosion of speculative art production by people of color across the globe, have led artists and scholars to update their ideas about Afrofuturism. One of the most immediate responses to these shifting technocultural landscapes has been to recognize Afrofuturism as one possible mode of storytelling in a much larger tradition of black speculative fiction. For instance, African American SF writer Nisi Shawl places classic Afrofuturist texts including Martin R. Delany's *Blake, Or the Huts of America* (1859) and Octavia E. Butler's *Kindred* (1979) in a larger history of "Black Science Fiction." For Shawl, "black science fiction" is a term that also includes black fantasy because "access to the scientific knowledge from which SF often derives has been denied to people of the African diaspora for much of history. And the classification of what is and is not scientific knowledge hasn't been under our control—it's frequently a matter of dispute" ("Crash Course"). In a similar vein, African American artist John Jennings and critic Reynaldo Anderson cast Afrofuturism as part of a larger Black Speculative Arts Movement that includes "Afrofuturism, Astro Blackness, Afro-Surrealism, Ethno Gothic, Black Digital Humanities, Black (Afro-future female or African Centered) Science Fiction, The Black Fantastic, and The Esoteric," all of which "overlap around the terms speculative and design; and interact around the nexus of technology and ethics" (*Black Speculative Arts Movement*).

Even as they position Afrofuturism within larger aesthetic movements, artists and scholars also nuance the term itself. Based on conversations with Alondra Nelson at Emory University's 2013 Alien Bodies Conference, Anderson coined the term "Afrofuturism 2.0" to "identify the twenty-first century contemporary expressions of Afrofuturism" that are found not just in literature and art, but that are also "emerging in the areas of metaphysics, speculative philosophy, religion, visual studies, performance, art, and philosophy of science and technology" (*Afrofuturism 2.0* ix). That same year, African American multimedia artist Martine Syms introduced the concept of "Mundane Afrofuturism." Much like Canadian author Geoff Ryman's 2004 "Mundane Science Fiction Manifesto," Syms's own work calls for SF that rejects the adolescent desire to run away from the world and its problems—often through scientifically implausible and worn-out tropes such as faster-than-light travel—and that instead focuses on the future of planet Earth as it might be changed by the sciences and technologies we already have.[3] Additionally, she argues, producers of black speculative fiction must avoid indulging in these exhausted concepts, including everything from "jive-talking aliens" and "white slavery" to "heavy-handed allusions to double-consciousness" and "Egyptian mythology and iconography" ("Mundane"). Instead, Syms recommends that Mundane Afrofuturists embrace "the possibilities of a new focus on black humanity: our science, technology, culture, politics, religions, individuality, needs, dreams, hopes, and failings" ("Mundane").

---

3. The text of Ryman's "Mundane Science Fiction Manifesto" is available on the *SFGenics* Wordpress page. For further information about the controversy it provoked within the SF community, see Ritch Calvin's article "Mundane SF 101."

The term "Afrofuturism" is particularly complex for first-generation Afrodiasporic artists who retain close ties to their African countries of origin. For example, while Nigerian American Deji Bryce Olukotun accepts the term as an important way to understand his fiction, he argues that Western white and black writers alike have historically played fast and loose with African art and mythology in ways that are often unrecognizable to Africans themselves.[4] Accordingly, it is the job of the contemporary black SF author to produce more nuanced representations of Africa: "We've come a long way since the days of Alan Quartermain slashing through the jungle, and it's been nearly 40 years since the release of Michael Crichton's *Congo*. . . . [The challenge now] is to craft an adventure story that embraces Africa in its 21st century complexity" (Olukotun, "Imagining the Future of Nigeria"). Other writers, however, generate new terms to solve this dilemma. Nigerian American author Nnedi Okorafor rejects descriptions of her work as Afrofuturist, using instead "Africanfuturism" and "Africanjujuism." As Okorafor puts it, these new terms more appropriately describe speculative fiction in which real African traditions are "woven in seamlessly with that which is made up" (@Nnedi Okorafor PhD). In a similar vein, Kenyan Canadian writer Minister Faust describes his own fiction, which draws inspiration from various ancient African civilizations to imagine futures where people of color struggle for justice, as "Imhotep-hop," because "I wanted something that would illustrate the attempt to connect the past with the future [and] Imhotep [the late twenty-seventh-century BCE chancellor to the Egyptian pharaoh Djoser] was the first recorded multi-genius in history" ("Afrofuturism"). For Faust, such terms are important because they distinguish between "Afrocentric" and "Africentric" speculative fiction: while the former describes stories engaging the Afrodiasporic experience of historical African Americans, the latter describes art with an African-focused context.[5]

Of course, black intellectuals descended from African slaves, and other black people who have lived in the West for generations also generate alternatives to the term Afrofuturism. Balogun Ojetade and Milton Davis are recognized leaders in the field of "Steamfunk," which Ojetade describes as a "style of writing and visual aesthetic that combines the African and/or African American culture and approach to life with that of the steampunk philosophy" in order to expose the "issues of racism, sexism, classism, colonialism, and imperialism" that are often erased in mainstream stories of

---

4. On his webpage *Returnofthedeji*, Olukotun uses "Afrofuturism" to tag posts about both American and African SF, including a post about his own fiction called "Major Film Company Options *After the Flare* and *Nigerians in Space*."

5. See Faust's contribution to the author roundtable in this volume for more details.

nineteenth-century Victorian England and the American Wild West ("What Is Steamfunk?"). In a similar vein, Charles R. Saunders is celebrated as the founder of "Sword and Soul Fantasy" or "heroic fiction/sword and sorcery/epic fiction based on African culture, traditions, and mythology" (K. Wright). Elsewhere, artists Camae Ayewa and Rasheedah Phillips use "Black Quantum Futurism" to describe creative projects inspired by "quantum physics and Black/African cultural traditions of consciousness, time and space" that explore "personal, cultural, familial, and communal cycles of experience [while] transforming negative cycles into positive ones" (Ayewa and Phillips). Taken together, these various kinds of black aesthetic production engender what Reynaldo Anderson calls "Astro-Blackness" or a "black identity framework" that emerges from "global technocultural assemblages, migration, human reproduction, algorithms, digital networks, software platforms, [and] bio-technical augmentation" (*Afrofuturism 2.0*). Even as they generate new and more precise terms to describe specific kinds of artistic and critical practice, then, black artists and scholars remain committed to the initial Afrofuturist project of reorganizing time and space in their work to challenge whitewashed narratives of history and imagine futures in full color.[6]

While we retain the original term "Afrofuturism" in this book, we define it in much the same way as other twenty-first-century intellectuals including Anderson and Syms. Afrofuturism represents a multigenerational, multigenre aesthetic and social movement that responds to/engages social media and Web 2.0, and that includes black authors stretching back to the beginning of modernity and spanning the entire globe.

Exploring Afrofuturism

Whether they call it Afrofuturism or something else, scholars and artists have long been interested in the meaning and value of black speculation. Leading SF journals *Extrapolation* and *Science Fiction Studies* have featured essays about black authors since their inceptions in 1959 and 1973, respec-

6. Significantly, many of the same artists and scholars who have generated new terms to describe speculative black art production still recognize a relationship between the terms they have created and Afrofuturism. For example, the *Black Quantum Futurism* Tumblr page positions its eponymous subject matter as "an evolution, or perhaps further exploration, of that term [Afrofuturism]" (*Black Quantum Futurism*). Meanwhile, Anderson casts Astro-Blackness as "an Afrofuturistic concept" (*Afrofuturism 2.0*). Whether or not they employ the term regularly, then, Afrofuturism remains an important touchstone in ongoing conversations about black speculative fiction.

tively, and as early as the summer of 1984, *Black American Literature Forum* devoted an entire special issue to the subject of race in SF. Throughout the 1970s and 1980s, however, there was little discussion of this fiction as a literary form with its own distinct themes, techniques, and relations to other kinds of black cultural production. This situation changed in the 1990s and early 2000s, when critics including Mark Dery, Kodwo Eshun, and Alondra Nelson began to map out the centrality of SF themes and techniques to Afrodiasporic artists. This period also saw the publication of the first black speculative fiction anthologies, most notably Sheree R. Thomas's *Dark Matter: A Century of Speculative Fiction from the African Diaspora* (2000) and *Dark Matter: Reading the Bones* (2004), which introduced readers to speculative stories by African American artists ranging from turn-of-the-century authors Charles W. Chesnutt and W. E. B. DuBois to contemporary writers Nisi Shawl and Kini Iburra Salaam. Meanwhile, Nalo Hopkinson's *Whispers from the Cotton Tree Root: Caribbean Fabulist Fiction* (2000) demonstrated the more global dimensions of Afrofuturism with stories by well-known Caribbean authors Jamaica Kincaid and Wilson Harris as well as tales from newcomers Tobias S. Buckell and Marcia Douglas. Taken together, these literary anthologies demonstrated how Afrofuturism manifests itself through time and space, thereby expanding Dery's initial conception of this aesthetic movement as a uniquely North American and postwar phenomenon.

Given the centrality of SF tropes and narrative techniques to classic definitions of Afrofuturism, it is no surprise that SF scholars were amongst the first to produce book-length studies of this phenomenon. Inspired by Dery's vision of a future-oriented black aesthetic practice as well as the proliferation of award-winning anthologies featuring speculative fiction by artists of color, groundbreaking studies including Elisabeth A. Leonard's *Into Darkness Peering: Race and Color in the Fantastic* (1997), DeWitt Douglas Kilgore's *Astrofuturism: Science, Race, and Visions of Utopia in Space* (2003), Sandra M. Grayson's *Visions of the Third Millennium: Black Science Fiction Novelists Write the Future* (2003), and Marleen S. Barr's *Afro-Future Females: Black Writers Chart Science Fiction's Newest New-Wave Trajectory* (2008) demonstrated the affordances and limitations of genre fiction—especially in its printed form—as a vehicle for imagining brave new futures in full color. Today, some of the best new investigations of literary Afrofuturism come from experts in black studies, including Esther L. Jones's *Medicine and Ethics in Black Women's Speculative Fiction* (2015) and Sami Schalk's *Bodyminds Reimagined: (Dis)ability, Race, and Gender in Black Women's Speculative Fiction* (2018). Considered together, these works emphasize the centrality of print fiction to the Afrofuturist project.

Over the past decade Afrofuturist scholarship has grown well beyond its initial mandate. While literary scholars continue to explore contemporary black artists in light of Dery's initial definition, they often do so from the new vantage points afforded by digitally enabled research and publishing practices. For instance, increased access to the archives of prominent African American artists have led scholars to rethink the role of scientific research in Octavia E. Butler's socially oriented SF, while the recent discovery of W. E. B. DuBois's turn-of-the-century science fantasy "The Princess Steel" (ca. 1908–1910) gestures toward the rich history of African American authors who have long used genre fiction to convey challenging political ideas to readers. Meanwhile, phenomenon including Ghanaian writer Jonathan Dotse's 2012 "Five Continent" science fiction event in Second Life and the publication of pan-African SF anthologies including Ivor W. Hartmann's *AfroSF* series (2012–present) and Nerine Dorman's *Terra Incognita* (2015) ask us if, when, and how it might be productive to consider Afrofuturism as a globe-spanning tapestry of creative voices and aesthetic practices linking historic African American, contemporary black Atlantic, and pan-African authors together in provocative new ways.

This anthology extends the work of its predecessors. Like Grayson, Barr, and Schalk, the authors featured here are interested in both established and new Afrofuturist authors. In the past decade there has been a veritable explosion of SF by authors of color, many of whom are not historic African Americans but first-generation immigrants who claim both America and other countries as home and who bring different concerns and different dreams to their chosen genre. Accordingly, authors in this volume pay homage to the richness of Afrofuturism with essays celebrating key figures associated with this literary movement and recovering those who have been lost to SF history. They also call attention to the new generation of authors who are currently revising, updating, and otherwise extending the Afrofuturist agenda in both the United States and abroad. Finally, the scholars featured in these pages explore if, how, and when African SF might be considered part of Afrofuturism. As such, our anthology sheds light on the complex ways artists of color stake claims for themselves in the global future imaginary.

Literary Afrofuturism in the Twenty-First Century also comprises a timely intervention into current critical conversations about speculative art by people of color. Not surprisingly, the rise of Web 2.0 and the increasing availability of affordable digital communication tools in recent years have encouraged scholars to turn their attention to Afrofuturism as it is expressed across media. In particular, works such as Adilifu Nama's *Black Space: Imagining Race in Science Fiction Film* (2008), Sandra Jackson and Julie E. Moody-

Freeman's *The Black Imagination: Science Fiction, Futurism, and the Speculative* (2011), Ytasha L. Womack's *Afrofuturism: The World of Black Sci-Fi and Fantasy Culture* (2013), Reynaldo Anderson's and Charles E. Jones's *Afrofuturism 2.0: The Rise of Astro-Blackness* (2015), and André Carrington's *Speculative Blackness: The Future of Race in Science Fiction* (2016) have been crucial for understanding the significance of Afrofuturism in media including film, comic books, and digital art.

While the impact of media Afrofuturism cannot be underestimated, this collection reminds readers that the printed word remains an important lens through which to understand the full dimensions of Afrofuturism. Building upon the work of their predecessors, the authors featured here provide protocols for reading Afrofuturism in the twenty-first century, especially as it expresses itself in black-oriented SF, fantasy, and comics. Taken together, they push generic boundaries; recover lost artists and introduce new ones; map the connections between black art, the environment, and public policy; connect the revival of old hate-based politics with the increasing visibility of imagined futures in full color; and explore how the seemingly meteoric rise of a new, pan-African speculative literary tradition may or may not connect with Afrofuturism under the umbrella of "black SF." Their essays are grouped into four conversations—about contemporary aesthetics, literary history, cultural history, and the relations of Afrofuturism and Africa—that are central to discussions of black speculative art in the current moment. All four of these conversations are framed by an introductory roundtable in which artists from around the globe exchange their own ideas about the promises and perils of Afrofuturism and an essay in which pioneering author and editor Sheree R. Thomas explores how black women are leading new developments in Afrofuturism today. Additionally, each conversation begins with original artwork by acclaimed artist Stacey Robinson, whose visual interpretation of the topic at hand orients—and reorients—readers to the issues considered therein.

Literary Afrofuturism in the Twenty-First Century: Section and Chapter Overview

Part One: Afrofuturism Now. While most of *Literary Afrofuturism in the Twenty-First Century* is dedicated to scholarly inquiry, we open this anthology with two pieces that explore the meaning and value of Afrofuturism from the perspective of fiction writers and editors themselves. The first, "An Author Roundtable on Afrofuturism," features African American artists Bill Campbell, N. K. Jemisin, and Nisi Shawl; Kenyan Canadian novelist and podcaster Minister Faust; Jamaican Canadian writer and editor Nalo Hopkinson; Nigerian author, editor, and journalist Chinelo Onwualu; and England-based South African writer and clinical psychology tutor Nick Wood. While all the artists involved in this conversation generally agree that "Afrofuturism" can be a useful critical filter and marketing tool, the US-based authors worry that all their creative output will be reduced to this single term, while those who are internationally based remain skeptical of recent critical and popular deployments of that term to describe speculative fiction that is produced in or oriented to Africa itself. As such, these artists stand in sharp contrast to contemporary scholars who are eager to include African speculative art in an expanded understanding of Afrofuturism. Even so, they agree with American artists and scholars who contend that black speculative fiction, whatever name it goes by, is an important way to re-present both Afrodiasporic and African history and culture to diverse audiences and to expand the scope of speculative fiction as literary practice.

Next, author and poet Sheree R. Thomas, editor of the groundbreaking Afrofuturist anthology *Dark Matter: A Century of Fiction from the African Diaspora* (2000) explores the past, present, and future of the aesthetic movement she helped introduce to the world. Thomas begins by identifying two key events that led to Mark Dery's fateful coining of the term "Afrofuturism": the meteoritic rise of Samuel R. Delany and Octavia E. Butler in the science fiction community of the 1960s and 1970s, and the celebration of black speculative fiction in black studies journals and conferences throughout the 1970s and 1980s. Thomas explains that women scholars were particularly instrumental in that process and, indeed, notes that it was yet another woman from academia—sociologist Alondra Nelson—who, in 1998, deployed Dery's term to create Afrofuturism.net, the first digital gathering space for black speculative artists and theorists. Since then, Thomas contends, black women writers including Nalo Hopkinson, Gloria Naylor, and Sofia Samatar have taken the lead in the Afrofuturism movement, creating works that evoke the past, critique the present, and challenge us to imagine a greater, more possible future.

Part Two: Afrofuturism in Literary History. The authors featured in the first section of this anthology show how Afrofuturism produced by black Atlantic authors enriches our understanding of contemporary science fiction. The section opens with De Witt Douglas Kilgore's "This Time for Africa!: Afrofuturism as Alternate (American) History," which juxtaposes alternate histories of the American Civil War written by authors such as Ward Moore and Harry Turtledove with two Afrofuturist novels from the turn of the millennium: Terry Bisson's *Fire on the Mountain* (1988) and Steven Barnes's *Lion's Blood* (2002). In doing so, Kilgore demonstrates how Afrofuturism can provide a necessary correction to the whitewashing of history while exploring what steps authors of all colors must take if they want to make Afrofuturism an "integral part of genre practice, allowing us to open up our speculations about the kinds of experiences that could determine human possibility."

In "Middle Age, Mer People, and the Middle Passage: Nalo Hopkinson's Afrofuturist Journeying in *The New Moon's Arms*," Gina Wisker demonstrates how authors who hail from outside the United States also participate in Afrofuturist aesthetic experiments. Wisker explores Caribbean Canadian Hopkinson's hopeful retelling of the terrible Middle Passage as an Afrofuturist tale that splices together the critical insights of the postcolonial gothic with the utopian dreaming of SF. Setting her 2007 novel on the fictional Caribbean island of Dolorosse, Hopkinson uses this imaginary space as the setting for an alternate past where enslaved Africans refuse the bad future set before them, choosing instead to seize agency, jump overboard, and become mer people. This alternate history inspires Hopkinson's aging heroine, who changes her own future for the better when she rescues a mer child, regains her childhood ability to find lost objects, and engenders the renewal of her father's long-barren garden.

Closing out this first section, Rebecca Holden's "Young Adult Afrofuturism" explores one of the most underappreciated subgenres in both Afrofuturism and SF: young adult fiction. Holden maps this growing subgenre of Afrofuturist literature through close examination of young adult tales written by well-known authors including Nnedi Okorafor's *The Shadow Speaker* (2007), Walter Mosley's *47* (2005), and Alaya Dawn Johnson's *The Summer Prince* (2013). These novels both connect their readers to the cultures and histories of the African diaspora and shows why those cultures and histories are still necessary in a supposedly deracinated technoscientific world. They warn readers about the danger of complacency with the present-day status quo while offering visions of the future where young black people who are indeed connected with each other, their pasts, and the world around them can build truly new and different futures.

Part Three: Afrofuturism in Cultural History. Much like their counterparts in the author roundtable, the scholars included in this section treat Afrofuturism as an important focusing lens through which to better understand black history and culture. In "Space/Race: Recovering John M. Faucette," Mark Bould reviews the brief but fascinating career of African American author John M. Faucette. Although Faucette wrote four SF novels in the 1970s and self-published a collection of thirty-nine short stories in 2002—a period when Afrofuturism was gaining significant recognition as an aesthetic movement—he has never been recognized as part of the literary generation that includes Samuel R. Delany, Jr., Octavia E. Butler, and Steven Barnes. Bould attempts to account for this aporia through close examination of Faucette's difficulty taking the literary conventions of his chosen genre seriously; his complex and sometimes-contradictory treatment of race, class, and gender; and his problematic relationship with SF editor Donald Wollheim.

Elizabeth A. Wheeler's chapter, "Runoff: Afroaquanauts in Landscapes of Sacrifice," demonstrates how the tropes structuring Afrofuturist fiction can be used to productively rethink the impact of real-world environmental disaster on black communities. She begins by reading Sherri L. Smith's young adult dystopia *Orleans* (2013) as a novel about both government negligence in the face of environmentally challenged black communities and as a celebration of the new cognitive and aesthetic practices that such communities develop to survive and even change the story of their future. Wheeler then applies a similar critical frame to the lead crises faced by African Americans in Sandtown, a neighborhood in Baltimore, and Flint, Michigan, showing how young people in these real-world dystopias parallel their fictional counterparts by becoming "Afroaquanauts" who have "the optimism to 'dance underwater and not get wet' and the strength to push for change."

Lisa Dowdall's "Black Futures Matter: Afrofuturism and Geontology in N. K. Jemisin's Broken Earth Trilogy," takes off from recent controversies in which conservative fan groups calling themselves "the Sad Puppies" and "the Rabid Puppies" tried to undermine the achievements of N.K Jemisin when she won back-to-back Hugo Awards for novels depicting Afrocentric futures. According to the Puppies, black, female authors such as Jemisin are grouchy "social justice warriors" out to ruin the fun of SF for everyone with their insistence on "literary affirmative action" that dilutes both the science and the action of their stories. Dowdall, however, overturns such claims with a reading of Jemisin's Broken Earth Trilogy that demonstrates how the author uses geology to craft an action-packed tale of murder, sabotage, and redemption that spans continents and centuries while questioning widespread cultural assumptions about the "natural" divisions between race, species, and matter. Not only does the Broken Earth series give lie to the claim that authors cannot write swashbuckling tales of social justice, but, as Dowdall argues, both the geological novum of Jemisin's series and the lines of inquiry it prompts in readers and characters alike are more timely, more innovative, and, ultimately, more science fictional than the kind of pulp writing celebrated by the Puppies.

Part Four: Afrofuturism and Africa. While authors in the first three sections of this anthology are primarily concerned with artists from and issues facing Afrodiasporic communities in North America, those featured in this final section turn their attention to the complex relations of Afrofuturism as literary practice and Africa as both a source of artistic inspiration and a space for the production of black SF itself. Since Dery first introduced the term in 1993, scholars assumed that one key component of Afrofuturist art is its embrace of African history, art, and cosmologies. And indeed, much like their counterparts in the opening author roundtable, the scholars included in this section recognize that representations of both imaginary and real African entities remain central to literary Afrofuturism in the twenty-first century. This section opens with "'We Are Terror Itself': Wakanda as Nation," in which Gerry Canavan looks at the fictional African nation of Wakanda, home to the Marvel Comics superhero T'Challa, the Black Panther, to investigate the spatial logics of nationhood. Canavan reads Wakanda as offering audiences an Afrofuturist reorganization of space that positions the imaginary country as an alternative political institution always both inside and outside the logics of nation, of coloniality, of empire, even of the idea of law itself.

While Canavan explores how Marvel writers use the fantastic African country of Wakanda to disrupt preconceived notions of technoscientific modernity as a Eurowestern phenomenon, Jerome Winter's chapter, "Global Afrofuturist Ecologies," shows how Afrofuturists Sofia Samatar, N. K. Jemisin, and Nnedi Okorafor use stories set in Africa to expose the colonial and postcolonial assumptions that have long driven environmental SF written from globally Northern perspectives. Focusing specifically on Samatar's *A Stranger in Olandria* (2013) and *The Winged Histories* (2016), Jemisin's *The Killing Moon* (2012) and *The Shadowed Sun* (2012), and Okorafor's *Lagoon* (2015), Winter demonstrates how Afrofuturist authors critique technoscientific dreams of environmental mastery that, in all of these tales, lead only to environmental disaster. At the same time, Samatar, Jemisin, and Okorafor offer readers hope that the ecological practices of indigenous people across Africa and across the global South might provide the foundations for a range of possible new futures—and new stories about those futures as well.

In "An Afrofuturist Reading of Deji Bryce Olukotun's *Nigerians in Space*," Marleen Barr explores how the eponymous author's own call for increasingly nuanced representations of Africa in Afrofuturism informs his own work. Focusing on Olukotun's *Nigerians in Space* (2014)—a book the author began writing to inspire thinking about the possibility of a Nigerian space program only to visit the country and learn that such a program had already been in place for a decade—Barr argues that Afrofuturism can and must be redefined to involve "realizing that Africans' involvement in space exploration is a present reality, not SF." Barr shows how Olukotun begins this process of redefinition in *Nigerians* by replacing conventional ideas about distinct Afrodiasporic versus African identities with the concept of an emergent "African global nomadism." This new identity formation connects African Americans and Africans from diverse countries as well as humans and nonhumans together in new ways that make clear Earth is our shared home—and the stars our shared destiny.

The last author in this section tests recent scholarly claims about the importance of including African SF authors in a new iteration of Afrofuturism—what Reynaldo Anderson argues might be best understood as "Afrofuturism 3.0" ("On Black Panther"). In "Faster than Before: Science Fiction in Amos Tutuola's *The Palm-Wine Drinkard*," Nedine Moonsamy explores the promises and perils of Afrofuturism 3.0 with her case study of Nigerian writer Amos Tutuola, particularly in relation to his best-known novel *The Palm-Wine Drinkard* (1952), which mixes the classic science fictional quest narrative with Yoruba folktales. While Moonsamy does find points of connection between Afrofuturism and the work of African authors such as Tutuola, she also notes that Tutuola grapples with geopolitical concerns that differ from those of his Western counterparts and proposes that intellectuals might well need to redefine Afrofuturism if they wish to include African authors.

Literary Afrofuturism in the Twenty-First Century concludes with "Coda: Wokeness and Afrofuturism," in which we consider the significance of this collection in terms of both science fiction history and present-day politics. We also identify authors and issues that emerged as we developed the current volume and suggest some paths for future research. Finally, we celebrate the ongoing usefulness of Afrofuturism as an aesthetically and socially provocative concept, while inviting readers to speculate about what might lie beyond Afrofuturism itself.

Works Cited

Anderson, Reynaldo, and Charles E. Jones, editors. *Afrofuturism 2.0: The Rise of Astro-Blackness*. Lexington Books, 2016.

Ayewah, Camae, and Rasheedah Phillips. "About." *Black Quantum Futurism.* https://www.blackquantumfuturism.com/about. Accessed 8 Feb. 2019.

Baraka, Amiri. "SOS." *The Norton Anthology of African American Literature,* edited by Henry Louis Gates, Jr., and Nellie Y. McKay, 2nd ed., Norton, 2004, p. 1942.

Barr, Marleen S., editor. *Afro-Future Females: Black Writers Chart Science Fiction's Newest New-Wave Trajectory.* The Ohio State UP, 2008.

Black Quantum Futurism. https://blackquantumfuturism.tumblr.com/. Accessed 8 Feb. 2019.

Black Speculative Arts Movement. "About." https://www.bsam-art.com/about/. Accessed 8 Feb. 2019.

Bould, Mark. "Revolutionary African American SF before Black Power SF." *Extrapolation,* vol. 51, no. 1, 2010, pp. 53–81.

Brown, Adreinne, and Britt Rusert. "Introduction to 'The Princess Steel.'" *PMLA,* vol. 130, no. 3, 2015, pp. 819–21.

Calvin, Ritch. "Mundane SF 101." *SFRA Review,* vol. 298, 2009, pp. 13–16. https://sfra.wildapricot.org/resources/sfra-review/289.pdf. Accessed 8 Feb. 2019.

Carrington, André. *Speculative Blackness: The Future of Race in Science Fiction.* U of Minnesota P, 2016.

Coker, Cheo Hodari, creator. *Luke Cage.* Netflix, 2016.

Coogler, Ryan, director. *Black Panther.* Marvel Studios, 2018.

Delany, Samuel R. "Racism in Science Fiction." 1999. *Dark Matter: A Century of Speculative Fiction from the African Diaspora,* edited by Sheree R. Thomas, Warner Aspect, 2000, pp. 383–97.

———. "Black to the Future: Interviews with Samuel R. Delany, Greg Tate, and Tricia Rose." *Flame Wars: The Discourse of Cyberculture,* Duke UP, 1994, pp. 179–222.

Desta, Yohana. "*Black Panther*'s Four-Day Total: $427 Million Worldwide and a Slew of Shattered Records." *Vanity Fair,* 20 Feb. 2018. https://www.vanityfair.com/hollywood/2018/02/black-panther-box-office-domestic-worldwide. Accessed 22 Feb. 2018.

Dorman, Nerine, editor. *Terra Incognita: New Short Speculative Stories from Africa.* Short Story Day Africa, 2015.

Du Bois, W. E. B. "The Princess Steel." 1908–1910. *PMLA,* vol. 130, no. 3, 2015, pp. 822–29.

Eshun, Kodwo. "Further Considerations on Afrofuturism." *CR: The New Centennial Review,* vol. 3, no. 2, Summer 2003, pp. 287–302.

Faust, Minister. "Afrofuturism, E-Town, Imhotep-Hop, and Me." *YouTube,* 1 Apr. 2013. https://www.youtube.com/watch?v=wv-IX2_vIhk. Accessed 8 Feb. 2019.

Gilroy, Paul. *The Black Atlantic: Modernity and Double Consciousness.* Harvard UP, 1993.

Grayson, Sandra M. *Visions of the Third Millennium: Black Science Fiction Novelists Write the Future.* Africa World Press, 2003.

Harper, Steven, creator. *Send Me.* True/Distance Productions, 2016.

Hartmann, Ivor W., editor. *AfroSF: Science Fiction by African Writers.* StoryTime, 2012.

———. *AfroSFv2: Five Novellas.* StoryTime, 2015.

Hathaway, Jay. "What Is Gamergate, and Why? An Explainer for Non-Geeks." *Gawker*, 10 Oct. 2014. https://gawker.com/what-is-gamergate-and-why-an-explainer-for-non-geeks-1642909080. Accessed 8 Feb. 2019.

Heller, Jason. "Why clipping.'s Hugo Nomination Matters for Music in Science Fiction." *Pitchfork*, 7 Apr. 2017. https://pitchfork.com/thepitch/1483-why-clippings-hugo-nomination-matters-for-music-in-science-fiction/. Accessed 8 Feb. 2019.

Hopkinson, Nalo, ed. *Whispers from the Cotton Tree Root: Caribbean Fabulist Fiction.* Invisible Cities Press, 2000.

Jackson, Sandra, and Julie E. Moody-Freeman, editors. *The Black Imagination: Science Fiction, Futurism, and the Speculative.* Peter Lang, 2011.

Jemisin, N. K. "Too Many Yesterdays, Not Enough Tomorrows." 2004. *Mothership: Tales from Afrofuturism and Beyond,* edited by Bill Campbell and Edward Austin Hall. Rosarium, 2013, pp. 12–21.

Jones, Esther L. *Medicine and Ethics in Black Women's Speculative Fiction.* Palgrave Macmillan, 2015.

Kilgore, DeWitt D. *Astrofuturism: Science, Race, and Visions of Utopia in Space.* U of Pennsylvania P, 2003.

Lavender III, Isiah. *Afrofuturism Rising: The Literary Prehistory of a Movement.* The Ohio State UP, 2019.

Leonard, Elisabeth A., editor. *Into Darkness Peering: Race and Color in the Fantastic.* Greenwood Press, 1997.

Mills, K. Nicole. "Tracie Thomas Receives Emmy Nomination for Role in Slavery Time Travel Web Series." *HBR: Women of the African Diaspora in Film and Television,* 14 July 2016. http://hollywoodsblackrenaissance.com/tracie-thoms-emmy-nomination/. Accessed 22 Feb. 2018.

Nama, Adilifu. *Black Space: Imagining Race in Science Fiction Film.* U of Texas P, 2008.

Nelson, Alondra. "Introduction: Future Texts." *Social Text,* vol. 20, no. 2, Summer 2002, pp. 1–15.

Nickalls, Sammy. "*Luke Cage* Is So Great That It Broke Netflix." *Esquire,* 2 Oct. 2016. https://www.esquire.com/entertainment/tv/news/a49165/luke-cage/. Accessed 22 Feb. 2018.

@Nnedi Okorafor, PhD. "This is why I call Akata Witch and Akata Warrior #AfricanJujuism. Some of the African traditions that many think r fantasy r real & it's woven in seamlessly with that which is made up & because these traditions are known by so so few, this isn't well understood." *Twitter,* 17 Nov. 2018, 8:39 am. https://twitter.com/Nnedi/status/1063834093660454912 Accessed. 8 Feb. 2019.

Ojetade, Balogun. "What Is Steamfunk? Exposing the Big Steampunk Lie!" *Chronicles of Harriet,* 5 Apr. 2013. https://chroniclesofharriet.com/2012/04/05/what-is-steamfunk-exposing-the-big-steampunk-lie/. Accessed 8 Feb. 2019.

Olukotun, Deji Bryce. "Afrofuturism: Major Film Company Options *After the Flare* and *Nigerians in Space.*" *Returnofthedeji,* 12 Sept. 2018. https://returnofthedeji.com/revamp/tag/afrofuturism/. Accessed 8 Feb. 2018.

———. "Imagining the Future of Nigeria: Accessing Africa though Sci Fi." *Lit Hub,* 18 Sept. 2017. https://lithub.com/imagining-the-future-of-nigeria-accessing-africa-through-sci-fi/. Accessed 8 Feb. 2018.

"On Black Panther, Afrofuturism, and Astro-Blackness: A Conversation with Reynaldo Anderson." *The Black Scholar*, 13 Mar. 2018. https://www.theblackscholar.org/on-black-panther-afrofuturism-and-astroblackness-a-conversation-with-reynaldo-anderson/. Accessed 8 Feb. 2019.

"Puppygate." Fanlore.org. https://fanlore.org/wiki/Puppygate. Accessed 8 Feb. 2019.

"RaceFail '09." Fanlore.org. https://fanlore.org/wiki/RaceFail_%2709. Accessed 8 Feb. 2019.

Ryman, Geoff, et al. "The Mundane Science Fiction Manifesto." 2004. *SFGenics: Notes on Science, Fiction, and Science Fiction*. 4 July 2013. https://sfgenics.wordpress.com/2013/07/04/geoff-ryman-et-al-the-mundane-manifesto/. Accessed 8 Feb. 2019.

Schalk, Sami. *Bodyminds Reimagined: (Dis)ability, Race, and Gender in Black Women's Speculative Fiction*. Duke UP, 2018.

Schaub, Michael. "N. K. Jemisin Makes History at the Hugos with a Third Win in a Row for Best Novel." *Los Angeles Times*, 21 Aug. 2018. https://www.latimes.com/books/la-et-jc-nk-jemisin-hugo-awards-20180821-story.html. Accessed 8 Feb. 2019.

Shawl, Nisi. "A Crash Course in the History of Black Science Fiction." 2018. *Nisi Shawl*, http://www.nisishawl.com/CCHBSF.html. Accessed 8 Feb. 2019.

Syms, Martine. "The Mundane Afrofuturist Manifesto." *Rhizome*, 17 Dec. 2013. http://rhizome.org/editorial/2013/dec/17/mundane-afrofuturist-manifesto/. Accessed 8 Feb. 2019.

Thomas, Sheree R., editor. *Dark Matter: A Century of Black Speculative Fiction from the African Diaspora*. Warner Aspect, 2000.

———. *Dark Matter: Reading the Bones*. Warner Aspect, 2004.

Wingfield, Nick. "Intel Allocates $300 Million for Workplace Diversity." *New York Times*, 6 Jan. 2015. https://www.nytimes.com/2015/01/07/technology/intel-budgets-300-million-for-diversity.html. Accessed 8 Feb. 2019.

Womack, Ytasha L. *Afrofuturism: The World of Black Sci-Fi and Fantasy Culture*. Lawrence Hill, 2013.

Wright, K. Ceres. "Sword and Soul." *Amazing Stories*, 3 Dec. 2013. https://amazingstories.com/2013/12/sword-soul/. Accessed 8 Feb. 2019.

Wright, Richard. *Native Son*. 1940. Harper Perennial, 2005.

Yaszek, Lisa. "An Afrofuturist Reading of Ralph Ellison's *Invisible Man*." *Rethinking History: The Journal of Theory and Practice*, vol. 9, no. 2/3, 2005, pp. 297–313.

———. "Afrofuturism, Science Fiction, and the History of the Future." *Socialism & Democracy*, vol. 20, no. 3, 2006, pp. 41–60.

———. "The Bannekerade: Genius, Madness, and Magic in Black Science Fiction." *Black and Brown Planets: The Politics of Race in Science Fiction*, edited by Isiah Lavender III, UP of Mississippi, 2014, pp. 15–30.

PART ONE

Afrofuturism Now

FACING: Stacey Robinson, "AfroVision," 2018

CHAPTER 1

Author Roundtable on Afrofuturism

Isiah Lavender III and Lisa Yaszek

While most of this edited collection is dedicated to scholarly investigations of Afrofuturism as a literary phenomenon, we wanted to first make space for the voices of artists who explore the intersection of science, technology, and race in their own work. Accordingly, we invited seven groundbreaking authors and editors from North America, Europe, and Africa to discuss their thoughts about Afrofuturism and the writing traditions with which they identify.

Bill Campbell is the author of *Sunshine Patriots* (2004), *My Booty Novel* (2007), and *Pop Culture: Politics, Puns, "Poohbutt" from a Liberal Stay-at-Home Dad* (2010), and *Koontown Killing Kaper* (2012). Along with Edward Austin Hall, he coedited the groundbreaking anthology, *Mothership: Tales from Afrofuturism and Beyond* (2013). Likewise, with Nisi Shawl, he coedited *Stories for Chip: A Tribute to Samuel R. Delany* (2015) and, with Jason Rodriguez and John Jennings, the Glyph Award-winning *APB: Artists against Police Brutality* (2015). Campbell lives in Washington, DC, where he spends his time with his family, helps produce audio books for the blind, and helms Rosarium Publishing.

Minister Faust is a Kenyan Canadian novelist, print/radio/television journalist, blogger, sketch comedy writer, video game writer, playwright, and poet. Faust first achieved literary accolades for his debut novel, *The Coy-*

ote *Kings of the Space-Age Bachelor Pad* (2004), which was shortlisted for the Locus Best First Novel, Philip K. Dick, and Compton-Crook awards. Faust is the critically acclaimed author of the Kindred Award–winning *From the Notebooks of Doctor Brain* (2007), retitled *Shrinking the Heroes* (2013), *The Alchemists of Kush* (2011), and the ongoing *War & Mir* series (2012). Faust hosts a weekly podcast, *MF Galaxy*, where he interviews writers on writing, pop culture, progressive politics, and Africentric culture.

Nalo Hopkinson, born in Jamaica, received an MA in writing popular fiction from Seton Hill University and a Doctor of Letters from Anglia Ruskin University, UK, and currently teaches at the University of California, Riverside. Her teaching specialty is creative writing, with a focus on speculative literatures. She is a recipient of the John W. Campbell Award, the World Fantasy Award, the Andre Norton Award, and Cuba's Casa de las Americas prize for literature written in Creole as well as a two-time recipient of the Sunburst Award for Canadian Literature of the Fantastic. Her novels include *Brown Girl in the Ring* (1998), *Midnight Robber* (2000), *The Salt Roads* (2003), *The New Moon's Arms* (2007), *The Chaos* (2012), and *Sister Mine* (2013).

N. (Nora) K. Jemisin is an author of speculative fiction who lives and writes in Brooklyn, New York. Her work has been multiply nominated for Hugo, Nebula, and World Fantasy Awards; shortlisted for the Crawford, Gemmell Morningstar, and Tiptree Awards; and she has won a Locus Award for Best First Novel as well as several Romantic Times Reviewer's Choice Awards. In 2016, she became the first black person to win the Best Novel Hugo for *The Broken Earth* (2015). In 2017, she won Best Novel again for *The Obelisk Gate* (2016). In 2018, she won for the third time in a row for *The Stone Sky* (2017). Her first eight novels, a novella, and a short story collection are out now from Orbit Books.

Chinelo Onwualu is a Nigerian writer, editor, and journalist living in Toronto, Canada. She is editor and cofounder of Omenana.com, a magazine of African speculative fiction. She is a graduate of the 2014 Clarion West Writers Workshop, which she attended as the recipient of the Octavia E. Butler Scholarship. Her short stories have been featured in several anthologies including Ivor W. Hartmann's *AfroSF: Science Fiction by African Writers* (2012) and Billy Kahora's *Imagine Africa 500: Speculative Fiction from Africa* (2015). Her writing has also appeared in *Strange Horizons, The Kalahari Review, Brittle Paper,* and *Ideomancer.*

Nisi Shawl's debut novel *Everfair* (2016) was a finalist for the 2016 Nebula Award. Her collection, *Filter House* (2008), was one of two winners of the 2009 James Tiptree, Jr. Award. Her work has been published at *Strange Hori-*

zons, in *Asimov's SF Magazine,* and in anthologies including *Dark Matter, The Moment of Change, Dark Faith 2,* and *The Other Half of the Sky.* Shawl was WisCon 35's Guest of Honor. Her edited works include: *The WisCon Chronicles 5: Writing and Racial Identity* (2011), *Bloodchildren: Stories by the Octavia E. Butler Scholars* (2013), *Strange Matings: Octavia E. Butler, Science Fiction, Feminism, and African American Voices* (2013) with Rebecca Holden, and *Stories for Chip: A Tribute to Samuel R. Delany* (2015) with Bill Campbell. Along with Cynthia Ward, Nisi coauthored *Writing the Other: A Practical Approach* (2005). She is a cofounder of the Carl Brandon Society and serves on the board of directors of the Clarion West Writers Workshop.

Nick Wood is a Zambian born, South African naturalized clinical psychologist with over twenty short stories previously published in international venues, including *AfroSF* and *AfroSF 2,* amongst others. He is the author of *The Stone Chameleon* (2004) and *Azanian Bridges* (2016), which has been shortlisted for four awards, viz. the Sidewise (Alternative History), Nommos (African), BSFA, and John W. Campbell (2016).

ISIAH LAVENDER III and LISA YASZEK (IL3 and LY): *Thanks to everyone for agreeing to participate in this roundtable. Now that Afrofuturism, as initially described by Mark Dery, has been in existence for over a quarter century, what do you think of the term—is it a movement, a moment, a marketing strategy, or something else? What relation, if any, do you see between Afrofuturism and the writing traditions with which you identify?*

NALO HOPKINSON (NH): You can now make a valid argument that it's a movement. At first it seemed to me to be more of a carrier bag into which scholars and artists were sorting art that shared closely allied sets of aesthetics and sensibilities about African diasporic speculative art-making. I don't at all see it as a marketing strategy, although that can't be far behind. That probably explains why I'm starting to hear scholars and students calling it a "genre," which frankly makes me shudder. It's a filter, a lens. In other words, I'm fine with the term being applied to my work and my sensibility, but not with it being used to define *me* as an artist and to essentialize my creative practice. I have enough of that when reviewers and readers assume that all my characters are black and that all my creatures come out of Caribbean folklore.

"Afrofuturism" as a notion is way useful, but it doesn't cover the landscape. It comes out of an African American experience. It doesn't completely contain or reflect those of us whose root context isn't American; for instance,

Caribbean artists, or those from the continent of Africa, or black European artists. When I write from a Caribbean place, it isn't solely black. It can be Afrocentric, but it's still rooted in a region that has been heavily creolized for centuries. A Jean Rhys ghost story isn't Afrofuturist, but it definitely contributes to the Caribbean fantastical tradition. (Afrofuturism is similarly an only partially adequate filter for those works that skew more toward the fantastical than the futuristic.) The term "Afrofuturism" can recognize work like mine, but it can't completely encompass it, nor should it have to. That's the value of a filter. As an analytical tool, you can choose to use it selectively, or to combine it with other filters. It all depends upon the light you want to cast on a particular work.

N(ORA) K. JEMISIN (NKJ): I don't really think of the term at all. It's always been something that other people applied to me and my work, not something I ever used or even fully understood. When I was younger, "Afrofuturism" meant music—Parliament Funkadelic, Roger and ZAPP, Pharoah Sanders. Maybe movies like *The Brother from Another Planet* (1984). So that's what it has remained in my head, updated now with Janelle Monáe and Missy Elliott and so on. I'm aware that the scholarly conception of the term has evolved and changed the Zeitgeist with time . . . but I'm too busy working on my next thing to take the time to catch up with the scholarship!

I *have* found lately that the term has become shorthand for "Science Fiction and Fantasy (SFF) by black people," in the media. But like any shorthand, that's a double-edged thing. On the one hand, reporters, etc. who've at least done some cursory Googling of the term are less likely to ask me stupid, racist questions about whether black people have a future. On the other hand, I constantly find myself lumped in with writers who are nothing like me in content or style or focus, just because we're black. Every other magazine or newspaper thinks it's got the hook when it decides to contact me and Nnedi Okorafor (it's usually her, since the Hugo) for a hot take on whatever—just like the other thirty-three magazines or newspapers that contacted the two of us for the same hot take.

On a positive note, though, at least Nnedi and I have fun commiserating about the problem over sushi and private messages.

NISI SHAWL (NS): Honestly, I think of the term "Afrofuturism" as a convenience for critics first, a marketing tool second, and third as a moment of attention in the stream of pop culture-consciousness. What Dery described had of course existed before he sought to label it, and in fact I believe the term Afrofuturism derived from his interactions with Samuel R. Delany, who at the time had been writing award-winning SF and fantasy for decades. Nor was Delany the first African-descended person to do so;

W. E. B. DuBois wrote SF well before Delany, and also well before Sun Ra performed his Afrofuturistic music.

The term Afrofuturism allows Dery and other critics and scholars to conceptualize the commonalities underlying the participation of Afrodiasporic people in the creation of speculative fictions. Following his analytical trail, we creators have adopted the term and have used it to publicize our work to those looking for pleasures familiar to them from their experience with other African-descended creators of speculative fictions. Hence its use as a tool for marketing our work. In trying to convey the aim of my novel *Everfair*, I combined two portmanteau words: Afrofuturism and Retrofuturism. Retrofuturism is the label many steampunks apply to their subgenre; I called *Everfair* a novel of AfroRetrofuturism, which is an unwieldy mouthful all right, but which seemed far more to the point to me than the publisher's descriptor of "Neo-Victorian alternate history." That latter phrase leaves out all blackness, and isolates me as a writer from one of my chosen communities, that of practitioners with similar backgrounds and goals. . . .

Our emergence as a black speculative fiction community has led to the entertainment establishment paying attention to our emergence, which means we now have a certain cachet. I hope this cachet is here to stay.

MINISTER FAUST (MF): For several reasons, I see no reason to accept the term "Afrofuturism." First, by definition as an Africentrist, I center my work on Africa and Africans, but a non-African coined the expression (please note the spelling; "Afrocentrist" refers to someone who adheres to the philosophy of Afrocentricity [incorrectly called "Afrocentrism" by its attackers] that Molefi Kete Asante articulated in his book of the same name). Self-definition is a prerequisite for self-determination. If Africentric SF and fantasy aren't (broadly speaking) liberationist, they aren't worth our intellectual energy or financial resources. Second, Africentric SF and fantasy are far older than the term "Afrofuturism," going back at least to Martin Delany's nineteenth-century novel *Blake: or, The Huts of America*, so why use such a recent term created by a non-African unless it adds significantly greater analytical value?

Third, much of Africentric fantasy is set in the past or the present, not the future, which makes the term "Afro*futurism*" a failure from the start. The term also implies a link—though nonexistent—to the Italian art movement *futurism*, which sought to separate early twentieth-century Italian culture from its focus on the past, especially Roman supremacy. Yet the Africentric project doesn't reject the African past, but instead draws its inspiration from it to innovate upon the present and thus create future. I would argue that Africentric SFF owes much to the visionary painting and black-and-white art of the African American artist Aaron Douglas whose style I describe as "Afriluminist"; many of Douglas's highly stylized works portrayed the glories of the African past—including those of Ancient Egypt—and fused them with images of industrial modernity and the technofuture.

As I see it used widely on the internet, the term "Afrofuturism" seems to be a catchy expression primarily for people who are not producing or reading Africentric SFF novels and short stories. Rather, those web-writers seem to focus their "Afrofuturism" articles primarily on US-based popular musicians, clothing designers, and occasionally movies, television, comics, and graphic novels.

To the extent that the term means Africentric SF and fantasy, I accept that some people classify my novels as "Afrofuturist." But we need a term of our own devising. Unfortunately, short of some bizarre alteration of planetary culture, my cumbersome term *Imhotep-hop* will never see widespread adoption.[1]

NICK WOOD (NW): I'm very much an outsider on this, so here's my outsider's perspective, both from a geographical and cultural distance. This label looks like an attempt to hang a conceptual umbrella over a range of cultural products (e.g., music, art, and writing) from across the African diaspora in North America. I guess the proof is in the pudding—how many of those ostensibly included underneath the label see this as a valid term for what they are doing, and, most importantly, does this concept enhance or hinder the production and reception of black American creative endeavors?

My distance from this movement is that I am a white African currently living in Britain, and so my intersection points are minimal, mostly along the African nexus. But for me this is a living, central nexus, so I have sought out and read (amongst others) Butler, Delany, Shawl, Hopkinson, Jemisin, and Okorafor.

Nnedi Okorafor is an interesting case in point, given her African ancestral roots are recent and linked to an explicitly dual American-Nigerian identity. I recently read an old interview of Samuel Delany by Mark Dery, and Delany makes the point about the systematic erasure and destruction of African history, heritage, and filial connections under American slavery—the attempt to wipe out identity, including all connections with family, language, and place (i.e., the brutal white destruction of history and any and all

---

1. Faust defines *Imhotep-hop* as an Africentric mode of literature that "draws from myriad ancient African civilizations, explores present realities, and imagines a future in which people struggle not only for justice, but the stars" (https://www.goodreads.com/author/show/15661.Minister_Faust).

prior sense of place or belonging). I've read Afrofuturism is seen as a way of naming and reclaiming the future by reconnecting to a long-destroyed past and multiple African heritages and, taking this forward, finding creative ways to reclaim a destroyed, emptied space—and to even move out into space, hitherto a very white space, at least from within the traditional Western canons of SF.

BILL CAMPBELL (BC): I've been having problems with this term since I first stumbled across it around ten years ago. Nothing irksome. More like, "What the hell is this?" I saw a bunch of other black writers around my age asking the same question across social media. When I started occasionally reading up on it (nothing too deep, mind you), I still had the same questions. The term seemed to be casting a pretty wide net across all sorts of media, and while I could possibly put George Schuyler next to, say, P-Funk, I have a problem relating him to Earth, Wind, & Fire or *The Brother from Another Planet*.

To me, a movement generally needs a doctrine or manifesto, a conscious decision to be a part of a group. It's probably a limited understanding, but it's mine. Afrofuturism as it stands seems to lack that. Dery came up with the term around the same time that I started writing SF, and I can tell you that, while some of the people and projects he mentioned influenced me, I never said, "I am an Afrofuturist!" I still don't.

When it came to [our fiction anthology] *Mothership*, Ed [Edward Austin Hall] and I definitely used "Afrofuturism" as a marketing tool. It was a simple way of saying, "Black folks are doing this." The diversity of topics, genres, and the people we included in the book was also very purposeful. I'm a firm believer that artistic movements (especially black ones) constantly have to fight being strangled in the crib. I think the process generally goes *Classify, Commodify, Codify, and Kill*. I hoped that, if we made the book as hard to pin down as possible, that we could help delay the codification process if the book gained any sort of importance.

In all honesty, I'm still not sure what "Afrofuturism" means or is supposed to mean. As an editor, publisher, and occasional writer, I'm not really sure it matters terribly much to me. For me, the most important thing is to continue to give brown folks the platform to share their voices.

CHINELO ONAWALU (CO): I don't know that I've spent very much time thinking about that term, to be honest. I first encountered it when I discovered Sheree R. Thomas's collection *Dark Matter: A Century of Speculative Fiction from the African Diaspora* in 2003. It pulled together all these amazing stories from black people in North America and the Caribbean over the last one hundred years, and it really opened my eyes to what could be done with writing. But it was clear to me, even then that this wasn't really an "African thing." These stories were dealing with racism and the longing for a safe space to call home, themes that simply weren't part of my own daily reality as an Igbo woman living in Nigeria. I understood the sentiment behind many of the stories because I had once lived in the United States, and I had personally experienced the pervasiveness of racial bias there, but it never struck me as personally relevant.

I certainly wouldn't call myself an Afrofuturist because I believe the term defines a particular type of literary, artistic, and musical aesthetic that is born out of the unique experiences of the African Diaspora. In fact, I would go so far as to argue that it is more specific to the experiences of African Americans in the United States.

When we started the African Speculative Fiction Society last year, there was a lot of internal debate as to what to call the kind of writing, art, and film aesthetic that we were producing. We settled on the term "African speculative fiction" or "AfroSF" because we recognized that we were preoccupied with very different themes and coming out of very different histories.

IL3 and LY: Many of the scholars featured in this anthology identify black speculative literary and cultural practices that are as old as SF—and indeed, as old as technocultural modernity itself. Are there specific moments in Afrodisaporic and/or African history that you wish were better known/have inspired you and your work?

CO: I don't know if I have any writing traditions with which I personally identify. I had a wide range of speculative influences growing up—though mostly by white creators. I read a lot of Golden Age SF as a kid and dipped my toe into the mainly white fantasy worlds of Tolkien, Jordan, and Le Guin. I started out by creating my own secondary world fantasy with sci-fi elements based on these influences. But I wouldn't say that there's any connection to the kind of writing that I personally do and Afrofuturism. We are concerned with very different things, I think.

I feel like Afrofuturism is primarily looking at the imagination of a technological future where blackness has a place, while I tend to be grappling with my personal concerns about religious and cultural degradation as part of the ongoing legacy of colonialism, familial connection, and changing gender roles amid rapid urbanization, and the future of political systems on the continent in the face of increasing economic inequality and a devastatingly changing climate.

NKJ: Specific moments: Margaret Garner's[2] mercy-killing of her own children to keep them out of slavery; the MOVE bombing,[3] the riot that destroyed Black Tulsa,[4] and other examples of hugely disproportionate violence inflicted on black communities for little more than their determination to exist; and generally, the constructedness of modern racism. I get flak sometimes for incidents in my fiction that are based, usually allegorically, on real incidents from history; people accuse me of being too over-the-top. Actual history is much, much more dramatic than most people seem to realize.

NS: Absolutely! In fact, if some of these moments were better known, they would be more accessible resources for me and other creators. But already, for instance, I've incorporated Azande metallurgical prowess into the design of the shonguns of my *Everfair* fighters.[5] And I've lectured at Stanford and Duke about social sciences and social technologies of the African diaspora. See, sometimes when you can't import material culture, you import immaterial culture. Systems of knowledge are immaterial, yet that's exactly what a science is: a system of knowledge. Also, a system of learning. Though enslavers are on record as having done their best to despoil their captives of such things, African-based sciences survived in limited forms. It's heartening to discover their roots when researching my work.

MF: As an Africentrist, I am inspired by more than five thousand years of African civilizations, cultures, languages, literatures, sciences, and technologies.[6] I am particularly fascinated by the Nilotic (sometimes called Kushitic) civilizations of Ancient Egypt, Sudan, and Ethiopia, but also the coastal Swahili civilization, the Mali empire, the Yoruba kingdom, and the Moorish civilization.

In the West, centuries-old liberatory traditions (including that of the African Methodist Episcopalian church and Marcus Garvey's Universal Negro Improvement Association) embraced identification with Africa and self-description by Africans as Africans. We're currently in a moment when US culture is fighting that identification, repealing, and replacing the con-

---

2. See Toni Morrison's *Beloved* (1987) or Nikki M. Taylor's *Driven toward Madness: The Fugitive Slave Margaret Garner and Tragedy on the Ohio* (2016).

3. For further details, see Jason Osder's 2013 documentary *Let the Fire Burn* (2013).

4. See Tim Madigan's treatise *The Burning: Massacre, Destruction, and the Tulsa Race Riot of 1921* (2013) and Rachel Lyon and Bavand Karim's documentary *Hate Crimes in the Heartland* (2014) for more information.

5. The Azande are an ethnic group of north central Africa with a metallurgical reputation known especially for the Kpinga knife. For more details, see Enid Schildkrout and Curtis A. Keim, *African Reflections: Art from Northeastern Zaire* (1990).

6. See Asante's *Afrocentricity: The Theory of Social Change* (2003).

cept of Africanity with "blackness," even though all successful national and international liberation movements succeed in large measure because of identification with ancestral homelands, not skin (which is *literally* the most superficial identification possible; there is no Yellow History Month; South Asians do not enroll in Brown Studies; the European Union is not the White Union; there is no language of Blackinese, no religion of Blackianity, and the two countries named for skin—Sudan and Ethiopia—had those names imposed on them by Arabs and Greeks; Nigerian and Niger likely owe their names to the Tuareg word *n-igerewen* meaning "river of rivers," not any European word meaning "black").

So it is my hope that through my work and that of comrade-creators of Africentric SFF (especially Charles Saunders, Nalo Hopkinson, and Milton Davis), readers of all backgrounds will understand two things: a) Malcolm X's proverb, "You can't hate the roots of the tree and not hate the tree. You can't hate your origin and not end up hating yourself"[7] and b) despite the truth of Malcolm's words, global African psychological, cultural, economic, and political liberation requires that we embrace Africa not out of fear of self-hate, but out of love. Why? For the same reason that "anti-racism" is a doomed project from the outset, whereas the successful, prosocial approach is simple: *show the beauty.*

For those of us who create Africentric SFF, showing ancient and contemporary African brilliance and beauty is our duty and our joy, because doing so spotlights the cosmic elements for creating the future in our own image.

NW: Africa has ancient astronomical heritages that are not well known (e.g., the Dogon people in Mali). Professor Thebe Medupi's *Cosmic Africa* (2003) film is a delight to watch on this. Professor Medupi also shares his expertise on this subject in *The Ancient Astronomers of Timbuktu* (2013), a documentary by Sharron Hawkes for which he served as associate producer.

Nisi Shawl's *Everfair* raises the genocidal legacy of Leopold II of Belgium in the "Congo" in the nineteenth and early twentieth century—he drove a massive Holocaust (ten to fifteen million murdered and counting) that is still not well known or talked about. Also, [he condoned] rape, looting, extortion—the colonial enterprise in all its "civilizing" glory.

The assassination/murder of the newly elected President Patrice Lumumba in the Congo—this Conradian "heart of darkness" has had savage barrages of "dark" acts dealt to it over the ages by pale hands—Tade Thompson and I used this as the set-up piece for our novella "The Last

---

7. See Malcolm X's February 13, 1965, Detroit lecture entitled "Speech at Ford Auditorium." The full text of his speech is available at http://www.blackpast.org/1965-malcolm-x-speech-ford-auditorium.

Pantheon" in *AfroSFv2* (2015). This act was apparently ordered by the then-US president Dwight D. Eisenhower. African and American history tied together again, by unacknowledged blood. The torture and murder of Steve Biko in South Africa 1977 was one of the key inspirations for my book *Azanian Bridges* (2016). The recent decolonizing movement sweeping South Africa, heralded by "Rhodes Must Fall"[8] should be better known, as should the (unfortunately so far unsuccessful) attempts to strike back into the heart of the Old but still active Empire embodied by Oxford University.

Finally, my new work in progress is "Water Must Fall," which looks at drought, climate change, the appropriation of land and water, and the need to highlight indigenous rights, resisting the capitalist commodification (and destruction) of fragile and vital resources.

BC: Damn near all of it. Hopefully, if Rosarium Press continues, the answer to this question will become more apparent.

IL3 and LY: Other scholars included in this anthology explore the role of Africa in Afrofuturist SF. Whether or not you personally define yourself as an Afrofuturist, all of you do indeed reference African history, mythology, science, and culture in your writing. What is the role of Africa, broadly defined, in your personal and/or imaginative lives?

NH: I am part African, part British, part Jewish, and part Taino, yet my features, history, and experience make me all black. This is what it means to be black and Caribbean. Africa shapes my physiognomy, my history, my experience in the world. Conversely, it's a continent I've never visited, so it still has a somewhat mythic status in my mind. That's a misapprehension I have to navigate.

NS: I've never gone to any African countries, but I'm keenly aware of the role the continent plays in my life. I practice a West African-rooted religious tradition—Ifa—and that colors and contributes to my understanding of the world. While writing *Everfair* I created a Pandora station to play background music. It evolved to include both Congolese artists and Afro-Caribbean liturgical music. Such a joy!

MF: As I describe above, global Africanity is my past, present, and future. I enjoy and celebrate the achievements and contributions of others, but not to the extent of decentering myself.

---

8. See Amit Chaudhuri's web article "The real meaning of Rhodes Must Fall" for further information at https://www.theguardian.com/uk-news/2016/mar/16/the-real-meaning-of-rhodes-must-fall.

CO: Africa doesn't have a broad definition for me because it's a real place not an imaginative placeholder or an idea. I am a Nigerian citizen. Until last month, I lived in Abuja. It is the messy contradictions of any home—with its glorious expressiveness and vibrancy, on one hand, and its heartbreaking brutality and inequity on the other.

It is the freedom to never have to worry about being the "only black person in the room" combined with the intense pseudocultural pressures that undergird a pervasive and toxic patriarchy. The power of belonging in which everyone can say my name right (including me) while still berating me for not being "Igbo" enough.

I think that there is an enormous amount of cultural and historical knowledge that has been completely erased from our sense of our history as Africans as a result of the systematic destruction of our heritage by European colonial powers. For instance, I had no idea just how devastating the sack of the Kingdom of Benin by British colonial forces in 1897 had been. In the history books, it's been mildly renamed "The Benin Expedition," a term which glosses over the scale and brutality of the destruction. Even today, no one talks about how the British Museum got its amazing collection of Benin bronzes because colonial troops committed an act of cultural genocide akin to the worst acts of ISIS or the Taliban when it burned and looted a centuries-old kingdom.

Another example is discovering that West Africans had many complex writing systems. I was always taught that of all the "major" civilizations, sub-Saharan Africans were unique because they'd never developed writing. All my life I had been taught to thank the white missionaries for deigning to transcribe my spoken language into a written form solely for my benefit. Imagine my surprise to learn that Nri, Nsibidi, and Adinkra were all West African writing systems that were widely in use right up until colonial invasion.

I don't know whether my ongoing learning about the scale of cultural loss that colonialism wrought on my people has *inspired* my work, but it has certainly sparked my imagination. Perhaps, as I continue in my own writing, this knowledge will take more of a front seat.

NW: Having been born and bred and living thirty-five years of my life in Africa, I plan to return eventually with my partner to help out with needed mental health projects. In September [2017] I presented at the first ever Pan-African Psychology Conference in Durban, first in an invited Symposium (with Professor Nimisha Patel) on developing anti-racist practice in British Psychology and then a paper on "Challenging Whiteness" during the training of clinical psychologists in the UK. I cowrote a paper with Nimisha on this, but no one in Britain would touch it—so we've ended up securing publication in the *South African Journal of Psychology* instead, despite it being about racism in the UK!

I'm hoping my personal and professional life will dovetail more in the years ahead. I've written stories set in the UK, but I write mostly about the "borders between" places and states. The white Afrikaners have a funny, derogatory term about the white, male English South African.

The derisory Afrikaner term for people like me? *soutpiel*, or "soutie" for short. In its English translation, "salty penis,"—a man who stands with one foot in Africa, one in Britain, and with his penis dangling in the Atlantic Ocean in between. Over time I've learned to accept I'm a "soutie"—of Africa, but not fully African. From Britain, but not fully British. So, I write about Africa and ways of striking back at enduring Empire, from without and within.

Why? In 1988, our eldest daughter was three years old, and we managed to get her in to one of the first "non-racial" nurseries opening up in Cape Town, despite apartheid's State of Emergency. But she came home one day sobbing, saying she wanted to be white, because "they all say, mommy, black is dirty, black is ugly." So, I write for a new world, where children everywhere might all just be happy, for who they are.

BC: Good question. I'm not really sure. Being from two strains of the African diaspora—American and Jamaican—Africa has definitely played a part in my cultural imagination. But to what extent, I couldn't really tell you. As a third culture kid, I've always had a strong interest in international affairs and history because, at an early age, I knew I was from somewhere else as well as from Pittsburgh. My main concern has always been African America and the Caribbean as a whole, but my interests are definitely more disparate than even that. I am currently working on a graphic novel project that I've written set in 1930s Eastern Europe. So, I'd definitely say that Africa is in the mix and probably floats somewhere near the top of the gumbo of my imagination, but that gumbo has a *lot* of ingredients.

IL3 and LY: Will Afrofuturism end? If so, what comes next and why?

BC: All things end. I am hoping that it won't be a corporate decision (though I constantly fear that it will be) that they're just tired of this whole "diversity" thing. What I am hoping is that it simply peters out because a strong black presence in literature is normalized and just stuff that everybody reads.

NH: I don't know, and I don't care to speculate. [Afrofuturism] might end as a notion, but as a record of a fruitful period of expression and thought, it won't disappear.

CO: I can't really answer this question because it's so far outside of my wheelhouse. I'm sorry!

NKJ: Can't answer the first part, either, given my answer to question 1 about not really even understanding the term. I don't know enough of what it is now to opine about what it might end as. As for what comes next, though—I would hope a broadening of literature so that it will no longer segregate "Africa" and "the future" from one another, and no longer lump Janet the steampunkista in with Jamel the literary zombie writer, just because the two share a color or an interest in protagonists who aren't white. I don't know what that period of broadening, which is already happening, will be called, though. That's up to the scholars to decide.

NS: I suppose someone will create a new buzzword or catchphrase or subgenre or some such label. I have no interest at all in what that could turn out to be.

MF: It may end, but no one can predict what will replace it. Whatever it is, it will partly bore us with its conventionality and partly outrage us by its defiance of our expectations. Both can add value.

NW: There's no easy "post-racial" future though, as I naively thought in that four-hour non-racial queue to vote for a new South Africa in 1994, when I believed that race and racism was starting to come tumbling down. More fool I—that's going to take much further long and hard work and probably the prizing open of (white) fingers too. [But as for Afrofuturism as an aesthetic movement,] all things end. Next, I hope we have just plain World-futurism—do we have any? If so, how do we make it happen, in the best and fairest way, for all remaining sentient life on this planet?

CHAPTER 2

Dangerous Muses

Black Women Writers Creating at the Forefront of Afrofuturism

Sheree R. Thomas

The works of novelists Andrea Hairston, Nalo Hopkinson, Nnedi Okorafor, Sofia Samatar, and other short fiction writers such as Alexis Pauline Gumbs, Kiini Ibura Salaam, and Nisi Shawl help frame black women's agency and aesthetics in a world that often denies the existence of both. Through investigating the relationship between indigenous and folk traditional culture, with its healing, rootwork, and sophisticated adaptations of technology, I show how each of these black women writers are taking the lead in the Afrofuturism movement, creating works that evoke the past, critique the present, and challenge us to imagine a greater, more possible future.

These black women speculative fiction writers are dangerous muses, women whose work is inspiring a new renaissance, a reemergence of Afrofuturism in all its many forms. They use and retool genre conventions to revise long held meanings that define community and communal storytelling. They defy old meanings imposed on black women's bodies and amplify their voices, creating characters that become the heroines of their own adventures, the creators of their own unforgettable tales. Their choice of characterization, language, themes, and setting do not reinforce traditional notions of whose stories are worth telling, nor even how stories should be told. They are dangerous to the status quo, destroying the old temples of golden ages past, and are stealthily building the world anew in their own remarkable image.

"Dangerous Muses" explores how these writers repurpose the speculative fiction genre to identify sites of intervention and reconnection. Through their imaginative works, they offer spaces for black women and other readers to inhabit, new dimensions of consciousness, and innovative new narratives to interrogate family, race, gender, class, and identity.

"Where there is a woman, there is magic," Ntozake Shange proclaimed, and these representative black women writers are no exception (1). If Samuel R. Delany ushered in a new pioneering path for black voices and black genius in science fiction, and Octavia E. Butler helped to widen and expand that grand path, then these magical black women writers are carving a path so strong, so bold, so beautiful that it is their voices and their visions that are shaping Afrofuturism today. The subgenre's controversial and complicated journey into the stars would be stunted and earthbound without their unique contributions. In Zora Neale Hurston's *Their Eyes Were Watching God* (1937), Nanny tells Janie that black women are the mules of the world. Well, if black women rise, so do we all. Once delegated to the back roads and the back rooms, black women writers are the leaders in the field of Afrofuturism—and they are not going back, not holding back, and their brilliant work will carry us with them, too. Each year sees a fresh new crop of black women's creations to explore. And as usual, black women have been hard at work. The intellectual, creative labor these writers have produced is understandably challenging, for they have not only been star-blazing a path for themselves but they are birthing a black womanist future for us all.

Almost two decades into the twenty-first century, with a historic first black presidency behind us, America is no closer to reaching the fabled Promised Land than before. Yet this is not only a time of intense political activism but also a time of shifting consciousness, historical revision, creative innovation, and cultural affirmation when sociopolitical norms once championed, if not in deed but by word, are being actively challenged and suppressed. We have been here before, fellow travelers, many times in the cynical cycle that is race relations and white supremacy in America, and yet we have never quite been *here*. It feels as if every dystopian novel ever written is happening all at once. We are the pattyrollers and the runaways, the abolitionists and the gradualists, the marchers and martyrs, the dreamers and the dreamed.

And yet there is hope. "*I got love for my folks / baptized when the levees broke.*"[1]

The waters rise, quick, quick, but we rise above them.

---

1. Hear Erykah Badu's song "Soldier" (2008).

Creators, and those who study them, those who are inspired by them, are rising to meet the challenge of giving verse and vision, a record of our time. The work today is built on a bridge from the past, and we who labor and love in the fields of the speculative fiction genre must all cross it. The 1970s and 1980s saw publications like *Black American Literature Forum, The Black Scholar, Callaloo, Drumvoices Revue, Obsidian, Transition,* and others featuring literary criticism on black speculative fiction from scholars like Frances Beale, Sandra Y. Govan, and Ruth Salvaggio. These women scholars helped to introduce Butler and others to a whole new generation of readers, placing their work firmly in a canon of black womanist writing. The 1990s and early 2000s was an exciting era when new nomenclature was designed to try to capture a centuries-old song. To be black and try to live fully as a human being with dignity and rights that are respected in a culture in which every natural resource and system is designed for your destruction, plunder and mayhem, maiming and dysfunction, is in itself an act of futurism. Accommodationists will suck their teeth. Colorblind folks will fan themselves, but no matter where you fall on the ideological spectrum, it's true—we were never meant to be free here. When you understand that, you can appreciate why the cycles remain, the pendulum in constant motion, two steps forward, fifty years back. You are the alien of the other shore, *The Brother from Another Planet* (1984), the *Sister Outsider* (1984) singing perpetual blues, attempting to live and inhabit a strange space and time that has not yet arrived, a future that seems to be forever moving just out of reach.

In 1992 Mark Dery interviewed pioneer Samuel R. Delany, scholar Tricia Rose, and cultural critic and journalist Greg Tate, coining the term "Afrofuturism" in an essay, "Black to the Future," named after Def Jef's track. His theoretical groundwork and musings were published the following year in a special guest-edited issue of *The South Atlantic Monthly* and in 1994 in his own book, *Flame Wars: The Discourse of Cyberculture.* Dery sought a term that would speak to African American themes and concerns in the context of twentieth century technoculture. He recognized that black artists had "other stories to tell" and was curious about what those might be. He wrote, "If there is an Afrofuturism, it must be sought in unlikely places, constellated from far-flung points." In 1998 sociologist Alondra Nelson later cofounded the Afrofuturism listserv with other scholars, musicians, artists, writers, gamers, and readers from around the world who shared an interest in exploring the intersections of race, art, and technology within speculative themes.

The conversations we had on the listserv were riveting, lively debates and a few kerfluffles, imaginative brainstorming sessions on a myriad of topics, resource databanks, artist critiques, and praisesongs. Even then there was a shared sense of excitement on what Afrofuturism had been and what it could be. These other tales were quietly being coded, painted, recorded, danced, and written all around—some within the big houses, studios, art world, and mainstream venues and others without. Untold volumes of creative work were critically neglected because it flew under the radar of what had already been canonized. While independent presses, small publishers, and self-published works were often left out of the "why aren't black people writing science fiction" conversations, the Afrofuturism listserv community recognized that there was a number of black creators innovating not just on American shores but in spaces and mediums all around the world.

In 1998 Afro-Canadian Nalo Hopkinson won Warner Aspect's first novel contest, launching her publishing career with *Brown Girl in the Ring*. Hopkinson's discovery ushered in a more urgent desire for readers to explore similar work. Two years later, the new millennium arrived with the fanfare of any year—with long spells of exhilaration, anxiety, and fits of watchfulness. Fresh on the heels of discovering an incredible new talent immediately celebrated as an heir to Octavia E. Butler, the imprint published in 2000 the first volume of my *Dark Matter* anthologies, where I had journeyed, "Looking for the Invisible," signaling an unprecedented period of discussion and production of fiction by black writers (*Dark Matter* ix).

Since that period, black women Afrofuturists have emerged as the leading voices creating bold, innovative works in this growing field. Writing tales that are often interstitial, these authors blur the lines between the science fictional and fantasy, the historical and futuristic, centering the interior lives and thoughts of black women in the action. And like some of their predecessors of the previous century who weaved fantastical, science fictional elements with the historical and contemporary in their work such as Alice Walker in *Possessing the Secret of Joy* (1992) or Lorraine Hansberry's invented African nation in *Les Blancs* (1970), these writers took traditional conventions and reshaped them, crafting stories that ring with imagination and feel like truth.

※

If fantasy and folklore are as Hurston said, "the boiled down juice of human living," then SF and Afrofuturism are the elixir of the gods (Hemenway 157). And what gods are more feared than black people? The fear of race and gender robs us of beauty, *Get Out* (2017) writer and director Jordan Peele said when speaking of "Noir Town," his photo shoot for the fashion magazine *W* starring the cyberqueen herself, musician and actress Janelle Monáe, whom Peele casts as an updated version of the (usually white and male) Hitchcock hero.[2] Peele speaks to what stories are stunted or left untold because the narratives are forced within an exploitative framework based on fear.

In *Black Panther* (2018), black women are fearless, seen in all their glorious genius and beauty—black women are portrayed as sisters, mothers, wives, lovers, warriors, and scientists. They are portrayed as healers, healing with roots and technology. The elders who tend the sacred purple blossoms that bestowed upon the lineage of Black Panther monarchs their supernatural strength and panther-like abilities are part of a long tradition of ritual herbalists. The flowers, once mixed into an unknown beverage, also hold the power to send one's consciousness to the realm of the ancestors. This realm, the world of those who came before, figures largely in the work of black women writers. Its borders are porous, pulling descendants back and forth, in mind and body, to reconnect with forgotten knowledge, to reveal hidden mysteries, and to guide generations. Some of the most iconic black women writers in literature share interpretations of this traditional power figure with today's most intriguing black women Afrofuturist writers. This narrative thread unites many of their works.

Conjurers and Seers

A gifted anthropologist who traveled throughout the American South and Haiti collecting oral histories and secret knowledge of spiritual practices, Hurston was well versed in the spirit of her people. From *Mules and Men* (1935), *Tell My Horse* (1938), and *Moses, Man of the Mountain* (1939) to her other nonfiction works based on her invaluable contributions to the Works Progress Administration's Federal Writer's Project research, *The Sanctified Church* (1981) and *Go Gator and Muddy the Water* (1999), Hurston reached back and preserved vital folk knowledge that may have been lost through the ages in the rush to assimilate to whatever current ideal of blackness persisted.

"I mean to wrassle me up a future, or die trying," Hurston once said (Walker, *I Love* 14). Sadly, it seems that she did both. But through her travels and folkloric study, Hurston knew firsthand, better than most, that sacrifice is part of some rootwork. And while we may never know the untold volumes of genius we lost when Zora Neale Hurston died, we do know how much she loved us. For the evidence is in the future she did "wrassle up" and the incredible treasures of the past she uncovered, honored, and preserved.

---

2. See Lynn Hirschberg's "Jordan Peele Reinvents the Hitchcock Heroine with the Help of Janelle Monáe" in the February 20, 2018, issue of *W Magazine*.

The herbs and herb doctors she recorded in *The Sanctified Church* represent a small portion of the considerable firsthand accounts, folklore and humor, oral histories, and other materials Hurston collected in her travels. Of the colorful cast of real-life characters she had the good fortune and remarkable social skills to meet, it is the conjurers and healers, Father Abraham, Daddy Mention, and the storied High John the Conquerors that stand out.

Perhaps the most recognizable conjurer besides those featured in Charles Chesnutt's *The Conjure Woman* (1899), Toni Morrison's Pilate in *Song of Solomon* (1977), or Gloria Naylor's *Mama Day* (1988), is Hurston's Moses, who appears in a work once described by a critic as a "noble failure" (270). In her beautiful novel, *Moses, Man of the Mountain*, Hurston offers a remarkable picture of leadership and human foibles by reimagining the iconic Biblical story told in the idiom and black vernacular of the South. While it received mixed reviews, Hurston brilliantly recasts the Jewish wanderers of the Old Testament with the philosophical story of Africa's "lost tribe," the descendants of enslaved people forced to work and wander in a nation where they lack citizenship, protection of the law, and freedom to name and claim themselves. Moses as a prophetic figure now recast with the vernacular of a hard shell Baptist preacher is fitting, as he, like the fabled founder of the Church of God in Christ, Bishop Charles Harris Mason, is said to have been a rootworker and healer, often using and recognizing natural objects and herbs as "earthly signs" from God (Chireau 111). African traditional religions such as Vodou of West Africa and Haiti, and African diasporic spiritual traditions such as Hoodoo, Candomblé, Santeria, Obeah, and so forth have been forced to wear many masks. To do otherwise is to invite erasure.

A people whose past was ruthlessly, strategically stripped from them in state-sanctioned violence and numerous perfidious tactics cannot be faulted for seeking ways to mitigate dire circumstances. Armed with the foreknowledge and assurance that comes with faith, some relied on the guidance of the divination, readings, and prescriptions prescribed by community healers. Unlike most traditional practices, hoodoo is nonhierarchal.

Conjurer, hoodoo doctor, rootworker, no matter what the name, these special people were said to be gifted with uncommon gifts and insights. They worked to heal "the sick and spellbound," addressing the ailments of a people denied proper medical care, denied the right to read or to be formally educated, and denied full agency over their own present and futures. In *Nineteen Eighty-four* (1949), George Orwell tells us that "who controls the past controls the future . . . who controls the present controls the past" (248). Despite brutal policies that attempted to strip kidnapped black people of all

African retentions, reshaping them from free, whole humans to tools, the bondspeople resisted and fought to retain the vestiges of their culture and past. Not all memories or gifts were stripped, suppressed, or stolen. Despite the forced migration and displacement of millions, despite the rapid acculturation, the violence of bondage, and the fear, these Africans forced across the big waters carried their knowledge and memories inside their hearts and heads.

Coming from long and ancient traditions of spiritual beliefs, the bondspeople of the African diaspora adapted their own faiths to the new environments they found themselves laboring and living in, creating something old and new at once. And with new roots came new spices and herbs, and with new recipes and rituals came new gods.

Ezili is said by some to be one of the lwa in Haiti that does not have an antecedent in West Africa. Born out of the experience of slavery, Ezili is the lwa of love, fertility, and motherhood. Known by several names and incarnations, her presence is symbolized by the heart, the hummingbird, the maiden, and the crone.[3] Nalo Hopkinson wrote a novel, *The Salt Roads* (2003), in which this lwa is "born from countless journeys chained tight in the bellies of ships. Born from hope vibrant and hope destroyed. Born of bitter experience. Born of wishing for better. Born" (40). Her journey mirrors those of the nineteenth century Afro-French mulatto, Jeanne Duval, courtesan/lover to the Bohemian poet, Charles Baudelaire, and two enslaved women, Thais/Meritet/St. Mary, a fourth-century Alexandrian girl sold into prostitution in Egypt, and Mer, a gifted healer trapped on a sugar cane plantation in late eighteenth-century Haiti.

Cultural hybridity and structural complexity are the hallmarks of Hopkinson's writing. In *The Salt Roads*, she interweaves the disparate voices and lives of three black women and a goddess and creates an alternate history (or alternate herstories) that spans time and three continents, traveling intermittently from the often carnal world of humans to that of the gods. Mer, who tells us that her "wishes can't fly freely. They're rooted to the ground like me, who eats salt," struggles for independence and freedom amidst daily horrors, trauma, and sociopolitical instabilities (*Salt* 349). The multiple narrative structure of this experimental novel reminded me of the dueling asphalt beats of jumping Double Dutch. Hopkinson takes multiple voices, sexualities, and storylines and twists them into a single rope, turning the story together in a pattern that allows the women in the novel and readers beyond to jump in and out over time.

---

3. See Donald J. Consentino's *Sacred Arts of Haitian Vodou* (1995).

For me, the twinned, roped narratives creates a greater space for understanding these women's similarly complex lives. Even the lwa's experiences of love, loss, and exile parallels the mortal women. While I see a kind of Double Dutch consciousness expressed in the work, scholar Leif Sorensen offers the whining sonic tapestries of Reggae dub music as a possible way of examining the novel's ever shifting terrain. Writes Sorensen, "Hopkinson adapts the sonic style of dub to create new Afrofuturist literary forms" (267). In the perspective of the goddess, lwa Ezili tells us, "*Music is the key, it seem; flowing as rivers do, beating like the wash of her blood in her body*" (*Salt* 116). With her breaks, beats, and blues, what Hopkinson creates is an experimental Afrofuturist lens that sees the lives of black women as critical sites for examination and vessels that are valuable enough to hold sacred knowledge and bear witness to the voice of gods. In Hopkinson's novel, black women's tears bring meaning in their salt. They are the "mothers of memories."

Cultural identity is a function of memory, history, and consciousness. Artists across media interrogate memory, renegotiate history, and evolve to arrive at new levels of thinking. They observe, listen to their inner muses, and work to bring their visions into our world. It can be challenging to create art under any circumstances, but imagine what that experience might mean when the artist's voice and vision are deemed trivial and their very bodies under constant attack. Black women artists face the slings and arrows of fortune like other artists but have also faced attacks and erasure from within and beyond their own communities—and yet they persist. The 1960s saw a radical redefinition of what scholar Madhu Dubey called "literary blackness" (153), while the 1970s saw writers such as Gayl Jones, Toni Morrison, and Alice Walker further redefine that with a black feminist/womanist aesthetic. But the speculative literature of pioneers Octavia E. Butler, Jewelle Gomez, and the black women writers that followed extended this cultural project to incorporate exploration of a genre that previously rendered them invisible. Writing works that placed recognizable black women as protagonists, as subjects of their own stories rather than objects and set pieces in those of others, black women speculative writers created a space where the ancient and the modern systems coexist. In their new works, intergenerational systems of knowledge and survival techniques help characters mitigate the historical, seemingly infinite onslaught of anti-blackness, misogyny, and erasure.

Set at the turn of the twentieth century, in the rural swamps of Peach Grove, Georgia, and Chicago, Andrea Hairston's *Redwood and Wildfire* (2011) explores and overcomes all of the aforementioned obstacles with an uplifting fantastical love story that encompasses hoodoo, history, heartbreak, and the magic of cinema. Redwood Phipps, a black woman, and Aidan Cooper Wildfire, an Irish-Seminole, are both gifted with intuitive powers that go far beyond their theatrical talents. Redwood can hold a tornado in her hand. Aidan's voice can sing the hurt out of a spirit, bring a change with a note in his songs. Both share family histories that are marked in part by trauma, a shared personal history that leads them out of the Georgia swampland to forge a new future for themselves in the North. Set at a time of rampant lynchings, before the Hollywood system is solidified in full play, readers see people of color attempt to inhabit a world of their own making, taking hold of the opportunities that present themselves despite very clear, sometimes violent warnings against such bold agency.

With a joyful conviction that is refreshing to read in the genre, Hairston does not sugarcoat the harsh realities of the era she explores. Instead she lays bare the grim blood and bones, then breathes life into scenarios that might fail in a lesser writer's hands. She infuses humor in her layered writing that's steeped in the culture of her characters. What gives the novel its power is Hairston's remarkably astute understanding of the true power of the ancient wisdom found in the conjure/hoodoo tradition: that one must want to heal, to be healed, that it takes a laying on of communal hands to do so, and to work your mojo, you got to move. Like Redwood and Aidan's journey to Chicago during the World's Fair, where wonders abound, readers of the novel undergo a restorative journey. The Afrofuturist work of Hairston's novel is transmigration—to restore history, to restore spirit. By reclaiming traditions that had been maligned and erased, co-opted and commercialized, *Redwood and Wildfire* restores the value of folk magic to its proper place of respect, restores the marginalized people of history to full color, full breadth and depth of life, and lifts them from being mere extras in another's dramatic story to full actors in their own life stories. This is no small feat when set against the racial tensions of the era. With a generous spirit, a master storyteller's skill, and a philosopher's mind, Hairston expertly creates a world peopled with characters readers are deeply invested in.

A novel of haints, healers, and new blues, Hairston's *Redwood and Wildfire* is what Hurston might have written had she completely embraced fantasy and the technological wonders of cinema in her day. In the novel, we watch society's transformation as the performance world shifts from the minstrel shows of slavery, to vaudeville, to films. *Will Do Magic for Small Change* (2016) is a meta-tale, a novel within a novel, both SF and fantasy, a family history and a revelation. In the book, wandering aliens reside alongside magic and Dahomey warrior women. Family history—the gripes, the disappointments, the secrets, and the love—are on full display as the backdrop of young Cinnamon Jones's coming-of-age in 1980s Pittsburgh and her family's hidden history connected to a West African empire of the 1890s. In this, her third novel, Hairston continues the story with Aidan and Redwood's granddaughter, Cinnamon Jones.

The story begins with a funeral and ends with Aidan and Redwood returning from the first book to sing more of their blackbird healing wisdom at the climax of the work. The novel explores gun violence, drugs, poverty, and the harsh consequences that face those who don't quite fit in the rigid norms of the day. "Normal is the secret weapon of empire," Hairston once wrote in an essay. "Invisible, taken for granted, running constantly in the background, normal is the default setting for the empire of the mind" ("Dismantling"). Bitten by the theater bug, Cinnamon dreams of following her gifted grandparents' theatrical footsteps, but her above-average height, big-boned body, and dark, melanated skin does not make that an easy prospect. Cinnamon is thick and black and female at a period when none of that is in style. A child from poverty, of myth and art, Cinnamon holds fast to her dreams with the help of new equally awkward friends, Klaus and Marie.

Homophobia and sexual fluidity are explored alongside anti-blackness and black communal responses to it. Young Cinnamon is bisexual and explores an early polyamorous romance. Taiwo, the Wanderer alien, is non-gendered, neither male nor female or perhaps both. Love in all its forms—communal, familial/sibling love, and intimacy in multiple iterations are examined with graceful nuance. And like the restorative project of *Redwood and Wildfire*, *Will Do Magic* attempts to restore the lost fragmented selves of its characters, their kinships and lost history. There is a great deal of self-discovery in the work, particularly in the Dahomey warrior character Kehinde, who seeks lost connections of her own.

And like Hopkinson's *The Salt Roads*, Hairston's *Will Do Magic* is non-linear in its structure. A journey/journal of lost souls found, *The Salt Roads* and *Will Do Magic* both explore a form of an alternate dimension. Pieces of Cinnamon's dead brother's story and that of Taiwo's appear mysteriously in their own time, and like Cinnamon, readers must reconcile who they are with what they bring to the page.

Ancestors and Witnesses

The opening to Gloria Naylor's *Mama Day,* is a tour de force, an incandescent river of history that begins on God's Seventh Day, explaining the origin of the family's name. With a family tree mapped out prior to this flood, Naylor evokes the Days' ancestry while making readers witnesses to the magic hidden in the plain view of generations in a Gullah family, situated somewhere between the Georgia and South Carolina Sea Islands, crowned by Sapphira Wade, the dangerous matriarch of the Day family who is said to have born seven souls by the plantation owner she is also said to have poisoned after getting him to sign over all the land to her and their children. At its heart, the novel is the story of a marriage, the relationship between Cocoa, a Willow Island native, and her New Yorker husband George. But *Mama Day* is also the story of an island and its culture, a people's centuries-old struggle to maintain autonomy and dignity, a future where black people are not tools and mules, but whole women and men. When Cocoa and George visit her great aunt Mama Day, a series of soul-deep changes are set in motion, and the women's personal magic rises, leaving readers as witness to a multiplicity of possibilities.

Miss Lissie from Alice Walker's *The Temple of My Familiar* (1989) participates in an African-derived matriarchy that witnesses the sweep of centuries. *Temple* is the story of the possessed and the dispossessed but also of those who survive despite bearing witness to great tribulations. Miss Lissie is an African/American/woman/goddess born and reborn through the ages. She is reincarnated many times, for reasons initially unknown, and her various lives create a limbic space for Walker to explore folk memory and to reimagine possible reiterations of utopic life. Miss Lissie, like Sapphira and Mama Day, and the women of Hairston's novels, shows that the black community is epic and universal enough to hold the dreams of a nation, the hopes of the future, bearing witness to the whole wide past.

Sofia Samatar, a Somali-American born in Indiana, writes beyond diasporas and through mirrors, creating speculative works that reflect her hybrid heritage and the journeys she and her family have made as they navigate life across many borders. In her stories, often told from the point of view of an observer, Samatar invites us to bear witness to the strange, dream-like far-flung settings she creates. In "The Red Thread" (2016), told from the perspective of the young child Agar Black Hat, readers are transported to an extraterrestrial colony in the wake of cataclysmic climate change. After the trauma, citizens suffer further indignity when a universal draft forces religious pacifists from Earth. Samatar's gorgeous storytelling allows us to experience the story as a witness while critical details are expertly revealed one by one. In fact, Samatar wrote the first draft of her debut novel, *A Stranger in Olondria* (2013) from Yambio, South Sudan. She describes it as "a distillation of everything that happened to me at that point" (Clarke). In the coming-of-age tale, young Jevick is haunted by an illiterate ghost as he travels through a strange land. The novel explores who gets to tell stories and how, who has a voice and who is silenced, what are the treasures and pitfalls of language, and how people are freed or imprisoned by the tongue. Writing on semiotics, selkies, jazz musicians, and refugees, Samatar is an exciting voice amongst black women Afrofuturists.

Alexis Pauline Gumbs's work expresses a commitment to indeterminacy, a kind of radical contingency, where readers are asked to follow multiple paths to a future connected by layered readings of the past. "Seven Possible Futures for a Black Feminist Artist" (2017) is a hybrid work, part prose poem, part historical notes taken from the future that has already happened in an alternate world. It begins with the study of the death of a black (woman) artist, and it is the questions that the futuristic scholar/anthropologist/archivist asks that resonates so powerfully in the series:

> What was in them that made work more food to them than food was? And tobacco?
>
> Was it indigenous memory? How often did they paint their insides with substance and strain? Is there an imprint that deepens in the face of repeated misunderstanding?
>
> And tokenization? Does it inoculate the blood? (114)

Gumbs continues her investigations in *M. Archive* (2018), which features a series of invented artifacts that show the resilience of black genius, black art in the wake of a cataclysmic disaster. Told from the perspective of a future researcher who discovers evidence of the value and resourcefulness of black feminist theory after the end of the world, Gumbs's revelatory writing like that of author Kiini Ibura Salaam's vivid, brilliant short stories in *When the World Wounds* (2016) represent a serious engagement with the breath, depth, and wealth of black women's lives on and off the page. These writers take us through dark, burnt out territory, but also guide us to the light, where we can witness our best selves.

Immortals and Muses

Bill Gunn's atmospheric black vampire film and love song to black spiritual traditions, *Ganja & Hess* (1973), offered a take on vampirism and black urban elite aspirations during the Black Arts Movement. The audience is treated to a cultured, confident black anthropologist whose cool exterior and inner wariness does not protect him from being attacked by a house guest and infected by an ancient African relic that holds a powerful, dark secret. Shot in Rochester, New York, in a stone mansion Gunn rented for the summer, *Ganja & Hess* was unusual not only for its intriguing displays of black wealth at a time when black people were equated with failure and poverty, but in its sensual portrayal of a black woman who begins as an accomplice and hustler who is tricked into a life she does not choose for herself, but ends as a creature of her own making based on a pivotal choice that seals her fate.

In *Ganja & Hess*, Gunn asks: how do we unburden ourselves of the weight of colonialism, particularly when the shackles placed on our limbs are placed by our own brethren? The ancient culture in the film that is the source of the cursed artifact and of the bloodlust that plagues the couple represents the long arm of history, complicated and twisted in its reach. The film has an almost mythical structure where Hess the anthropologist is visited by one admirer who wishes to kill him and another—Ganja—who wants to love him. The first visitor kills Hess with a curse that forces him to live eternally with an unspeakable thirst for blood. In the end, Hess's lover Ganja returns his life to him by killing him but chooses another fate for herself. Thus Ganja, who arrived seeking a wayward lover, also arrives at the space where she bears witness to herself.

For Hess, immortality becomes a burden he can no longer bare. His inescapable blood lust, the craven murders of his fellow brothers and sisters, weigh on him, a curse he would rather die than live with. For Ganja, immortality comes to mean something else—freedom and absolute agency—perhaps the first time she has experienced such things in her entire life. The film is an allegory of the internal conflicts and contradictions inherent in black liberation movements, including the micro-civil wars, the drive to idolize visible leaders, and the tendency to cannibalize the very people you seek to liberate.

In Jewelle Gomez's *The Gilda Stories* (1991), the initiation into vampirism is a mercy. Rather than committing senseless murder and mayhem, the vampires of Gomez's novel and linked stories barter with humans, trading the peace and healing born from their telepathic and intuitive powers for the life blood of humans. This parity of resources would have been unknown to Gilda, who embraced vampirism after she fled the abusive small farm where she was enslaved. Rather than a life of servitude in the fields, Gilda finds freedom in the most unlikely place, Woodard's Bordello. Like Ganja, life as an immortal represents true freedom and to some extent, renewed purpose. Rather than a life spent as a tool for someone else's profit, Gilda becomes a free woman with the freedom to enter when and where she chooses.

The new Gilda story Gomez wrote for the first volume of *Dark Matter: A Century of Speculative Fiction from the African Diaspora* (2000) was set in the Jazz Age. "Chicago 1927" sees Gilda, a former Louisiana slave turned vampire in 1850 as an act of freedom, travel to a blues club to meet Lydia Redmond, an intriguing songstress whose music carried only a little of the sorrow of the blues, her strength drawn from something else. Gomez's Gilda is significant because she draws her power from herself and not from a powerful male in her life. Moreover, the person who introduces her to her new immortal life is a woman, not a man. She does not need to use seductive womanly charms to feed but uses her own physical strength and intuition to do so. Gilda's intuitive, telepathic powers are similar to the intuitive gifts of a seer's most astute reading. In Gomez's stories, Gilda moves through the earth on her own terms, and gives as much as she takes in life force.

Alaya Dawn Johnson's novel, *Moonshine* (2010), also set in the 1920s, imagines a world where vampires live alongside djinni, feminists, and fae. Zephyr Hollis, the daughter of a demon hunter and an underpaid, underfed New York City educator, is drawn into the world of the "Others" by Amir, a djinn with his own agenda. Johnson's paranormal story explores social justice issues from the perspective of an obsessive do-gooder who is best described as a vampire suffragette. Zephyr is intelligent, resourceful, and philanthropic without being pretentious. Through the plight of the "others," Johnson successfully inverts some of the class, race, and gender assumptions found in more traditional vampire tales while delivering a fast-paced, entertaining story.

Tananarive Due's bestselling four-novel series, African Immortals, begins with the unforgettable novel *My Soul to Keep* (1997) and ends with *My Soul to Take* (2011), Dawit/David, the 500-year-old immortal in the first book, who has loved and lost at least three different wives, had a noble purpose that has become distorted over time. After a series of loved ones and associates begin to die mysteriously, his wife, Jessica, discovers his secret and learns that David is part of an ancient Ethiopian sect of scholars that traded their mortal humanity and vowed eternal secrecy. Unfortunately for Jessica and her daughter, Dawit decides to ritually initiate Jessica as well, launching her into a race to save herself and her family. Each volume of the series takes readers deeper into the Ethiopian sect, and the storytelling becomes more science fictional as it progresses. Due's biological and historical extrapolations make the series a thrilling and riveting mystery as well.

Celebrated for her provocative SF and memorable, often black women protagonists, Octavia E. Butler was a pioneer in the world of Afrofuturists who proved comfortable writing in multiple generic forms. She often challenges notions about what it means to be human and explores human sexuality and notions of community when set against the backdrop of competition for resources and survival. The vampires or *Ina* in Butler's final novel, *Fledgling* (2005), are as intriguing as any other characters Butler has penned. They are ruthless and uncompromising in their agenda, while Shori, the 53-year-old genetically engineered child protagonist in the body of an 11-year-old child, embodies Butler's signature troubling of traditional sexual mores and values. *Fledgling*, a work Butler said she wrote for fun while taking a break from the third volume in the *Parable* series—what had been tentatively titled *Parable of the Trickster*—is a work that is unsettling, deeply disturbing in the best ways, and challenging. Butler places Shori, an amnesiac, in the path of danger as she struggles to discover her true nature as a human-Ina hybrid as well as her real family/communal center. She does not fit comfortably in either the human or Ina worlds, and she grapples with fierce desires and needs. Butler does not allow readers the comfort of a moral high ground, instead pulling them into Shori's experiences and implicating them in the choices she makes as she determines to survive on her own terms.

Travelers and Jigganauts

The time travel novel *Kindred* (1979) is one of Butler's most well-known works and, like Walter Mosley's young adult slavery novel *47* (2005), Kiese Laymon's *Long Division* (2013), or the *Brother Future* (1991) film starring Moses Gunn, Carl Lumbly, and Vonetta McGee, her protagonists remain earthbound, navigating time against their will (much like the black supermodel in Haile Gerima's classic film *Sankofa* [1993]). There are implications that this is just a metaphor, no pithy "it was all a dream" rejoinders. When people travel in these stories, they are truly there, "returning to the source" (*Sankofa*).

Using Afro-Caribbean magic and folklore as well as a hybrid of Jamaican, Haitian, and Trinidadian roots and culture, in *Midnight Robber* (2000) Nalo Hopkinson reimagines the Black Atlantic off planet to create Toussaint, a vibrant future where the descendants of formerly enslaved Caribbean people colonize a planet, transforming it with nanotechnology and peopling it with their own rich culture. On Toussaint, steel pan music, majestic pageantry, and the ingenious creativity of black people is on full display. The story begins on Jonkanoo at Carnival time. Hopkinson's novel has the bones of classical, "hard" SF with the muscle, heart, and spirit of the African diaspora, and the storytelling skills of a master at her craft. She remixes the traditional trickster Anansi tale and the figure of Eshu from the Yoruba religion with a glorious supercomputer, the *Matrix*-like AI Granny Nanny, to create force that reckons. Predating the invention of Apple's Siri, Hopkinson's Granny Nanny influences fates and wields power over the whole colony, monitoring activities, addressing most needs, and controlling Toussaint's citizens with a mostly benign efficiency.

Like Gayl Jones's classic novels *Corregidora* (1975) and *Eva's Man* (1976), Hopkinson's *Midnight Robber* explores the trauma and darkness associated with the sexual abuse of girls and women. The heroine, Tan-Tan, is forced to atone for the sins of her corrupt father, exiled to the wilds of yet another world, New Half-Way Tree, named after the lively Jamaican crossroad. There she encounters the haints of dreams, folkloric characters who walk and breathe of their own accord, creatures with their own agendas and secrets. Tan-Tan and her father have their own secret, and it is their abusive relationship and Hopkinson's skillful exploration of it that is the heart of the novel. In particular, the teenaged Tan-Tan negotiates this relationship by running away and discovering other exiles who have eked out an existence in their own enclaves. In the high-tech wonderment that is Toussaint, Tan-Tan's coming-of-age is a turbulent one shadowed by abuse and fear. In the jungled, untamed terrain of New Half-Way Tree, Tan-Tan learns that "when you take one [life], you must give back two" (320–21). Forced to live in a penal colony amongst outsiders and the aliens, Tan-Tan becomes the stuff of legends. She dons the mask of the Robber Queen, and her journey there forces her to face her inner pain while carving out a space for healing, redemption, and fresh hope. Invoking the lore and language of the diaspora, replete with tremendous world-building, *Midnight Robber* is a novel of transformation and communal justice, an Afrofuture where trauma is not the end of the tale but the beginning of a new adventure.

While Nnedi Okorafor has a complicated, if not ambivalent relationship to the Afrofuturist, her *Binti* series, like Hopkinson's *Midnight Robber*, is a quintessential example of Afrofuturism. *Binti* (2015) is the maturation tale of a young Himba girl from the future who discovers that her heritage, her self-worth, and her culture's gifts are valuable tools for forging life-saving connections with an alien culture. Okorafor's novels and recent contributions to Marvel's *Black Panther* comic series make her the most prolific and recognizable African speculative fiction writer of our day. As both her accomplishments and those of the many other authors listed on the African Speculative Society's website indicate,[4] Okorafor's prescient call may be answered sooner than she thinks.

---

4. See http://www.africansfs.com.

Hairston's debut novel, *Mindscape* (2006), takes negative assumptions about black women's worth and reshapes them with Hairston's ensemble cast of unusual and unforgettable characters. Captain Lawanda, bearer of one of the delightfully blackety-blackest black names and an expert code switcher of the highest order, is considered an ethnic throwback by her colleagues because she refuses to engage in their limited notions of what a black woman of intellect can and cannot be. Besides shattering respectability politics and the incessant policing of black people's tongues, minds, and manners with the character of Lawanda, Hairston further defies convention with Elleni, a shamanistic black woman who holds one of the lone keys to navigating and communicating with the strange, alien barrier that has divided the entire planet Earth into four nearly impenetrable zones. Hairston writes robust, real women, muscular in mind and body. In *Mindscape,* we find women who lead, nurture, heal, fight, create art, love, and sweat. Equipped with almost-sentient hair that is beyond Medusa, Elleni struggles to perform wonders in a world where she is both valued and scorned for her ability and where she must also struggle out from under the shadows of her mentors Celestina and Femi. In this first novel, as with the others that followed, Hairston writes the world. Intersectionality and queerness are represented fully, and no one in her ensemble cast of unforgettables is without their flaws and challenges.

Black women writers, innovators in the field of world-breaking and world-making, have created and are still creating some of the best, most memorable speculative fiction of the twentieth and twenty-first centuries. Their work is exhilarating and imaginative, well-crafted and conceived, and often beautifully written. These writers have captured the human spirit on the page, while delving into Afrodiasporic ancestral roots. Their stories and novels are written in the tradition of black feminism, and they continue to expand our understanding of Afrofuturism and what this exciting body of work can be. These black women writers, dangerous muses all, write stories set amongst the stars peopled by women and communities we not only know, but love.

Works Cited

African Speculative Fiction Society. 2016, http://www.africansfs.com/. Accessed 1 Mar. 2018.

Badu, Erykah. "Soldier." *New Amerykah Part One (4th World War)*. Universal Motown, 2008.

Bordelon, Pamela, editor. *Go Gator and Muddy the Water: Writings by Zora Neale Hurston from the Federal Writers' Project*. Norton, 1999.

Butler, Octavia E. *Fledging*. Seven Stories, 2005.

———. *Kindred*. Doubleday, 1979.

Campanella II, Roy, director. *Brother Future*. Wayne Morris, 1991.

Chesnutt, Charles W. *The Conjure Woman and Other Tales*. 1899. Houghton Mifflin, 1926.

Chireau, Yvonne. *Black Magic: Religion and the African American Conjuring Tradition*. U of California P, 2006.

Clarke, Nic. "Ways of Knowing: An Interview with Sofia Samatar." *Strange Horizons*, 24 Jun. 2013, http://strangehorizons.com/non-fiction/articles/ways-of-knowing-an-interview-with-sofia-samatar/. Accessed 1 Mar. 2018.

Consentino, Donald J., editor, *Sacred Arts of Haitian Vodou*. U. of California, Los Angeles, UCLA Fowler Museum of Cultural History, 1995.

Coogler, Ryan, director. *Black Panther*. Marvel Studios, 2018.

Dery, Mark. "Black to the Future: Interviews with Samuel R. Delany, Greg Tate, and Tricia Rose." 1993. *Flame Wars: The Discourse of Cyberculture*, edited by Dery, Duke UP, 1994, pp. 179–222.

Dubey, Madhu. *Black Women Novelists & the Nationalists Aesthetic*. U of Indiana P, 1994.

Due, Tananarive. *My Soul to Keep*. Harper Voyager, 1998.

———. *My Soul to Take*. Washington Square, 2011.

Gerima, Haile, director. *Sankofa*. Channel Four Films, 1993.

Gomez, Jewelle. "Chicago 1927." *Dark Matter: A Century of Speculative Fiction from the African Diaspora*, edited by Sheree R. Thomas, Warner, 2000, pp. 19–34.

———. *The Gilda Stories*. 1991. City Lights Publishing, 2016.

Gumbs, Alexis P. *M Archive: After the End of the World*. Duke UP, 2018.

———. "Seven Possible Futures for a Black Feminist Artist." *Speculating Futures: Black Imagination & the Arts*, special issue of *Obsidian: Literature & Arts in the African Diaspora*, vol. 42, nos. 1–2, 2016, pp. 114–20.

Gunn, Bill, director. *Ganja & Hess*. Kelly-Jordan Enterprises, 1973.

Hairston, Andrea. "Dismantling the Echo Chamber: On *Africa SF*." *Los Angeles Review of Books*, 16 Jan. 2014, https://lareviewofbooks.org/article/dismantling-echo-chamber-africa-sf/#!. Accessed 1 Mar. 2018.

———. *Mindscape*. Aqueduct, 2006.

———. *Redwood and Wildfire*. Aqueduct, 2011.

———. *Will Do Magic for Small Change*. Aqueduct, 2016.

Hansberry, Lorraine. *Les Blancs: The Collected Last Plays: The Drinking Gourd/What Use Are Flowers?*. 1970. Edited by Robert Nemiroff, Vintage, 1994.

Hemenway, Robert E. *Zora Neale Hurston: A Literary Biography*. U of Illinois P, 1980.

Hirschberg, Lynn. "Jordan Peele Reinvents the Hitchcock Heroine with the Help of Janelle Monáe," *W Magazine*, 20 Feb. 2018, https://www.wmagazine.com/story/jordan-peele-janelle-monae-hitchcock. Accessed 1 Mar. 2018.

Hopkinson, Nalo. *Brown Girl in the Ring*. Warner, 1998.

———. *Midnight Robber*. Warner, 2000.

———. *The Salt Roads*. Warner, 2003.

Hurston, Zora Neale. *Moses, Man of the Mountain*. 1939. Harper Perennial, 1990.

———. *Mules and Men*. 1935. Harper Perennial, 1990.

———. *The Sanctified Church: The Folklore Writings of Zora Neale Hurston*. Turtle Island, 1981.

———. *Tell My Horse: Voodoo and Life in Haiti and Jamaica*. 1938. Harper Perennial, 1990.

———. *Their Eyes Were Watching God*. 1937. Harper Perennial, 2006.

Johnson, Alaya Dawn. *Moonshine*. St. Martin's Griffin, 2010.

Jones, Gayl. *Corregidora*. Random House, 1975.

———. *Eva's Man*. Random House, 1976.

Laymon, Kiese. *Long Division*. Agate Bolden, 2013.

Lorde, Audre. *Sister Outsider*. Ten Speed Press, 1984.

Morrison, Toni. *Song of Solomon*. Alfred Knopf, 1977.

Mosley, Walter. *47*. Little, Brown, 2006.

Naylor, Gloria. *Mama Day*. Vintage, 1988.

Okorafor, Nnedi. *Binti*. Tor, 2015.

Orwell, George. *Nineteen Eighty-Four*. 1949. Signet Classic, 1961.

Peele, Jordan, director. *Get Out*. Universal Pictures, 2017.

Salaam, Kiini Ibura. *When the World Wounds*. Third Man Press, 2016.

Samatar, Sofia. "The Red Thread." *Lightspeed Magazine*, June 2016, http://www.lightspeedmagazine.com/fiction/the-red-thread/. Accessed 28 Feb. 2018.

———. *A Stranger in Olondria*. Small Beer, 2013.

Sayles, John, director. *The Brother from Another Planet*. Cinecom, 1984.

Shange, Ntozake. *Sassafrass, Cypress & Indigo*. St. Martin's, 1982.

Sorensen, Leif. "Dubwise into the Future: Versioning Modernity in Nalo Hopkinson." *African American Review*, vol. 47, nos. 2/3, 2014, pp. 267–83.

Thomas, Sheree R., editor. *Dark Matter: A Century of Speculative Fiction from the African Diaspora*. Warner, 2000.

Walker, Alice, editor. *I Love Myself When I Am Laughing and Then Again When I Am Looking Mean and Impressive: A Zora Neale Hurston Reader*. The Feminist Press, 1979.

———. *Possessing the Secret of Joy*. Harcourt Brace Jovanovich, 1992.

———. *The Temple of My Familiar*. Harcourt, 1989.

PART TWO

Afrofuturism in Literary History

FACING: Stacey Robinson, "Radical Imagination," 2018

CHAPTER 3

This Time for Africa!
Afrofuturism as Alternate (American) History

De Witt Douglas Kilgore

Afrofuturist narrative places the persons and ambitions of the African diaspora at the center of history. What kind of difference this action makes is important to our understanding of science fiction (SF) as a genre that often defaults to a liberal-leaning but Eurocentric view of history and social change. This chapter will argue that an Afrofuturist perspective makes a critical difference in alternate history, an important subgenre of SF. It focuses on two alternate history novels in which the American South is radically changed by the cultural and political dominance of Africa's New World immigrants. In the first of these two novels, *Lion's Blood* (2002), Europe never achieves global hegemony. Instead, Steven Barnes gives that troubled achievement to the peoples of an Islamic Africa. Egypt and Abyssinia (Ethiopia) are the great powers that conquer significant portions of the Western Hemisphere and use enslaved whites to create large and prosperous plantations. The second novel is Terry Bisson's *Fire on the Mountain* (1988), a critical utopia in which John Brown's 1859 Harper's Ferry raid opens the way to a future in which the American South is home to a socialist, Africentric nation.[1] While a black American authors the first novel and a white Ameri-

---

1. Some readers might wonder why we have included studies of earlier works in a collection called *Literary Afrofuturism in the Twenty-First Century*. As noted in the introduction to this volume, our primary goal as editors is to showcase the ideas about and

can writes the second, both writers create alternate histories in which African peoples are in control of global technology, culture, and politics.

The approach of this chapter is to examine Africentric work by black and white authors alike so we might gain a measure of how influential Afrofuturism, as a "quintessentially black" practice, has been on SF as a whole (Dery 13). These storytellers assume that peoples and cultures of African descent may be active historical agents in the past and future. This presumption is not, however, sufficient to make a novel or story Afrofuturist, even if it uses knowledge of Africa, its peoples, cultures, and diaspora. SF is littered with tales of futures in which people of African descent are marked as enemies of a benevolent, legitimate, and white *civitas*. King Wallace's *The Next War: A Prediction* (1892) and Larry Niven and Jerry Pournelle's *Lucifer's Hammer* (1977) are representative of the species. In this strand of thought, it is only when people of color serve or are allied with white-dominated regimes that they become "good." By way of contrast, an Afrofuturist narrative assumes no such racial subordination. Instead, Afrofuturist writing: 1) seeks to switch the order of received racial hierarchy, thereby undermining the naturalness of our customary pecking order (Barnes) and/or 2) allows for the emergence of an Africentric fusion politics that links people across class and race lines against the feudalism inherent in capitalist economies (Bisson). Each aspect proves anti-racist in its subversion of whiteness as a virtue that orders all our social relations.

As SF, Afrofuturism has found itself in a genre that seems ill suited to its purposes. For much of its history, SF paid obeisance to the notion that whiteness is a sign of the most advanced human class. Its writers assumed that any good future would be an invention of the West's white-dominated technoscientific elite. Under this paradigm any future history that placed African or Asian civilizations at the wheel of destiny would be dystopian at best, apocalyptic at worst. This presumption drives the narrative of *Farnham's Freehold* (1964), Robert A. Heinlein's anxious speculation about the danger of a black-ruled future.[2]

---

issues in Afrofuturism that concern artists and scholars alike in the present moment. While these twenty-first-century concerns map most clearly to twenty-first-century texts, our authors demonstrate that such concerns can also be used to recover and reread earlier Afrofuturist texts as well (especially as many of those texts anticipate the issues that have become central to creators and scholars of black speculative fiction today).

2. The centrality of white patriarch Hugh Farnham's perspective indicates that Heinlein's Afrofuture is only a way of delivering his character (and by extension author and reader) from imbrication in contemporary racism. Hugh and his family escape to an alternate reality where they establish a libertarian domain that we can assume is post-

By contrast, the number of SF stories endorsing futures led by benevolent African and Asian civilizations is small. A. M. Lightner's *The Day of the Drones* (1969), Mack Reynold's North Africa Trilogy (1961–1978),[3] Michael Moorcock's *The Land Leviathan* (1974), and Kim Stanley Robinson's *The Years of Rice and Salt* (2002), the last two of which are adventurous alternate histories, are notable exceptions to the rule.[4] The reluctance to see human civilization as a collective endeavor across our differences means that, despite its press, SF's social ambitions are often quite modest. Before the flowering of Afrofuturist writing by black authors, Africanist speculation amongst white writers leaned toward pessimistic forecasts at worst and extrapolations in which an African culture is "saved" as a utopian enclave at best, as in Mike Resnick's *Kirinyaga* (1998). All too often the habit of whiteness evident in SF's mainstream restricts its writers to projecting a whitewashed history into the future (Young 10–11).[5] However, as the novels above indicate, this imaginative lack does not exhaust the genre's potential. It has a formal malleability that leaves room for alternatives other than those that make whiteness the requirement for human progress.

Appreciating Afrofuturism's potential as a persuasive part of SF's imaginative toolkit requires that we consider it an extrapolation not only of present potential but also of history, a past that is prologue to what we could be. Despite our understandable insistence that history is a stable monument—the faithful record of things past—our telling and writing of it is as vulnerable to our desires and interests as the futures we create. Professional history does have evidentiary protocols that differentiate it from fiction as a mode of writing. However, our evidence is never complete, and how we organize and interpret it shifts according to our angle of vision.[6]

---

racial or, at least, color-blind. In any case, Farnham's eventual goal is to make sure the novel's nightmare of black supremacy never happens.

3. That trilogy includes *Blackman's Burden* (1961), *Border, Breed nor Birth* (1962), and *The Best Ye Breed* (1978).

4. For more on the incipiently Afrofuturist strand of Africentric speculative fiction written by white British and American authors see Kilgore's "Afrofuturism" (2014).

5. Helen Young's diagnosis of the ways in which preoccupation with whiteness influences the creation of fantasy applies to its generic neighbor. She argues that "Habits of Whiteness in Fantasy . . . simultaneously influence who can be present, and what is seen, thought, and done, by creating patterns of bodies and spaces alike" (11).

6. Hayden White's thoughts on how we interpret historical storytelling is of great value in understanding how playful fictions of past events might help remind us of how "our own culture can provide a host of different meanings for the same set of events" (125).

If we accept that history is an artful science, then we can appreciate the stakes when a fiction writer plays with it. The counterfactuals of alternate history embody thought experiments that help us value the history we have. If things could have happened differently what does that teach us about the past we accept as nonfiction? Allohistorical narratives do not replace actual history but throw it into relief. If the game is well played, we receive an invitation to perform a narrative inquiry that reflects on what our histories mean and how they are used. If history is a foretaste of things to come—arguably the grounding assumption of SF—then creative engagement with it may open up neglected aspects of our common heritage. As a fantastic recasting of the past, alternate history helps transform "what if" into "what then."

In turn if Afrofuturism gives us permission to dream worlds in which African diasporic cultures determine the nature and direction of human civilization then it also prompts us to reimagine the past. Any future we expect is always only an extrapolation of the histories we tell. Until the mid-twentieth century, American academic and popular historians were strongly influenced by the post–Civil War ideology that celebrated the defeated Confederacy as a valiant Lost Cause in defense of an honorable way of life. As David W. Blight argues, the explicitly racist caste of this narrative was a critical feature of reconciling Northern and Southern whites. It was also a powerful ideological tool for Americans "determined to control, if not destroy, the rise of black people in the social order" (*Race and Reunion* 266). That race-based reunification devalued the historical experience of African Americans, the trauma of slavery, and the ways they struggled for freedom (Hall 449). Black Americans as active agents of history had to be written out of it. While this pernicious historiography has been challenged and overturned, it continues to haunt our political culture. Breaking with this emphasis has been hard work, to be accomplished not only by assertions of its explanatory inadequacy. A partial solution lies in the crafting of belief and evidence through affective counternarratives that reject white supremacy as an attractive frame for national identity. That is what Steven Barnes and Terry Bisson achieve in the Afrofuturist alternative histories they have written.

Reversing Racial Hierarchies in Steven Barnes's *Lion's Blood*

Steven Barnes's *Lion's Blood: A Novel of Slavery and Freedom in an Alternate America* is unique in using alternate history as a vehicle for imagining an

American South that eliminates Europe as a dominant force in its history. While his historical world does contain Asian and indigenous peoples, they are mostly mentioned to illustrate a world order in which African, Asian, and Indigenous American civilizations are great powers. Barnes's main strategy in this novel is to flip the historic relationship between black and white, the assumed hierarchy that places one race over another. In a very different nineteenth century, technologically and culturally advanced Africans have colonized what in our history is the Old South. It is a colony that owes fealty to the Islamic thrones of Egypt and Abyssinia, the dominant world powers of this timeline.

In this world Europe develops neither the cultural nor technological innovations that made some of its nations world powers. It is divided between a fairly unified Viking civilization and tribal societies—the Irish, the Franks, the Germans huddled in defensive crannogs—which the Northmen raid for goods and slaves. Islam is the dominant global religion while Christianity has few adherents beyond Europe's native tribes. As Isiah Lavender III notes, "'America' has been settled by Islamic Africa, not by Christian Europe" (81). This critical change carefully delineates the ethos of Barnes's alternate history even if it does not change the structural similarities between the novel's slave system and that of our own history.

By making a deliberate break with the familiar story of European expansion, Barnes makes room for a novel in which Africans take the lead, resulting in a narrative that is both celebratory and cautious. His rhetorical strategy invites us to celebrate African, Arabic, and Islamic derived knowledge and achievements. However, his alternate New World is a profoundly conservative theocracy that limits self-governance to an aristocratic class of black male landowners. Chattel slavery is the foundation of Bilalistan's economy and the institution that organizes relations between black masters and white servants. Thus, Barnes designs his fiction as a direct counterpoint to the actual history of slavery and freedom in America. As Lavender argues, the familiar "racialized formations of American culture" are thereby upended (80). The contrast is so obvious that we cannot help but take on a kind of historical double-consciousness. *Lion's Blood*'s reversal of racial polarity prompts us to consider the wrongs of slavery and freedom from a vantage that does not privilege whiteness. To be white is to be abject in a history that has been blackwashed.[7]

---

7. The world that Barnes creates for *Lion's Blood* and *Zulu Heart* (2003) is also in direct conversation with Heinlein's *Farnham's Freehold*. The African colonists of both novels are aristocratic slaveholders, masters of what we recognize as an evil system. Barnes's critique of that order is in ideological sympathy with Heinlein's own.

The length of Barnes's narrative attests to the effort he puts into lending his Africentric alternate history a realistic feel. It shows in the lives he chooses for his characters, the language they use, and how they understand their positions within the social order. The first novel of Barnes's two-book project is a kind of Prince and Pauper *bildungsroman*. Its principal players are Aidan O'Dere, a white Irish slave, and Kai Jallaleddin ibn Rashid al Kushi, the second son who inherits his father's princely estate—and all its slaves, including Aidan—when his father and older brother are killed. Barnes establishes an uneasy friendship between the two that highlights the stark rules of a rigid racial hierarchy. Their relationship invokes a Kiplingesque logic in which two strong men come together "though they come from the ends of the earth," their masculinity and common valor overcome the divisions of border, breed, and birth (Kipling 1–3).[8] Readers easily sympathize with the wrongs done to the Irish slave and his dreams of freedom. The narrative challenge is to understand Kai's position and accept his evolution toward the idea that whites may have rights to independence that a black man is bound to respect.[9]

When Kai first meets Aidan, he is a lonely if privileged boy. In Aidan he finds a playmate that helps relieve his alienation. The relationship is, however, not equal. Kai initially sees Aiden as little more than a pet with whom he can while away time between the studies required of Bilalistan's Muslim aristocrats (113, 136). As they grow older, their relationship evolves to the point where Kai is willing to see Aidan as "exceptional," a slave who is a bit better than the other whites his family owns (214). Young Kai understands their relationship as part of a perfect world ordered "by Allah's design" (87). He believes that whites should be grateful to a society that has rescued them from savagery and embrace their station in it (184). When Aidan rebels against the restrictions that would deny him his choice of mate (Sofia, a slave who is also Kai's concubine), Kai attempts to assert his dominance by force (303). And remember that Kai *is* one of the novel's most sympathetic and moral characters.

As a youngster Kai learns and believes that African achievements are superior to those of Europe (214). More often than not, white "genius" is

---

However, while Heinlein's New World Africans are almost childlike in their vile decadence, Barnes's Bilalistani are mature agents of the most advanced civilization on the planet.

8. See Kipling's "The Ballad of East and West" (1889) in *Selected Prose and Poetry of Rudyard Kipling* (1937).

9. See Paul Finkelman's study *Dred Scott v. Sandford* (1997) for an explanation of Chief Justice Roger B. Taney's famous turn of phrase.

dismissed as a bizarre exception, as in the case of Leonardo Da Vinci, who is called the "the Mad Frank" (272). At other times, it gets "blackwashed" to sustain the metanarrative of black superiority, as with the fact that Alexander the Great, the founding Pharaoh of the modern Egyptian empire, was Greek and not African (140). Kai, who is naturally inspired by black Africa's glorious history, sincerely hopes to make his own contribution (142). Through Kai's internal understanding, Barnes illuminates the almost insuperable differences that exist between white slaves and their black masters. In *Lion's Blood* the bedroom and the battlefield are the only places where these differences break down. In these arenas, white women (bedroom) and white men (battlefield) achieve some measure of autonomy and even the promise of manumission (524).

What makes Barnes's effort incipiently Afrofuturist is both the wealth of cultural detail he brings to Bilalistani society and the clear implication that the people of its ruling classes actually deserve their high status. Let us take these two in turn. First, high status: In *Farnham's Freehold*, Heinlein signals the illegitimacy of the New World African culture by its decadence and cannibalism. By contrast Barnes produces an episteme that is characterized by high levels of intellectual and martial accomplishment. It is a world that is ruled by laws and mores that make it no less livable or admirable than life in our own history. While Barnes implies that some form of racial egalitarianism is possible for this world, any conceivable future derived from it would be ineradicably Islamic and African in character. Second, this forecast becomes credible with the wealth of cultural detail that Barnes creates for Bilalistan. In our own world we are intermittently aware that African Americans are a composite group composed of a wide variety of African, indigenous, Asian, and European ethnicities. This results from a peculiar institution that routinely stripped enslaved Africans of language and culture. *Lion's Blood*'s slaves are similarly handled and herded together to take up their role as living tools. (Aidan and his folk prove exceptions to this rule because the Wakil of Dar Kush is more enlightened than his neighbors. He allows his slaves to keep their names and allows a measure of religious independence [153].) Bilalistan's African colonialists, however, remain connected to their cultural roots. Ancestries invoked in major or minor ways include Zulu, Dogon, Yoruban, Nigerian, and Ethiopian lineages. As writers such as Nalo Hopkinson and Nnedi Okorafor have shown, futures extrapolated from these backgrounds would organize the world differently. This comports well with Barnes's presentation of blackness as a cornucopia that contains multitudes instead of a singular exotic dystopia. Afrofuturism imagines those differences as an ordinary good.

The episteme that Barnes crafts for *Lion's Blood* is a thickly described and functional secondary world. However, the sociopolitical order of his creation has more in common with the feudal aristocracies of modern fantasy than the historical United States, a putatively modern democratic republic. This move lessens the political and ideological pressure on his imaginary plantocracy. The existence of chattel slavery does not seem out of character in a monarchal system that determines social and political rank (economic power) almost exclusively by heredity. In Barnes's world the political arguments that challenged the royal and noble regimes of Europe in the eighteenth and nineteenth centuries seem not to exist. The writer emphasizes the achievement of liberty through the action of male and female bodies. Freedom becomes less a political issue than a personal one, to be recognized or granted not as a matter of rights conferred by political theory but by affinities secured through personal relationships. Barnes creates no ground in which a robustly democratic revolutionary movement could flower.

His black elite is, for the most part, not confused by any political philosophy that undermines the morality of a system that gives them clear physical as well as emotional benefits. Barnes's secondary world functions as a critique of our own world, up to a point. Its bifurcated personal narrative undermines the legitimacy of a slave power that secures black dominance. However, it is also clear that the Bilalistan aristocracy has earned its primacy. Barnes constantly reminds us that the Bilalistani are a martial as well as a highly cultured and religious people, and are the subjects of a powerful, global civilization. Enslaved whites are right to rebel against their condition—and seek to preserve their folkways—but must learn from their masters if they truly seek liberty and prosperity. Rebellion of the kind we know in our own world seems out of reach. An independence movement founded on abstract principles like the rights of man make little sense in a world that can articulate no alternative to the feudal relations of blood and soil. This is the core absence in Barnes's Afrocentric timeline. It organizes the ethos in which his characters act and through which readers are prompted to endorse both sides of the master-slave paradigm. The conservative character of this conception should be apparent. Barnes may accept the idea that "all men are created equal," but he certainly does not create an episteme in which all people can think themselves self-evidently equal.

Some crucial points exist that we must recognize before we move to our model of a full-blown science fictional Afrofuture. Barnes's emergent Afrofuturism establishes a world in which black people (especially the upper class) never labor under any presumption of social, political, or economic disability. This does not mean, however, that the writer gives us an Afrofuture whose politics we easily agree with or admire (even as we enjoy the ride). This world may contain "revolutionary manumission abolitionists," but we are not shown those disreputable people (Miranda and McCarter 27). The republican traditions that created our own democracies have no real meaning in a nineteenth century completely controlled by aristocratic slaveholders (there are no classes of Northern industrialists and shop keepers to serve as a political counterweight to the Barnes plantocracy). *Lion's Blood*'s white slaves have less philosophical cover than the black slaves of our own history. The latter had access to a political tradition and a language that could challenge the hypocrisy that attended the founding of a "free" nation. Even as we struggle with the hypocrisies that blunted the best ideals of our own revolutionary tradition, we would be very different without it. A future in which that particular history does not exist is unlikely to be guided by ordinary men or women of any race.

While Barnes proffers a future in which racial reform comes from the top down, Bisson proposes one that rises from the bottom. His Afrofuture results from a successful slave rebellion that gives birth to a black nation founded on the revolutionary tradition absent in Barnes's allohistory. Bisson's counterfactual also challenges us with a more direct address and commentary on the real history of American white republicanism, slavery, and civil war. The writer imagines a turning point where a crusading anti-slavery, anti-racist movement allied to the international left decisively defeats America's Southern plantocracy before it can metastasize into the Confederacy and Jim Crow. He then unveils a historical alternative that seems better than our own comparatively compromised reality.

Africentric Fusion Politics in Terry Bisson's *Fire on the Mountain*

What makes *Fire on the Mountain* Afrofuturist is author Terry Bisson's use of an historical and narrative strategy that satirizes our own history. It takes on the historical revisionism that followed Reconstruction and championed white supremacy as the price of union between North and South. It is told primarily from the viewpoints of an ex-slave, his Nova African granddaughter, and a white Southern abolitionist. As part of his project, Bisson mostly avoids the individualist warrior ethos that characterizes Barnes's counterfactual. When civil war comes, it recedes into the background. This opens us to what an alternate history looks like from the perspective of the initially ordinary people who move to fight America's white plantocracy. Liberty is not conferred by a supreme power that finally recognizes the valor and sexiness of their subalterns; instead, former slaves and their allies wrest it from the plantocracy itself. Freedom also emerges from political philosophies directly articulated by both historical and fictional characters.

The resulting utopian alternate history serves as a useful model for the "visionary fiction" advocated by Adrienne Maree Brown and Walidah Imarisha (4). Such fiction is "science fiction that has relevance toward building new, freer worlds from the main strain of science fiction, which most often reinforces dominant narratives of power" (Brown and Imarisha 4). This way of seeing the strand of Afrofuturism that Bisson models links the form to an explicitly progressive political agenda, one that seeks to change the world as we know it.[10]

Bisson takes as the turning point of his novel the historical reality of John Brown's raid on the Harper's Ferry Armory. In Bisson's alternate history, Harriet Tubman joins Brown and the attack is successful. That success sparks a slave rebellion that energizes the abolition movement and an international socialist crusade. The slave rebellion evolves into an independence movement and the founding of a new nation, Nova Africa, in the territory that actually harbored the Confederate States. In this history John Brown, Frederick Douglass, and Harriet Tubman are honored as the founders of a wealthy, prosperous, and socialist nation that becomes a world power. Bisson thus produces a sharp break from conventional alternatives that can only imagine fascist or liberal Confederacies in which white nationalism secures a capitalist future.[11]

In *Fire on the Mountain*, Captain Brown and General Tubman take the heroic moral space that General Robert E. Lee occupies in Lost Cause revision as well as in most alternate Civil War stories.[12] In a key passage, Bisson has Douglass give a speech that spurs Northern abolitionists into active support of the rebellion against slave power. This speech establishes the immediatist philosophy driving Bisson's alternate history:

> Some of you whites would give the African his freedom, but not give him the gun with which to take it.

---

10. Brown and Imarisha include an excerpt of *Fire on the Mountain* in an anthology of "visionary fiction" that "highlights that change is collective; and is not neutral—its purpose is social change and societal transformation" (279).

11. For example, Ward Moore imagines an expansive, imperialist Confederate States of America in *Bring the Jubilee* (1953).

12. In his chronicles of a world in which the Confederacy wins the Civil War, Harry Turtledove maintains the legend of Lee as a heroic, toughly moral character.

Not Brown.

Some of us Africans would ask for freedom, but not take up a Sharps and fight for it.

Not Tubman.

Not those of us who are with them tonight, either in spirit or On The Mountain . . . those of us who are True Abolitionists . . . sons of Man and Reason, whether African or European, white or black, slave or free . . . (52–53)

Here Bisson ventriloquizes a full-throated abolitionism of a kind that is either defeated or virtually irrelevant in the counterfactual mainstream.[13] Douglass's invocation of "Man" and "Reason" takes us back to the radical rhetoric of Thomas Paine and the other founding writers of the American republic.[14] Within Bisson's continuity, it replaces Douglass's actual 1852 speech, "What to the Slave Is the Fourth of July?" Following the logic of Bisson's counterfactual, Douglass may still give a version of this speech, but it would celebrate the independence of a Southern nation ruled by the descendants of African slaves, not a requiem for betrayed ideals. (Bisson makes sure that Nova Africa also celebrates its Independence Day on 4 July. Like so many of his wry jokes, this challenges us to reevaluate sacralized events in our own history.) Thus, Bisson provides an allohistorical salvation of what, as David Blight has argued, was the project of Douglass's later years: giving speeches "about trying to hold onto an emancipationist, abolitionist memory of the Civil War and Reconstruction" in a nation that wanted to forget.[15]

Conventionally, an alternate history that does not valorize our familiar world is bound to be bad, especially if people of color gain directive power within it. Bisson counters this pessimistic scenario and builds an allohistory in which a multiracial international left builds a finer world. As a result, the Civil War looks quite different:

---

13. The gradual emancipation of the slave is a hallmark of liberal allohistorical narratives like Harry Turtledove's *The Guns of the South* (1992). The novel's triumphant Confederacy abolishes slavery in deference to what it learns of our own history. Black liberation remains, however, contingent on white assent and regulation (500–503). This is very different from the "if not now then when" sensibility that fired the Civil Rights movement of the 1960s, for example.

14. Thomas Paine, in his pamphlet *Common Sense* (1776), declares, "The cause of America is in a great measure the cause of all mankind" (2).

15. See David W. Blight's Lecture 26, entitled "Race and Reunion: The Civil War in American Memory," in his Open Yale Course podcast.

> Not only Brown but Tubman lived; our gallant Tubman, it was in fact she who . . . broke the encirclement with the first international detachment of Haitian cavalry, of Garibaldini in their red silks, of Cherokee and Creek warriors, and Pennsylvania Molly Maguires. . . . Meanwhile, to the south, Atlanta was burning, and the Cherokee courthouse raid has filled Asheville with troops. . . . Like a fire, abolition was consuming the South. (131)

The result is not a racial holocaust but an accomplished present in which Africa is a continent of "sweeping highways" and "soaring cities" as well as "grand plains" (38), there is a space station named Kilimanjaro (23), and PASA (the Pan Africa Space Administration) puts the first humans on Mars to mark the centenary of the victory at Harpers Ferry (63). And since—in this world—socialism is hegemonic, universal health care guarantees human dignity. There are no bad teeth even in the backward border regions of the USSA [United Socialist States of America], the northern remnant of the old Union (60).

Our own history is represented as trashy fiction in *John Brown's Body*, a half-century-old speculative fantasy that the inhabitants of Bisson's alternative see as a species of vulgar white nationalism. The alternative history it imagines is our own. The North wins the Civil War against "the slave owners, who are trying to set up a separate country—like Nova Africa, as a matter of fact, on pretty much the same territory" (81). When the paperback's plot is explained, the black woman through whose eyes we see much of the present is incredulous: "'Ridiculous!' said Yasmin. 'The author would have all of history hanging on a rope with poor old Captain Brown'" (154–55). Her daughter supplies the punchline: "That's why I don't like science fiction. It's always junk like that. I'll take the real world, thanks" (155).

In *Fire on the Mountain*, Bisson creates not only an alternate history but also an Afrofuturist emplotment that diverges from the common fictional treatment of the Africentric future as something to be feared and fought. Through his critical utopian vision, the world finally slips the bonds of a benighted feudalism for a socialist world order whose plasma airship technology seems to sing for joy (132). The salvation of a capitalism freed from the economic and moral reality of slavery is exchanged for a socialism that can fulfill (small-d) democratic promise, creating lives and states that are released from gross inequality. Everyday life, permanently organized around what Raymond Williams might call a new "structure of feeling," disposes of feudalist class and race hierarchies (82). Bisson's Afrofuturism challenges the complacent assumption that our own history has led to the best of all possible worlds. Experimenting with historical continuity in this way allows us to test our understanding of the past and the plots we make from whatever evidence it leaves behind. Taking seriously the alternate history genre as a necessary resource for Afrofuturism may help us with the continuing struggle to open up new interpretive ground and to see the liberatory potential in sensibilities far from today's conservative leaning political center.

The Afrofuturism modeled in Barnes and Bisson's alternative histories have the following features in common: 1) It places black people in control of the dominant record of important public events and significant persons and proposes that cultures, beliefs, and techniques of African origin could unleash the human mind and spirit. 2) It takes as a given that African dominance could lead to a world in which *everyone* has a shot at life, liberty, and happiness. 3) It explores beyond the imaginative anemia that predicates human historical progress on a primarily Anglo-Saxon, Teutonic, or more expansively, Celtic ascendancy. 4) It dispenses with the liberal, meritocratic notion that blacks must always prove themselves worthy of equality in a white-dominated world order. 5) It may produce, for the reader, what Walter Benjamin calls "presence of mind . . . an extract of the future, and precise awareness of the present moment more decisive than foreknowledge of the most distant events" (98). In other words, Afrofuturism attempts to produce knowledge of a reality that is often and usually overlooked: the active history and affirmative presence of people of color in the making and maintenance of life. This is essential if we wish to break the habit of whiteness Helen Young cites as a feature of fantastic literature and its discursive communities in *Race and Popular Fantasy Literature: Habits of Whiteness* (2016). What we may infer from these points is a way of Afrofuturist thinking that could make solutions necessary to human progress possible.

Works Cited

Barnes, Steven. *Lion's Blood*. Warner, 2002.

———. *Zulu Heart*. Warner, 2003.

Benjamin, Walter. "Madame Ariane: Second Courtyard on the Left." *One-Way Street*, NLB, 1979, pp. 98–99.

Bisson, Terry. *Fire on the Mountain*. Arbor House/William Morrow, 1988.

Blight, David W. "Race and Reunion: The Civil War in American Memory." *The Civil War and Reconstruction Era, 1861–1877*, http://oyc.yale.edu/history/hist-119/lecture-26. Accessed 22 Jun. 2017.

———. *Race and Reunion: The Civil War in American Memory*. Harvard UP, 2001.

Brown, Adrienne Maree, and Walidah Imarisha, editors. *Octavia's Brood: Science Fiction Stories from Social Justice Movements*. AK Press, 2015.

Dery, Mark. "Black to the Future: Afro-Future 1.0." *Afro-Future Females: Black Writers Chart Science Fiction's Newest New Wave Trajectory,* edited by Marleen S. Barr, The Ohio State UP, 2008, pp. 6–13.

Finkelman, Paul. *Dred Scott v. Sandford: A Brief History with Documents.* Bedford Books, 1997.

Hall, Jacquelyn. "'You Must Remember This': Autobiography as Social Critique." *Journal of American History,* vol. 85, no. 2, 1998, pp. 439–65.

Heinlein, Robert A. *Farnham's Freehold.* G. P. Putnam's Sons, 1964.

Kilgore, De Witt Douglas. "Afrofuturism." *The Oxford Handbook of Science Fiction,* edited by Rob Latham, Oxford UP, 2014, pp. 561–72.

Kipling, Rudyard. *Selected Prose and Poetry of Rudyard Kipling.* Garden City Publishing Company, 1937.

Lavender III, Isiah. *Race in American Science Fiction.* Indiana UP, 2011.

Lightner, A. M. *The Day of the Drones.* Bantam Books, 1970.

Miranda, Lin-Manuel, and Jeremy McCarter. *Hamilton, the Revolution.* Grand Central Publishing, 2016.

Moorcock, Michael. *The Land Leviathan.* Doubleday, 1974.

Moore, Ward. *Bring the Jubilee.* Ballantine Books, 1953.

Niven, Larry, and Jerry Pournelle. *Lucifer's Hammer.* Playboy Press, 1977.

Paine, Thomas. *Common Sense.* 1776. Dover, 1997.

Resnick, Mike. *Kirinyaga: A Fable of Utopia.* Del Rey, 1998.

Reynolds, Mack. *The Best Ye Breed.* Ace Books, 1978.

———. *Blackman's Burden.* 1961. Ace Books, 1972.

———. *Border, Breed nor Birth.* 1962. Ace Books, 1972.

Robinson, Kim Stanley. *The Years of Rice and Salt.* Bantam Books, 2002.

Turtledove, Harry. *The Guns of the South.* Ballantine Books, 1992.

Wallace, King. *The Next War: A Prediction.* Martyn Publishing House, 1892.

White, Hayden. *The Fiction of Narrative: Essays on History, Literature, and Theory 1957–2007.* John Hopkins UP, 2010.

Williams, Raymond. *The Long Revolution.* 1961. Parthian, 2011.

Young, Helen. *Race and Popular Fantasy Literature: Habits of Whiteness.* Routledge, 2016.

CHAPTER 4

Middle Age, Mer People, and the Middle Passage

Nalo Hopkinson's Afrofuturist Journeying in *The New Moon's Arms*

Gina Wisker

In her introduction to the coedited anthology *So Long Been Dreaming*, Nalo Hopkinson tackles head on the main issue that troubles black writers of speculative fiction: the invading, colonizing, and othering imperatives that underlie so much of the genre. As Hopkinson notes in terms of her own creative practice:

> Much of the folklore on which I draw is European. Even the form in which I write is European. Arguably, one of the most familiar memes of science fiction is that of going to foreign countries and colonizing the natives, and as I've said elsewhere, for many of us, that's not a thrilling adventure story; it's non-fiction, and we are on the wrong side of the strange-looking ship that appears out of nowhere. To be a person of colour writing science fiction is to be under suspicion of having internalized one's colonization. I knew that I'd have to fight this battle at some point in my career. (7)

One thing Hopkinson does so well is to utterly undermine some of the premises on which European folk tales, the fantastic, and science fiction (SF) are based, premises of Otherness and absence informing texts that fail to represent African-originated people or only cast them as aliens to be changed, colonized, and destroyed.

Fighting battles of absence in history and of internalized colonization is a strategy successfully used by Caribbean artists such as performance poet Merle Collins since the 1980s. Collins talks of the need to refuse history and grand historical moments so that the stories of those who do not identify with the invader, settler, colonizer, enslaver are heard above those historically embedded narratives. Accordingly, she uses Anansi storytelling time, folk characters, and the supernatural to retell history from other points of view than that of white, male colonialists, as in "Crick Crack, Monkey" (1985), where Collins uses a myth of a tree cracking each time a monkey lies to rewrite history from the perspective of the silenced. As such, the poem shows how history has been twisted. Abolitionists are celebrated, but had there been no transatlantic slavery, they would not have been necessary in the first place. As she puts it in the poem, the hunter is not the one whose story should be told, but rather that of the hunted: the lioness. Collins untwists the twisted history and looks forward to the moment when the "lioness will be her own Historian," reempowering the silenced, persecuted, and hidden, indicating the perspective of those once Otherized, telling a different story than that of the lioness—and of Black women ("Crick Crack").

Like Merle Collins, Hopkinson aims to produce both a new narrative perspective and a new literary form, not just to write the new vision within the constraints of an older form rife with misrepresentation. In the introduction to *So Long Been Dreaming,* she responds thus to a friend's question about her work:

> "What do you think of Audre Lorde's comment that massa's tools will never dismantle massa's house?"
>
> "In my hands massa's tools don't dismantle massa's house—and in fact I don't want to destroy it so much as I want to undertake massive renovations—then build me a house of my own." (7)

Hopkinson's commitment to making SF new is expressed in both her editing practices and, of course, her own fiction writing. In *The New Moon's Arms,* she specifically combines the critical insights of postcolonial literature with the utopian bent of SF to rewrite the horror of the Middle Passage as a transformative moment that can usher in new futures where people of color celebrate their multiple, hybrid connections to one another and the world at large.

Afrofuturism, Postcolonial Literature, and SF

Afrofuturism is closely related to African and postcolonial speculative fiction in its challenge to the imperialist assumptions that guide so much of the genre. In a special issue of the *Cambridge Journal of Postcolonial Literary Inquiry*, Moradewun Adejunmobi maps a history of SF, African magical realism, and postcolonial horror that disturbs the complacency of colonial narratives alongside formulae for writing SF and begins to recognize as related to SF a feature of African magical realist and fantasy narratives. So, Adejunmobi recalls and highlights the recognition of these characteristic in texts "ranging from D. O. Fagunwa's *Forest of a Thousand Demons* to Amos Tutuola's *The Palm-Wine Drinkard* and Ben Okri's *The Famished Road*," arguing "it becomes increasingly clear how long African literature has been on the cusp of SF" (265).

In that same special issue, Magali Armillas-Tiseyra notes more specific connections between Afrofuturism and postcolonial SF:

> The continual invitation to conjecture in turn produces speculative histories, which point to possible alternatives (alternate histories and futures) at the same time as they call for critical reflection on history itself as narrative, the construction of which conditions our understanding of both the present and future. Speculative here is not only a synonym for conjecture; I also draw on the transitive sense of the verb "to speculate," as in: to consider, examine, reflect, or theorize upon something with close attention. Speculative histories do not just produce conjectural alternatives; in so doing, they further compel a critical analysis of the past, the present, and its possible futures. (273)

This invitation to speculate about other pasts, presents, and futures powerfully informs recent films such as American James Cameron's *Avatar* (2009) and South African Neil Blomkamp's *District 9* (2009), both of which serve as critical allegories of colonial encounters and offer a postcolonial critique of the misunderstanding and destruction at their hearts.

Given that Afrofuturism invites readers to consider other pasts as well as other presents and futures, it is no surprise that authors often draw upon another related literary genre in their creative enterprises: the postcolonial Gothic. Postcolonial Gothic writers dramatize, then move beyond, the oppressive misrepresentation of people who have historically been constructed as different, "otherized" in a colonial and imperial past that haunts those whose ancestors were oppressed; the oppressors themselves; and the places, spaces, and language involved in that history of oppression. Such authors seek to explore the melancholic mourning and loss, the invasive violent disturbance of those colonially affected histories and lives that have been hidden and denied. The postcolonial is, in a way, always well understood through the Gothic—so that the ever-present colonial past can be ironized and exposed, dubious histories can be uncovered, and wrong potentially righted through events in the text and suggestions beyond it. Postcolonial Gothic writers deal with issues of difference, otherizing, and acceptance, as well the need to address racism and reinstate the histories and myths of a largely hidden ancestry, and they do so by using the characteristics of their genre to reclaim the past, to revision a lived present, and to speculate about the future.

Wilson Harris emphasizes the power of imagination and writing, noting that the prison house of history can be destroyed and rebuilt in a liberating form by "the imagination of the folk involved in a crucial inner re-creative response to the violations of slavery," and that "the possibility exists for us to become involved in perspectives which can bring into play a figurative meaning beyond an apparently real world or prison of history" (27). The figures who convey such perspectives in the postcolonial Gothic include such postcolonial versions of classically horrifying, metamorphosizing, boundary-crossing creatures such as the vampire, the zombie, and, as we shall see in Nalo Hopkinson's fiction, the mermaid.

While postcolonial speculative storytelling provides Afrofuturist authors with tools to rethink our stories of the past, SF provides writers with techniques for dreaming of new futures. The value of SF is that it offers us the seemingly familiar, then emphasizes instead the strange, and that one of its orientations is toward an alternative, positive future—possibly even a utopia. Pioneering SF studies scholar Darko Suvin's notion of "cognitive estrangement," developed from Bertold Brecht's observation that "a representation which estranges is one which allows us to recognize its subject, but at the same time makes it seem unfamiliar" is central to this project (Brecht). Suvin explains, "In SF the attitude of estrangement—used by Brecht in a different way, within a still predominantly 'realistic' context—has grown into the *formal framework* of the genre" (11–12). This attitude couples with the story types most commonly associated with the genre—including "the Islands of the Blessed, utopias, fabulous voyages, planetary novels, *Staatsromane*, anticipations, and dystopias"—enables authors to seek "the ideal in the unknown" (11–12).

Some of these story types are mythic, some are fabulous, and some are based in popular culture. However, the underlying similarity seems to be estrangement from a commonly accepted norm and the imagining forward of a positive alternative future. Considered in these terms, Afrofuturism is predicated on a double estrangement because it estranges us from both our commonsense assumptions about the world and about the norms of much SF, which is often unquestioningly white, male, and imperialist in its base and direction. Such voyaging, imagining and seeking can be put to work to reinforce then validate embedded inequalities as if they were essential or even divine. This is a familiar colonizing technique. In Afrofuturism, it is exposed as a construct, a deadly technique, but exposing the constructedness opens the way to imagine forward differently.

Suvin treats SF as "a literary genre whose necessary and sufficient conditions are the presence and interaction of estrangement and cognition, and whose main formal device is an imaginative framework alternative to the author's empirical environment" (11–12). Myth is different, has a certain permanence, and for many fantastic forms the empirical environment can actually be quite limited and limiting. Cognitive estrangement is a key here. An essential element of both SF and the Gothic, cognitive estrangement might well be also seen as a version of defamiliarization. Such estrangement—from both history and futurity—teaches us that things, thoughts, and ways of being could be otherwise. This experience is not always positive at first for readers, since estrangement at first disturbs complacency and established (safe for some) but limiting readings of events, places, and people. However, such estrangement is a first necessary step toward enabling new energies, new modes of problem-solving, and new modes of imagination that enable authors to depict ways of being and seeing.

Hopkinson's splicing of folklore and myth with the postcolonial Gothic and SF in *The New Moon's Arms* can be seen as a movement beyond Suvin's position into something more hybrid, rich, diverse. In this she can be aligned with African and postcolonial SF writers, some of whom also merge the folktale and the mythic with SF, part perhaps of the challenge to the fixed versions of SF that they recognize as always casting African-originated people and often women, too, as threatening to an ethnic and gendered norm, as the Other, subordinate.[1]

---

1. For further discussion of African authors as both engaging and revising the thematic and stylistic conventions of SF, see Jessica Langer's *Science Fiction and Postcolonialism* (2011); Eric Smith's *Globalization, Utopia, and Postcolonial Science Fiction: New Maps of Hope* (2012); and Mark Bould's "African Science Fiction 101" (2015) as well as the special issue of *Paradoxa* that Bould edited on "African SF" (2013).

A major achievement of Hopkinson's writing is her refusal to be pigeonholed culturally and in terms of the forms of her writing. Her work is truly hybrid, diverse, rich and ever morphing, a characteristic most suitable for Afrofuturist work (even if that is a label I expect she would both recognize and find limiting).[2] It is alive, it draws in the postcolonial vision of not merely disinterring and condemning the ills of the past but of actively rewriting it, revaluing the marginalized and silenced and offering speculative visions of new futures that do not merely substitute the historically otherized for the historically centralized. Hopkinson's work is in a rich vital liminal intersection with, and relationship with, a range of writing approaches and genres or subgenres. It can be appreciated as postcolonial or diasporan because she speaks from, with, and through Caribbean and other African-originated folktales, and she uses imagery and language to create new worldviews and expressions that splice together our forgotten pasts and revitalize our dreams of the future.

When we think about Afrofuturism, we must consider the politics, practice, and imaginative representations of colonialism. Decolonization affects practices from everyday behavior to language expression to representations of history. Such efforts surely started in Africa, but they are now worldwide, and they attempt to free people from mind-sets that were developed and bolstered up in colonialism in its broadest sense—the concepts of domination and subordination of others, including their behaviors, beliefs, expressions, values, and rights. While it has a much longer history, decolonization in common parlance usually focuses on reacting against the effects of the Atlantic slave trade and the imperial control of Africa, India, and the Asian subcontinent.

There is an important point to be made to unravel and critique oppressive value systems, hierarchies of imagination and oppression enshrined in laws and language, but there is also a duty of care to consider how other constructions, representations, and behaviors can move on from this. Afrofuturism, in its focus on revising and undermining the legacies of imperialism and colonial world views that underpin so much SF, deliberately decolonizes those spaces, places, and expressions. Hopkinson's work recognizes the burden and freedom of varied traditional modes of expression that predate colonization and imperialism, or that have revisited it, or that have developed behind and in spite of it, or that are based in reaction to and rejection of it.

---

2. For more detail about Hopkinson's ambivalence toward the term "Afrofuturism," see the "Author Roundtable on Afrofuturism" included in this volume.

The New Moon's Arms: Righting Wrongs, Writing Forward

Nalo Hopkinson's fantastic Afrofuturist novel *The New Moon's Arms* is a story of recuperation, renewing energy, and celebration. In this novel, Hopkinson revisits a history of slavery and then rewrites and reimagines it forward. Here, the horrific experiences of the Middle Passage of transatlantic slavery that recurs so often in Caribbean and African American writing is transformed into a magical story of multigenerational survival, triumph, and connection. Marvelously energetic and creative, *The New Moon's Arms* focuses on the character of Chastity Lambkin, a middle-aged, menopausal woman who fights loudly for her right to be seen and who defiantly renames herself "Calamity" while secretly mourning the loss of the magical finding powers she had as a child. Calamity is in a liminal space, resentful and confused, struggling to retain her rather overdressed, highly sexualized, youthful sense of self while refusing the roles of mother and grandmother. In addition to juggling her own changing life, Calamity must deal with a recalcitrant lover, her daughter Ifoema's frustration with her, and her own anger toward Ifeoma's father, her gay teenage sweetheart/best friend Michael.

The disarray of Calamity's life is mirrored by the disarray of her home, the fictional Caribbean island of Dolorosse. The island has been taken over by multinational hotels and other businesses interested in exploiting Dolorosse's natural resources. The toll on the island and its inhabitants is formidable. For example, characters lament the loss of native bats, noting that "you don't see so many anymore" because "they used to roost on Tamany Heights [and] fill up the whole cliff wall," but sadly, "Tamany Heights was now the Grand Tamany Hotel" (28). Similarly, other characters mourn the loss of indigenous fish, explaining that the "saline plant been messing up the water from since. Only few little snappers in the nest nowadays. Going to be worse now we have two plants" (28). Conversations about these changes indicate only loss and a shrinking small world of pollution, takeovers, erasure, and absence.

But as the title of Hopkinson's novel suggests, life is cyclical, and the new moon brings with it the hope of a new and better future for Calamity and her island. Indeed, much like the story itself, *The New Moon's Arms* might be a rereading of the past and an imagining of a new future. The title has several potential sources, one a folk ballad, "Sir Patrick Spens," in which a deadly storm is foretold:

> "For late yestere'en I saw the new moon
> the auld moon in her arm"

"Oh no, alas," says Patrick Spens
"That means there'll be a deadly storm." (Childs)

There is indeed a storm in Hopkinson's story, but it does not foretell death. Instead, it washes up the mysterious child Agway, whose presence enables Calamity to connect with her past and turn her life around. This relationship turns the negative threat of the deadly storm into an omen of positive change.

Another possible source for Hopkinson's title is a symphonic piece called *The New Moon in the Old Moon's Arms* by contemporary composer Michael Kamen. Kamen explains that this work was "inspired by the industrious Anasau tribe, which inhabited the American Southwest" and "disappeared around 1300 AD." According to Kamen, his piece "evokes the spirit of the people who passed this way a thousand years ago." The moon—old and new—is a "glimpse of the future in the light of the past" (qtd. in Anderson). Each suggests change, and, in the Kamen piece, that history is being renewed and rewritten from a non-European perspective.

Whatever the source of her title, the project of renewing and rewriting history from non-European perspectives is indeed central to Hopkinson's novel. Much Afrofuturist criticism questions the absence of black humans in imaginative depictions of alternative worlds. By way of contrast, I see Hopkinson as speculating forward from absence, silence, and a variety of literary victim positions into positive and future adventures characterized by alternative power and values. This is not just a matter of ensuring we see cultural variety in a future state, but more a re-scrutiny of a longer span of time and representation, mixed with a very positive, often comic, and surprisingly bawdy celebration of disruption and change. In this Hopkinson resembles the energies of carnivalesque feminist writer Angela Carter, who talks of putting new wine in old bottles and enjoying the explosion (37).

Hopkinson's own carnivalesque bawdiness is apparent at the beginning of the novel when Calamity Lambkin finds a tragic passage of her life disrupted by a moment of high comedy. At Calamity's father's funeral, a loud local woman bursts her elastic and her drawers fall down around her ankles. In this liminal space between life and death and burial, the energy of the comic blurts in. Around the same time, Calamity recovers a brooch that was clearly stolen from her years ago. What follows soon after is the return of her own magical ability to find lost objects. The carnivalesque, bawdy comic causes a breach of order in the everyday and a breach in a constrained narrative. The moment represents a liminal space, one which opens up the opportunity of a new energy and the power of finding what was lost—the ability to rethink, reclaim, and revitalize what was suppressed and to move forward.

But *The New Moon's Arms* is more than just the story of how one particular black woman gets her groove back. Hopkinson links Calamity's reclaimed magical powers to her reclamation of Afrodiasporic history, reminding readers of the harsh silencing and official absence of African Americans from centuries and decades in history. Like the early pages of Toni Morrison's *Jazz* (1992), which opens a window on a vibrant creative period in African American history during the Harlem Renaissance, Hopkinson's *The New Moon's Arms* reimagines a particularly poignant moment in Afrodiasporic history.[3] It reopens the history of Dolorosse and its people, reimagining the arrival of the slave ships that brought Calamity's people to Dolorosse as well as the escape of the slaves overboard to a new freedom as they voluntarily transform themselves into free-ranging mer people rather than suffer as enslaved humans.

The mer people of Dolorosse's waters represent a creative transformational response to an intolerable death in life. The story of their origins is told from the perspective of a kidnapped African woman called the "dada-hair lady":

After a lifetime of misery she could never have imagined before this, the sailors came down one day and took them out of the hold, those who could stand. So long the dada-hair lady's eyes have been yearning for the sight of the sky, but now the light pierced them like knives (255). . . . *She nodded and smiled. "We are leaving now!" she shouted in Igbo, for those who could understand. Some of those raised up cheer, which became a high piping. The people were changing.* . . . *The people's arms flattened out into flexible flippers. The shackles slipped off their wrists.* . . . *Some of the people who had been forced back into the holds were making their way out, now that their shackles had slid off. The ship was so far tilted that they didn't have to climb; just clamber up the shallow incline that led to the hatch.* . . . *The people's faces swelled and transformed: round heads with snouts. Big liquid eyes. Would she not change, too? Was this Uhamiri's price?* (255, 316; italics in the original)

The past and present of the dada-hair lady and her comrades was one of brutality and dehumanization, but their decisive action in jumping over-

---

3. *Jazz* explores the history of the southern United States with its oppressive myths and realities in relation to early twentieth-century Harlem, New York. For the Harlem-based characters, there is always the danger of selling out to cosmetic beauty and artifice, of violence, of losing one's self-worth and roots.

board signals a positive choice for a speculative, magical, and liberated future. The descendants of these first mer people help Calamity similarly rewrite her own past, present, and future as she comes to terms with both new and recovered powers.

Throughout Hopkinson's novel, the story of the mer people both echoes and extends other stories of jumping and/or drowning that represent either death or escape into a new version of being. Hopkinson writes:

> Was under cover of a night like this that Potoo Nelson and eighty-two other slaves climbed up the mountain and threw themselves off the cliffs into the sea at Rocky Bottom and drowned. In jumbie breath weather, people said the dead slaves came up out of the water and walked, looking for the man who had led them to their doom. (39)[4]

While this tale underscores the horror of the Middle Passage, treating the drowned slaves as zombies, other stories are more ambivalent. This is particularly true in regard to the tale of two lovers who jump off the cliff to escape slavery. This story is variously seen as a tragic loss of life or a romantic desire to join the freedom of the mer people should they exist:

> "You know the legend about Captain Carter?"
> Her face brightened. "Yes. Such a beautiful love story."
> "I guess. Except the lovers throw themselves into the water and die."
> She kissed her teeth. "You have to have a little romance, man. The story says they transformed."
> "They adapted to living in the sea."
> . . .
> "When I was a girl," I said, "I used to try to figure out how I could go and live with the dolphins." (134)

Here, Calamity connects the stories of escaped slaves and Afrodiasporic mer people to her own past. As a child, Calamity played and swam with a little blue girl whose home was the sea, and who led her into deep water,

---

4. The fictional tales of black people who escape slavery by jumping or drowning offered by Hopkinson in *The New Moon's Arms* have numerous real-world counterparts. For instance, in May 1803, approximately seventy-five Nigerian Igbo slaves who were chained and packed below deck on the *York* rose up and drowned their captors, grounding the ship in Dunbar Creek on St. Simons Island in the state of Georgia. Legend has it they then marched into the marshes and committed mass suicide. While the state of Georgia still refuses to officially commemorate this site, the local black community does so by refusing to fish in Dunbar Creek (Powell).

where she glimpsed another sea-based life and, though tempted to join these mer people, was too human, not enough of a mer person herself to do so safely.

As she confirms the mer people's existence, Calamity reevaluates her own magical powers and how they link her to them: She recalls that as a child:

> I found little things: dropped paper clips, lost keys, the change that slid down behind the sofa. Made sense for a little girl to find little things, nuh true? Once in a while I would get a pricking in the fingers of my left hand; the last two fingers that were fused together at the lowest joint. Sometimes when that happened, I could just put my hand on something that had gone missing. Not every time. But often enough that Dadda used to joke about his little finder girl. Often enough that my school friends would beg me to help them look for things that they had lost. (73)

Calamity's prickling occurs in the web of her fingers—and that web is much like the one between the mer-boy Agway's fingers and toes and behind his knees: "In the glow from the flashlights," Calamity "see[s] the webbing between his fingers, like a duck's" (93). Noting this connection prompts Calamity to recall the time she met the other mer child. This recollection both allows her to appreciate Agway for what he is and to recognize her kinship to him.

And indeed, Calamity is a descendant of slaves who were brought to Dolorosse, some of whom leaped overboard to become mer people and whose existence is kept secret except amongst those who live by fishing or patrolling the waters. Talking with an old rival/friend, she realizes that what she thought were mythical stories about the sea people are true:

> "You know the one about the blue child?" she asked me.
> . . . Evelyn nodded. "When the blue baby hits the water, it grows huge, turns into the devil woman of the sea who drags ships down. That's what the baby had wanted the whole time; to reach the sea." (133)

What seems to be simply local myth turns out to be the rich, true history of finding and befriending a mer person and joining the sea people.

When Calamity's magical powers return after her father's death, she is finally ready to embrace new opportunities for life. Agway the mer child needs her nurturing; realizing that is a recognition of her own maturity. The return is not just of her own magical powers but the magical richness of

Dolorosse itself, symbolized by the seemingly magical return of her father's long-gone cashew grove. Calamity remarks, "It was me. Every time I had a power surge. I shuddered, not burning up any longer. Chilled. . . . [my] skin pimpled at what I saw out the car window. Our cashew grove. From Blessee. Resurrected" (157–58). The island, like Calamity, may be aging, but for both, that aging is now marked by positive growth and change.

Hopkinson comments on the vital changes of writing from an African-originated perspective rather than one based in European culture:

> When I write science fiction and fantasy from a context of blackness and Caribbeanness using Afro-Caribbean lore, history, and language, it should logically be no different than writing it from a Western European context: take out the Cinderella folk tale, replace it with the crab-back woman folk tale; exchange the struggle of the marginalized poor with the struggle of the racialized marginalized poor. And yet, it's very different . . . with love and respect for the genre of science fiction that makes it possible to think about new ways of doing things. So long. (*So Long Been Dreaming* 8–9)

Of course, as *The New Moon's Arms* makes clear, it is not so much that Afrofuturist authors part ways with SF altogether, but more precisely that they let go of those aspects that simply reiterate the bad past of slavery and colonial relations without imagining truly new futures in full color.

So Long to the Past; Welcome to the Future

The postcolonial gothic and SF combine provocatively in *The New Moon's Arms.* As Hopkinson notes elsewhere:

> Postcolonial writers have given contemporary literature some of its most notable fiction about the realities of conqueror and conquered, yet we've rarely created stories that imagine how life might be otherwise. So many of us have written insightfully about our pasts and presents; perhaps the time is ripe for us to begin creating. (*So Long Been Dreaming* 270)

In many ways, Hopkinson's novel dramatizes the transformation she describes in this passage. Haunted by a personal and cultural past that alienates her from both her family and her own supernatural power, protagonist Calamity Lambkin faces those harsh histories and experiences a rite of passage, a renewal that is both her own and one inherited from others, taking richness from it, embracing her own hybrid identity, and moving on into a new period of revitalized magical powers, self-worth, and agency.

With *The New Moon's Arms*, Hopkinson demonstrates the real political and aesthetic potential of a hybrid story form such as Afrofuturism, which can bring together the narrative techniques of the postcolonial Gothic and utopian SF to rewrite the paralyzing past and create new and better personal and community futures. Ytasha Womack comments:

> Afrofuturism is often the umbrella for an amalgamation of narratives, but at the core, it values the power of creativity and imagination to reinvigorate culture and transcend social limitations. The resilience of the human spirit lies in our ability to imagine. The imagination is a tool of resistance. Creating stories with people of color in the future defies the norm. With the power of technology and emerging freedoms, black artists have more control over their image than ever before. Welcome to the future. (24)

This quote represents precisely what Hopkinson invites readers to do through the character of Calamity Lambkins. Much like her protagonist, readers are invited to confront the harsh truths of history, to see the beauty and power in stories of survival, and to take a proactive stance on an imagined possible set of Afro futures.

Hopkinson's Afrofuturism is aligned with this use of the magical, supernatural, and Gothic to create new versions and perspectives, to rewrite histories and imagine forward into different ways of being, different stories to tell of each other. *The New Moon's Arms* provides readers with a speculative recuperation of history that turns out to be—like the recuperation of lost things for Calamity herself—an important reinvestment in the magical; a crack in time and space where alternate stories and beings and objects and even ways of seeing can be explored. This embrace of the liminality from which new positive attitudes and behavior can follow is Afrofuturist speculative fiction. It is a radical, revolutionary, visionary practice, revealing practical ways forward, and new ways of thinking and being.

Works Cited

Adejunmobi, Moradewun. Introduction. *African Science Fiction*, special section of *Cambridge Journal of Postcolonial Literary Inquiry*, vol. 3, no. 3, 2016, pp. 265–72.

Anderson, Colin. "Michael Kamen—The New Moon in the Old Moon's Arms," *Classical Source*, Apr. 2001, http://www.classicalsource.com/db_control/db_cd_review.php?id=102. Accessed 15 Feb. 2018.

Armillas-Tiseyra, Magali. "Afronauts: On Science Fiction and the Crisis of Possibility." *African Science Fiction*, special section of *Cambridge Journal of Postcolonial Literary Inquiry*, vol. 3, no. 3, 2016, pp. 273–90.

Blomkamp, Neill, director. *District 9*. TriStar Pictures, 2009.

Bould, Mark. Introduction. *Africa SF*, special issue of *Paradoxa*, vol. 25, 2013, pp. 1–16.

———. "African Science Fiction 101." *SFRA Review*, no. 311, 2015, pp. 11–18.

Brecht, Bertolt. *Brecht on Theatre: The Development of an Aesthetic*. Translated by John Willett, Hill and Wang, 1964.

Cameron, James, director. *Avatar*. Twentieth Century Fox, 2009.

Carter, Angela. *Shaking a Leg: Collected Journalism and Writings*. 1968. Vintage, 1998.

Childs, Francis James. *The English and Scottish Popular Ballads*. 1890. Houghton Mifflin, 2017.

Collins, Merle. "Crick Crack Monkey." *Because the Dawn Breaks: Poems Dedicated to the Grenadian People*. Women's Press, 1985.

Harris, Wilson. *History, Fable & Myth in the Caribbean and Guiana*. Calaloux Publications, 1970.

Hopkinson, Nalo. Introduction. *So Long Been Dreaming: Postcolonial Science Fiction & Fantasy*, edited by Hopkinson and Uppinder Mehan, Arsenal Pulp Press, 2004, pp. 7–9.

———. *The New Moon's Arms*. Grand Central Publishing, 2007.

Kamen, Michael. "The New Moon in the Old Moon's Arms," uploaded by MusicianML, 25 Dec. 2010. https://www.youtube.com/watch?v=FFSrgOlnKJs. Accessed 20 Feb. 2018.

Langer, Jessica. *Science Fiction and Postcolonialism*. Palgrave Macmillan, 2011.

Morrison, Toni. *Jazz*. Knopf, 1992.

Powell, Timothy B. "Ebos Landing." *New Georgia Encyclopedia*. 15 Jun. 2004. http://www.georgiaencyclopedia.org/articles/history-archaeology/ebos-landing. Accessed 20 Feb. 2018.

Smith, Eric. *Globalization, Utopia, and Postcolonial Science Fiction: New Maps of Hope*. Palgrave Macmillan, 2012.

Suvin, Darko. *Metamorphoses of Science Fiction: On the Poetics and History of a Literary Genre*. Yale UP, 1979.

Womack, Ytasha L. *Afrofuturism: The World of Black Sci-fi and Fantasy Culture*. Lawrence Hill Books, 2013.

CHAPTER 5

Young Adult Afrofuturism

Rebecca Holden

> We need diverse stories, we need a million mirrors of different shapes and sizes. Not just so we can see ourselves. So that they can see us through our own eyes.
>
> —ALAYA DAWN JOHNSON, "A MILLION MIRRORS"
>
> Another strategy is to sometimes refuse to write yet another plea to the dominant culture for justice, and instead to simply set the story of the "othered" people front and center and talk about their (our) lives and their concerns.
>
> —NALO HOPKINSON, "MAKING THE IMPOSSIBLE POSSIBLE"

As science fiction (SF) author Alaya Dawn Johnson points out, people of all colors need diverse stories, including Johnson's Afrofuturist ones, to better understand one another's experiences of the modern world. At the same time, fellow Afrofuturist writer Nalo Hopkinson claims Afrofuturist stories have a specific value as stories by black people, for black people, about black people that foreground the concerns of a black audience with little concern for nonblack readers' reactions. While Johnson and Hopkinson's comments on SF by black authors might seem to point to diametrically opposed visions of the cultural work and audience for Afrofuturism, these two visions come together meaningfully in one of the most exciting developments in recent SF history: the rise of young adult (YA) Afrofuturism.

The now hip term "Afrofuturism" appears at times to refer to anything that depicts black people in any futuristic world—or as writer Sheree R. Thomas said recently, to "anyone black who is doing anything weird" (Thomas).[1] Almost every piece on Afrofuturism reminds us that the term

---

1. For further discussion of "Afrofuturism" as a term applied indiscriminately to a wide range of black speculative artistic productions, see the "Author Roundtable on Afrofuturism" included in this collection.

was coined in 1993 by cultural critic Mark Dery, who happens to be white.[2] Since then, it has been redefined, reappropriated by current writers and artists, applied to works of speculative and SF of the past, taken up by scholars from various fields and of varying ethnicities, and continues to be reshaped and retooled by many. In 1998, a group of African American scholars led by Alondra Nelson created a listserv dedicated to exploring Afrofuturism in multiple arenas. Nelson hoped "to find discussions of technology and African diasporic communities that went beyond the notion of the digital divide" (9). More recently Reynaldo Anderson and Charles E. Jones, seeking to further broaden the definition, note the new global nature of what they call "astro-blackness" and take it beyond the artistic fields into "metaphysics, speculative philosophy, religion, visual studies, performance, art, and philosophy of science or technology" (ix). Regardless of how any writer or critic feels about this movement, SF and fantasy by and about those of African descent clearly revitalizes the landscape of speculative and even "mainstream" fiction—from Colson Whitehead's *The Underground Railroad* (2016) to N. K. Jemisin's *The Obelisk Gate* (2016) to Nnedi Okorafor's *Binti* (2015).

While focused on entertainment, good storytelling, and artistry, Afrofuturism's project is to *change* its readers' views of the world; as the young artist June Costa from Alaya Dawn Johnson's *The Summer Prince* (2013) notes, art that "changes nothing at all . . . wouldn't really be art, would it?" (129). In a recently published essay, Esther Jones looks to Afrofuturism for a particular type of change when she prescribes novels by Nalo Hopkinson and Octavia Butler for nonblacks in medical professions. Noting both the historical and contemporary treatment of blacks and poor people as less than human in the medical field, Jones suggests that these Afrofuturist novels could help "non-black others in their roles as doctors and healthcare practitioners . . . mitigate the conscious and unconscious biases and stereotypes that inform their interactions with black people and the poor" (204). Jones argues that Afrofuturism allows its nonblack readers to see outside their limited world views, creating empathy for the other, who in this case are African Americans. We might extrapolate further and argue that reading SF stories centered on the black experience and black culture, might do what Johnson outlines in the epigraph to this piece: "So that they can see us through our own eyes," creating a kind of reverse "double consciousness" (DuBois 3).

---

2. Like Dery, I too am a white Euro-American scholar deeply interested in the SF of African Americans and others of the African diaspora and acknowledge that this fiction draws on traditions outside those of my ancestors.

Afrofuturism as tied to black creativity and agency and to the project of teaching readers about lost black histories and cultures helps us to see the special role that YA Afrofuturism could play for its readers. In general, YA speculative fiction continuously breaks genre boundaries, mixing fantasy, SF, horror, the supernatural, and mystery with little fanfare or complaints from its readers. At the same time, YA fiction, as discussed by authors, librarians, and teachers, has always had a didactic function. The Afrofuturist YA stories I investigate here—including Okorafor's *The Shadow Speaker* (2007), Walter Mosley's *47* (2005), and Johnson's *The Summer Prince*—break down our notions about how science, history, and technology might be defined and what effects those new versions might have on our potential future worlds. These novels not only connect their readers to the sometimes hidden or ignored cultures of the African diaspora, but they also reimagine those pasts making them all the more relevant to today's young adults, both those of the African diaspora and all others who live in the global twenty-first century. Afrofuturist YA texts, as such, may outline a new curriculum for today's youth that goes beyond the "race-less" futures envisioned in much supposedly progressive SF.

YA Literature and the Didactic Function

YA literature was first set up as a distinct category by the American Library Association in 1957. However, most scholars of this literature see S. E. Hinton's *The Outsiders* (1967) as the first novel written for and marketed to the young adult reader—and thus the first true YA novel and the beginning of the first golden age of YA fiction. These scholars debate specific definitions about what YA literature is, but no matter the subject of the YA novel, most note its didactic function.[3] In an essay from 1988, library scholars Barbara Baskin, Betty Carter, and Karen Harris discuss how teachers turn to "values-oriented" young adult literature that can appeal to the teenage audience and still teach morality, ethics, and societal values (67–68).

The often-dystopic SF and fantasy dominating the current, second golden age of YA appears to take on such molding of individual teenagers *and* their possible futures. While early SF written for adults, as C. W. Sullivan notes, was written off as "'escape literature' or worse" (1), scholars and writers point out how YA SF, perhaps even more so than its realist counter-

---

3. See Baskin, et al; Cart; Carlsen; Chisholm; and Edge for some definitions and histories of the genre.

part, entertains its readers at the same time that it teaches young adults useful information for the readers' personal success as well as for the success of their collective future. Robert Heinlein's juvenile SF series (1947–1960), published before YA fiction was a generally accepted category, anticipates the later boom in such fiction for teens as well as YA literature's propensity to "train" its readers. Heinlein argues that SF for young people "has prepared the youth of our time for the coming of the age of space" (qtd. in Sullivan 1)—presumably so that they can use the advanced technologies of such an age successfully.

Later scholars, such as Noga Applebaum, argue that many YA SF dystopias after 1980 alternatively warn young people about the dangers of advanced technology, teaching them to embrace nature in opposition to science and thus not preparing them for their futures (12). However, we might read such stories as arguments for a more ethical use of technology, in an effort to protect our future. Carrie Hintz and Elaine Ostry argue that YA SF dystopias engage the teen angst of their readers and encourage those readers to turn outward; as such, YA SF dystopias help children "learn about social organization, . . . view their society with a critical eye, sensitizing or predisposing them to political action" (7). For Hintz and Ostry, these novels act as cautionary tales "warning [young readers] to take care of the Earth and each other" (12) and thus are often about protecting a future instead of simply promoting an anti-technology or anti-science bias.

The prepping-for-the-future function of YA SF and dystopias, however, is not all about encouraging young adults to pursue meaningful STEM careers or participate in political movements. As Kay Sambell argues, the YA dystopic "text itself becomes a space that sometimes tries to create conditions for young readers to rehearse, actively, almost playfully, a way of reflective thinking that focuses on asking questions, discovering analyses, and hypothetically testing out solutions at their own pace in an imaginative environment that is affirming and supportive, but which also articulates dark truths" (173). Thus, these YA stories about an as-yet-unrealized future encourage their readers to rehearse possible futures in a space where they are invited to think creatively about their own place within such futures and think about how they might work toward solutions. Certainly not all YA SF is progressive, nor does it all promote the same messages about what type of future we might hope for. The novels reflect both the varied hopes and fears of the adult authors (and arguably of the scholars writing about YA fiction) for both what SF should be about and what children should be learning and thinking about in order to make their way successfully in the present world and into possible futures. However, as with much SF of the twentieth century, YA SF futures have been primarily imagined by white authors, and while the supporting characters may represent different minority groups, the protagonists are also most often white, and prior to 2000, most often male. The lack of variation in many authors' and protagonists' positions affects the lack of variation in the shape and size of the mirrors they use to reflect certain futures to readers.

YA Afrofuturism, as Johnson alludes to, can expand our perceptions by giving us more mirrors of different shapes and sizes that can reflect more varied perspectives of the future. While YA Afrofuturism is a relatively recent phenomenon, it has been taken up by well-respected authors both inside and outside the SF community—including Nalo Hopkinson, Steven Barnes, and Tananarive Due as well as Mosley, Okorafor, and Johnson—and provides an alternative to the white-centered futures in much YA SF. YA Afrofuturist stories provide young black readers with a novel learning environment: future worlds where people who look like them not only exist and teach the lessons but also determine what those lessons should be. One of the underlying thrusts of Afrofuturism is that it remains connected to the "dark truths" of the past of slavery and of the racism pervading the present and most likely the future. Thus, what I see as one of the hopes and "lessons" of much YA Afrofuturist is in its various models of how young black people can bring those dark truths as well as African American culture into imagined futures in meaningful ways. The YA protagonists I examine here, like all YA protagonists, are learning their place in the world, but because the world we know does not seem to think they belong, these young black protagonists cannot simply "grow up" and find their place in society. As such, the protagonists here must bend traditions to forge a future that can allow them some agency.

Such a learning environment is novel in a different way for nonblack young readers; more than simply creating empathy for and acceptance of the "other," YA Afrofuturism stories can help all young adult readers ask questions about what a truly diverse future might look like and what their place within that future might be. In all its iterations, Afrofuturism does not embrace any race-blind vision of the past, present, or future where all of us can take on the persona of or relate in the same way to the experience of say, Janelle Monáe's female android Cindi Mayweather, without having the lived experience of being a descendant of the African diaspora. At the same time, these novels can provide meaningful lessons and models of futures to all readers growing up in the twenty-first century, so as YA SF writer Alaya Dawn Johnson states, "We can *all* learn the second sight, to have double—hell, triple and quadruple consciousness" ("A Million Mirrors" 12). And so, we can see futures visible only when we can see those who are constantly othered in our society "through [their] own eyes" (Johnson, "A Million Mirrors" 14). Ultimately, like the YA SF that came before it, YA Afrofuturism prepares its readers for the future, a future that comes out of a world where slavery existed and where people of multiple backgrounds, ethnicities, races, and religions must learn to coexist and hopefully thrive.

Reformulating History and the Stories We Tell About It

One of lessons in YA Afrofuturist stories involves a reimagined notion of the "facts" of history and the necessity, especially today, of understanding the mutability of history as recorded, as well as the role accepting certain "facts"—alternative or otherwise—may play in limiting our visions of potential futures and advanced technologies.[4] Most Americans educated in the United States' public-school system have been taught that history is fact and progresses in a linear fashion. In addition, the scientific and technological histories we learn are primarily those that come out of white Western culture centered in Europe. Okorafor's *The Shadow Speaker* (2007) complicates this notion of history in two ways: by showing that history may not be entirely fixed, and that there might indeed be multiple histories of progress, including those connected with the innovative technologies produced by African cultures.

The Shadow Speaker is set in Niger, West Africa, in 2070, some thirty plus years after the "Great Change," the product of a nuclear war and so-called Peace Bombs. The Peace Bombs were supposed to counteract the effects of nuclear missiles and "create where the nuclear bombs destroyed and cause so many 'glorious' mutations amongst the humans . . . that no one would want to fight each other" (55). In addition to bringing magic (accepted as real in many non-Western traditions and within the past of this novel) back into the world and causing the birth of metahuman children (including shadow speakers, windseekers, rainmakers, and shape-shifters), these bombs set off earthquakes, tsunamis, tornadoes, and opened up boundaries between worlds. This story follows fourteen-year-old shadow speaker Ejii, who is just beginning to understand the shadows who speak to her, as she

---

4. Recently, several history, geography, and US government textbooks proposed and used in Texas public schools have been in the news for their less than accurate information. Some proposed books questioned the role of humans in climate change, suggested that Moses influenced the Founding Fathers, and that slavery was not a primary factor in the Civil War (Jervis).

travels with Jaa, the legendary warrior queen of her village; Jaa's husbands; and Dikéogu, an emerging powerful rainmaker who is Ejii's age. The group travels to the world of Ginen through a breach between the worlds to try and stop Ginen's Chief Ette from declaring war against Earth.

Part of revising history in this novel is making those who were previously invisible in society visible. In the opening of the novel, after Ejii's class watches a "digital" about the French, "people who colonized our country long ago," her history teacher questions the ways in which "history" ignores or misrepresents huge chunks of actual history: "Most of our history books are about foreigners or royalty or the wealthy or the murderous, they rarely focus on people like the farmer who lived and died on his farm or the mother who raised her ten children, the majority of people" (6). The teacher explains that the students must understand the past and their place within that past in order to move forward. In many ways, the novel represents Ejii's effort to complete her history assignment to "write [her]self into history because no matter what history books say, even [she is] a part of it" (6). Ejii investigates personal stories, histories, and the truths both society and individuals come to embrace based on various "facts" as she attempts to figure out where *she* fits in and what kind of future she might help forge.

Throughout the book, Okorafor uses the SF setting to underscore the false histories about race perpetuated throughout the nineteenth and twentieth centuries in bringing to life the recent scientific discoveries about early humans and the effects of human migration. For example, Ejii learns that all the humans of Ginen "look like black Africans" (215) because they chose not to explore the rest of their planet:

> On Earth, the first humans left Africa and explored other places. . . . The different environments and demands gave them different outside features, ways of thinking, cultures. So there were some with blue eyes, others with brown eyes, dark skin, light skin, woolly hair and silky hair, big noses, thin noses, brawny bodies, sinewy bodies. (215–16)

The alternative world of Ginen serves as a control for the evolution of race(s) on Earth, highlighting for the readers how we, like those on Ginen, were all once one people.

Similarly, in the future Okorafor creates, Niger—one of the driest, poorest, and least literate nations in Africa today—remakes itself; instead of continuing to sell its "greatest resource" (116), enriched uranium, to Western nations, in Okorafor's future Niger, "the government decided to make use of its own resource for once" (116) using its enriched uranium to power the "powerful yet so small and reasonably priced" (116) water capture stations that had been invented before the Great Change by a Nigériens scientist. These capture stations sell all over the world and have transformed the Niger of this novel into a much more hospitable and economically stable landscape.

Okorafor further highlights how the stories we are told to be true affect our views of ourselves and our place within the world. For Ejii, that means subconsciously accepting her father's views about the proper place for women. Before Ejii is born Jaa—the village chief and unofficial queen—leaves Kwàmfà village, and Ejii's father becomes chief. He brings back "the old way" (14), requiring women to wear burkas and refusing to allow them to ride camels, rebuild computers, or hone their metahuman skills (13).[5] When Jaa returns to Kwàmfà nine years later and assassinates him, Ejii is overjoyed but chafes at the new expectations; now she has to *choose* whether or not to wear her burka and is expected to speak up and improve her shadow-speaking skills (39). Her mother notes how Ejii has let her father's prescriptive version of the world define her, pointing out how with her male shadow speaker friends, "you walk behind them, you ask them what you should do instead of deciding for yourself, your lower your voice" (49). Later, when Ejii marvels at her newly discovered abilities, she thinks "just a few weeks ago, I only wished to be a good wife" (258). Being invisible had become second nature to Ejii; she had become what her father's narrative cast her to be and was not even aware that she had done so. Her father's death is not enough to overcome the way *his* view of the world shaped her—in the same way that the underlying messages about being black in our world, and the lasting effects of slavery, continue to affect black communities around the world.

To forge a new future for herself and her world, Ejii must not only learn to embrace change, but she must also teach others to do so. Ejii learns from her teachers to celebrate the accomplishments of Nigerians, to question the "old ways" that kept women subservient, to attend to her gifts as a shadow speaker, and to appreciate the living technology of Ginen. Ultimately, she also learns that while her father's "truth" is part of who she is, she does not have to be constrained by that past, nor must she take on the warrior queen Jaa's destructive methods of solving problems. Jaa and the Ginen ruler, Chief Ette, are intent on killing each other because each believes that the other's technology will be deadly to their respective worlds. In creating

---

5. Interestingly, Ejii's father—unlike all the rest of the characters in the book—is never named, effectively erasing him or at least his legacy from the history set down in this novel.

Ginen, Okorafor explains that she imagined "a perfect marriage between the ancient and the modern, nature and technology" where "the people live in houses that are grown" and "computers germinate from CPU seeds" ("Organic Fantasy" 281). Ginen weapons are far superior to those of Earth; as Jaa explains, "They can make the very trees and ground attack you" (268). At the same time, Earth's technologies "spew . . . smoke and fumes, poison to [Ginen]" (276). In the end, Ejii and Dikéogu, self-named "children . . . of change" (301), use their powers to force a temporary truce between Jaa and Ette. Like her fellow Nigériens who refigured enriched uranium from a source that powers killing to one that powers life in the water capture stations, Ejii asks Jaa's Ginen-grown sword to remember that it wasn't *"put in the world to only feed. You also are to grow"* (italics in original, 322); the sword sprouts a soft round end and no longer can be used to kill. Dikéogu similarly uses his rainmaking powers to cut off both Jaa and the Chief Ette's access to their armed allies. These actions force the leaders into a temporary truce. Ejii thus writes herself and her fellow "children of change" into history and calls on all the leaders to imagine new (Afrofuturist) histories and new hybrid technologies that benefit both worlds.

Reclaiming African American Folktales for the Present and Future

History, in terms of many Afrofuturist stories, involves more than the supposed "facts" we are taught in our history lessons; it is also connected to the folktales and oral traditions that grew alongside those histories. A brief look into African American folklore studies demonstrates the interest in preserving, studying, and even reveling in this cultural past. Virginia Hamilton's award-winning books, *The People Could Fly: American Black Folktales* (1985) and *Her Stories: African American Folktales, Fairy Tales, and True Tales* (1995), as well as the many other children's books of African American folktales, aim to make the old stories come alive again for young children, connecting them to the rich traditions of their ancestors. I argue that YA Afrofuturist retellings of these stories do not simply revive the old stories, but seek to alter them, revising them to make them meaningful and useful in defining agency for black young adults in futures that are yet to come. Such lessons extend the previous aim of Afrofuturism to help new generations connect to their cultural past or to tell tales that serve as a "testament to the millions of slaves . . . who only had their imagination to set them free" (Hamilton et al. 173).

Walter Mosley's 47 (2005) engages in such an Afrofuturist revamping of the High John the Conqueror slave folktale. Mosley explains that "in mythology among the slaves ... High John is a spirit who comes from Africa to free the slaves, and also to confound the master" (Bates). Although Mosley's retelling of this folktale is meant to teach about "the barbaric practice of slavery" (vi), it is not anyone's grandmother's slave narrative, but instead brings aliens and alien technology onto the plantation. Interestingly, the book's publisher created a lesson plan for 47 that sells it just that way. According to Hatchette Book Group PR, in Mosley's novel, "Young readers will find little here of the pathos of slavery that so easily bores and tires" (Hatchette). Instead, the lesson plan notes, because it revolves around "scientific vision and highly imagined hardware," the "book will attract young urban males and suburban ones who aspire to the image, with its unforced inferences to the contemporary enslavers of prison and intra-group violence" (Hatchette). While the notion that young readers are bored by the "pathos of slavery" may not ring true for me or even Mosley, in an interview with NPR, Mosley notes that "many black people, young and old, are afraid to read about slavery ... because it's just too heartbreaking" (Bates). Mosley clearly wants to update the lessons about slavery and teach young African American readers not only about the damages done to the bodies of slaves, but even more importantly for these readers, to the psyche of *all* African Americans in the past and in our present. At the same time, his novel encourages those readers to find the High John the Conqueror spirit within themselves and thus create new futures for African Americans.

By invoking the story of High John, Mosley taps into a longstanding African American storytelling tradition.[6] Zora Neale Hurston highlights the power of the High John myth in a 1943 magazine essay, where she quotes "Aunt Shady Anne" who claims that young African Americans in the 1940s "talk about the war freeing the Negroes, but Aye, Lord! ... 'Course, the war was a lot of help, but how come the war took place? They think they knows, but they don't. John de Conquer had done put it into the white folks to give us our freedom, that's what" (453). Hurston goes on to explain that High John lives on: "High John de Conquer went back to Africa, but he left his power here" and that "he can be summoned at any time" (452). While Hurston's essay aims to provide hope to white Americans during World War II, it teaches both young African Americans and all European Americans about the lingering power of this myth and High John's unconquerable spirit.

---

6. For more information, see John W. Roberts's classic *From Trickster to Badman: The Black Folk Hero in Slavery and Freedom* (1989).

In *47*, Mosley summons High John in his character of Tall John. The novel is a first-person narrative told by Forty-seven, a boy from 1832 with only his slave number for a name. When Forty-seven is sent into the fields to pick cotton as a teenager, he meets "amazing Tall John from beyond Africa, who could read dreams, fly between galaxies, and make friends with any animal no matter how wild" (vi). Tall John arrives as a supposed runaway slave boy who insinuates himself into Forty-seven's life. Actually an alien, Tall John has traveled hundreds of thousands of light years from his home planet and has lived on Earth for three thousand years waiting for Forty-seven because, as Tall John tells our narrator, Forty-seven is the hero who will defeat Tall John's enemy—also an alien—and save the whole universe. Tall John takes Forty-seven running on the wind, heals Forty-seven's infected hands and wounds, and makes the slaves laugh. In the end, Tall John's enemy does indeed attack the plantation. Many on the plantation die but Tall John helps Forty-seven liberate Forty-seven's friends; in return Forty-seven helps Tall John defeat the alien enemy. Tall John's miscalculations about humanity's brutality ultimately lead to his death, but before he dies, he passes his "cha," and thus all of his knowledge and power, into Forty-seven. Forty-seven no longer ages and thus, as he tells us, continues the fight against Tall John's enemy into the future and relates his story to us in 2005.

While Tall John starts out as the mystical High John character in this story, his task is to teach Forty-seven to take on this mantle—thus creating new African American myths and futures. The oldest and most respected slave on the plantation asks Tall John if he has heard of High John the Conqueror who "was sent by ancient African gods to bring us slaves back home to where our mothers' still waitin' for us" and notes that "If'n I put high in yo' name instead'a tall dat might jes be you" (63). Tall John admits, "At some othah time High John's spirit might'a passed through me" but claims that Forty-seven "has more interest in freeing the slaves than do I" (85, 63). Later, Tall John directly states that Forty-seven is "High John" even if he does not know it yet. Tall John explains that the Conqueror is "a spirit from the homeland. He burrow down here or there for a while, do his business, and then he move on" (85).

While most of the plantation slaves dismiss Tall John's notions as crazy, Forty-seven learns to see himself and his fellow slaves in a new light. Tall John admonishes Forty-seven throughout the book, "Neither nigger nor master be" (66). At first, even though he avoids referring to others as "nigger" or "master," Forty-seven does not understand the point: "Who would take care of us an' feed us if'n we didn't have no mastuh?" (94). Forty-seven, like Okorafor's Ejii, has been conditioned to see himself in a particular way, that "being black meant poverty, slavery, and all things bad" (30). When Tall John and Forty-seven are locked in a punishment box, Forty-seven comes to understand the meaning of Tall John's "Neither master nor nigger be"; he explains, "I realized that I was free even though I was clamped in chains and locked away. I was free because I had made the decision to run away if I could . . . and I could see that the real chains that the slave wore were the color of his skin and the defeat in his mind" (146). The color of his skin is what makes others, both black and white, see Forty-seven as a slave and the defeat in his mind is what makes the teenager see himself as a slave. Thus, Tall John successfully teaches Forty-seven—and by extension the readers of the book—to take on the spirit and power of High John the Conqueror.

This power allows Forty-seven to see himself and his fellow African Americans as free, beautiful, and capable. The High John who frees the slaves in this Afrofuturist slave narrative is not the African prince trickster figure, or even the seemingly magical Tall John, but instead is a slave boy who accepts the extraterrestrial Tall John and his futuristic technology as real. He is able to do this because, as Tall John tells him, "your mind dares to consider new ways" (96). The SF elements of the story, somewhat ironically, allow Mosley to make the High John spirit concrete in ways that the folktale may not for today's youth. We learn, along with Forty-seven, that Tall John is from a race of tiny, multi-colored people called the Talam and that his human body "was created by what my people call science" (105). Tall John can heal both Forty-seven and others because his people have studied human anatomy, and this knowledge enhances their understanding of the healing herbs used by African American healers (105). Tall John has devices that allow Forty-seven and his friends to hide from the slave catchers as well as the means to grant Forty-seven the power to run on the wind and what seems to be everlasting youth. Neither Forty-seven nor twenty-first-century readers have to accept Tall John's powers as magic or on faith, but simply as the products of science and technology that we have yet to develop or discover, and thus potentially "real" and even part of our actual future.

Forty-seven, the unschooled African American slave boy who initially buys into white society's negative view of blackness, becomes the teacher of both his fellow ex-slaves and Tall John. While Tall John has advanced technology and teaches Forty-seven to see himself as other than a slave, the alien jeopardizes the whole universe because of his outsider status; unlike Forty-seven, he could always "shrug off my chains and escape" (141). Tall John lacks the lived knowledge and drive for survival of those who have lived as slaves. After he loses his power, Tall John understands more clearly the plight and strength of Forty-seven's people: "You know how to survive against forces much greater than you. You are the teacher and I am the dunce. Without you there can be no future for anyone" (142). Forty-seven's story demonstrates that successful futures for African Americans lie not only in embracing the opportunities enabled by future technologies but also in accepting the sometimes difficult to understand choices made by their slave ancestors. Tall John fails to learn from Forty-seven how to *survive* the brutality of slavery in time—but Forty-seven does learn how to exist outside of the world defined by the master/slave relationship, which enables him to survive into today's world and share his story. Forty-seven successfully calls into being his own High John the Conqueror spirit because he can accept the effects of his slave past *and* the promise of Afrofuturist perspectives. He is no longer primarily defined by his slave status or the way that white society sees him, but neither does he use his new powers to become the master, subjugating those who enslaved him. Thus, while this book makes the brutal experience of slavery real for *all* readers, Mosley embeds a special lesson for those of African descent about slave histories, advanced science, mythology, and the necessary melding of all three to prepare for the future. Forty-seven's story exhorts these readers to remember their ancestors' slave past and at the same time escape the slave mentality in which the dominant society defines their value as people or, more pointedly, as commodities, and not as innovators or successful wielders of advanced technology. The fantastic elements of this novel make it clear that no easy formula exists to engage the necessary High John spirit, but it involves seeing outside of the possibilities of the accepted reality as defined by those in power, because as Afrofuturist stories show us, reality itself is continuously shifting.

Creating Afrofuturist Art from Afrofuturist Histories

This desire and aptitude to combine advanced technology with powerful histories to create something transformative is also at the heart of Alaya Dawn Johnson's complex Afro-Brazilian SF novel, *The Summer Prince*. Set in the futuristic pyramid city of Palmares Três four hundred years after nuclear wars have ravaged the Earth, this novel tells the story of the city's popular summer king, Enki, and an aspiring artist and finalist for the prestigious Queen's award, June Costa. The city is run by women, called "Aunties," and a queen, who is chosen from among the Aunties by a summer king every five years. Elected by the people, the summer king serves for a year, and at the end of his term chooses the next queen before being killed by the Aunties in a ritual sacrifice. This tradition began because the nuclear wars that so radically changed the Earth were initiated by men who wielded unchecked power: men, as history bears out, "can't be trusted to give up power once they have it" (Johnson, *Summer Prince* 197). Because queens can serve for two terms, the alternating cycle "moon year" king—chosen from among the wakas or those under thirty—has no actual power as he must select the queen "in gesture or in blood" (20) after his throat is cut with only the existing queen allowed in the room.

The story opens with June's childhood memory of going to see the sacrifice of a moon year king. The present time of the novel follows seventeen-year-old June through the year of the next moon king, Enki. June and her best friend Gil catch Enki's attention, who unlike anyone else in Palmares Três is "born as dark as molasses" because his pregnant mother entered the city too late for the gene mods that would ensure he "conform[ed] to our appearance regulations" (12). Enki grows up on the bottom level of Palmares Três in the verde, "which means he grew up poor . . . with the ever-present stink of hydrogen-producing algae" vats that provide power for the entire city (13). Gil becomes Enki's lover, and June becomes Enki's collaborator in a number of political art projects that bring to light the costs and power imbalance of the supposed utopia of Palmares Três. Toward the end of the year, June escapes with Enki in an effort to save him; however, this fails because when he is first elected king, he is injected with nanotech mods that guarantee his eventual death. In the end, Enki uses advanced technologies and illegal body mods he obtains from the ambassador from Tokyo 10—where most people have left their bodies and exist in a data stream—to subvert the summer king system and choose June as the next Queen before dying himself.

Like the other authors I examine here, Johnson creates a seemingly strange new future stemming from the African diaspora to make her readers curious about the history of that diaspora and the cultures produced by it. The city of Palmares Três and its summer king ritual are both products of Afrofuturism, coming out of the forceful imagination of its first queen and available technology. Enki imagines himself as that first Queen:

> *So I take my lover, my king, and I put him on a pedestal and I cut him down. A man, like the ones who ruined the world.*
>
> *I take from the world I know: Candomblé, which always respected a women's power. Catholicism, which always understood the transformation of a sacrifice. And Palmares, that legendary self-made city the slaves carved themselves in the jungle, proof that a better world can be built from a bad one.* (19)

Like the original "'Negro Republic' of Palmares," which was the largest settlement of escaped African slaves in Brazil and lasted for the entirety of the seventeenth century despite frequent attacks by Dutch and Portuguese slave owners (Kent 162–63), Johnson's Palmares Três serves as a utopian beacon to those seeking refuge in a world destroyed by war and a plague (127).

The resulting city that "sparkle[s] on the bay" (29) is a triumph of technology and design: "The clear dome soars above us, high enough that on some days wispy clouds can form, obscuring from sight the pulsing, glowing city rising into the distance above" (9). At the same time, as June learns and Enki knows too well, the city's success rests on the verde and those forced to live and work on the bottom tier. The ritual words in the summer king's sacrifice ceremony pay homage to "our ancestors who were slaves" (6), but the meaning has been lost. Enki shocks the Aunties and invigorates the wakas when he provides a more visceral reminder of their slave past and the present degradation of those in the verde. For his final performance as a summer king finalist, "he walks into the spotlight dressed like a slave in old-Brazil. . . . His feet are bare, like the poorest refugee from the flat cities" (25–26). When the Queen says, "You are dressed in the manner of a slave . . . in a city where there are none" (26), he answers, "But there is the verde" and claims that he is "dressed in the manner of my people" (27). While this is a performance, a piece of art, it is one that highlights how the upper-tier residents have closed their eyes and more importantly, their noses to the reality of the verde or as they call it, the *catinga*, Portuguese for "the stink" (13), upon which this supposed utopia is built. By becoming the "masters," the Aunties have brought the brutality of Old Brazil into Palmares Três and risk its integrity on multiple fronts.

Both June and Enki love Palmares Três, but they also want to see the city move forward—Enki so much so that he takes on gene modifications that wreak havoc on his body but enable him to connect to the city, become the city's voice, and take on the city's pain. Together June and Enki create an ambitious art project, which involves months of stringing lights throughout the four islands in the bay surrounding the city, that pays homage to the city. This art is ephemeral—an extensive lightshow to a soundtrack that includes "Roda Vida," a traditional song about the wheel of life, overlapping everyday conversations of the city's inhabitants, and Enki's addition of a recording of the Queen in which she admits she "allowed" the election of Enki for "the wakas and the verde" (130). Without Enki's damning addition to the show, June knows that the light show, while spectacular, might have boosted her chances for the Queen's Award and may have been remembered for a short while, but "it would change nothing at all . . . and so it wouldn't really be art, would it?" (129). Enki's version, which may keep her from winning the award, changes something, even if it is just people's *perceptions* of the Queen and the current system.

Ultimately, June and Enki's actions stir up an ongoing debate between those who want to open up the city to new advanced technologies and the Aunties who want to keep what they see as dangerous technology out of the city. In a technophile protest gone wrong, two city residents are killed by an illegal weaponized nanobot cloud. June feels torn between the horror of the death cloud and the Aunties who have manipulated June, the city, and the technophiles to maintain their control on what technology is permitted within the city. Some in Palmares Três find Tokyo 10, where millions have downloaded themselves into the data stream, alluring, but June comes to see that both cities are stagnating. As the Japanese ambassador tells her, those in Tokyo 10's data stream "think they've gone to heaven . . . [and] don't realize that means they're dead" (234); similarly, the once vital summer king ritual that allowed Palmares Três to become a stable refuge has become a meaningless and damaging ritual. Of course, as June tells Enki, she never wanted to be Queen and, in the end, it is still unclear what exact changes she will make in Palmares Três. However, Johnson does make it clear that June's empathy for others, commitment to past histories and cultures, and feelings about embodied art and technologies will indeed lead her to direct changes, bringing her beloved city into another new future.

Multifold Futures

YA Afrofuturist stories do not embrace any one future, technology, or even lesson for young adults of the African diaspora or the nonblack young adults that may people the future with them. We might ask if YA Afrofuturism pushes into the future and the fantastic more than other YA SF because the present continues to be oppressive for people of the African diaspora or because it seeks to make real futures that might have come out of different pasts, ones where African nations and peoples did not become pawns in the white man's power plays. Like the best of all speculative fiction, I believe YA Afrofuturism does both. It provides hope for the future, warnings about complacency with the present, and fascinating new modes of being or interacting with the world as well as new futures or worlds to explore—worlds with black young people as central to the story, which are particularly exciting for young adults of African descent but intriguing and necessary for *all* readers. Such stories reflect truly diverse futures, hopefully millions of them, and can broaden all of our minds in ways that help prepare us for those diverse futures we must, if we are to survive, learn to imagine and then live in.

Works Cited

Anderson, Reynaldo, and Charles E. Jones. *Afrofuturism 2.0: The Rise of Astro-Blackness.* Lexington Books, 2016.

Applebaum, Noga. *Representations of Technology in Science Fiction for Young People.* Routledge, 2010.

Baskin, Barbara, et al. "The Search for Values: Young Adults and the Literary Experience." *Library Trends*, vol. 37, no. 1, 1988, pp. 63–79.

Bates, Karen G. "Walter Mosley: A Slave's Flight to Freedom in '47.'" *NPR.org*, 8 Jun. 2005, https://www.npr.org/templates/story/story.php?storyID=4694437. Accessed 31 Aug. 2017.

Carlsen, G. Robert. *Books and the Teenage Reader: A Guide for Teachers, Librarians, and Parents.* 2nd rev. ed., Harper & Row, 1980.

Cart, Michael. *From Romance to Realism: 50 Years of Growth and Change in Young Adult Literature.* HarperCollins, 1996.

Chisholm, N. Jamiyla. "The Surprising, Short History of Young Adult Fiction | Real Simple." *realsimple.com*, n.d., https://www.realsimple.com/work-life/entertainment/history-of-young-adult-fiction. Accessed 16 Sept. 2017.

Dery, Mark. "Black to the Future: Interviews with Samuel R. Delany, Greg Tate, and Tricia Rose." 1993. *Flame Wars: The Discourse of Cyberculture*, edited by Mark Dery, Duke UP, 1994, pp. 179–222.

DuBois, W. E. B. *The Souls of Black Folk: Essays and Sketches.* A. C. McClurg, 1903.

Edge, Kristen. "Fantasy to Reality: The History of Young Adult Literature." *History Cooperative*, 16 Jan. 2015. http://historycooperative.org/fantasy-to-reality-the-history-of-young-adult-literature/. Accessed 9 January 2020.

Hamilton, Virginia, et al. *Her Stories: African American Folktales, Fairy Tales, and True Tales.* Blue Sky Press, 1995.

———. *The People Could Fly: American Black Folktales*, 1st ed., Knopf, 1985.

Hatchette Book Group. *47 Teacher's Guide.* Hatchette Book Group, https://www.hachettebookgroup.com/category/educator-guides/. Accessed 30 Jul. 2019.

Hinton, S. E. *The Outsiders.* Viking Press, 1967.

Hintz, Carrie, and Elaine Ostry. *Utopian and Dystopian Writing for Children and Young Adults.* Routledge, 2003.

Hopkinson, Nalo. "Making the Impossible Possible: An Interview with Nalo Hopkinson," by Alondra Nelson, *Social Text*, vol. 20, no. 2, 2002, pp. 97–113.

Hurston, Zora Neale. "'High John de Conquer' by Zora Neale Hurston, The American Mercury, October 1943." *UNZ.Org*, http://www.unz.org/Pub/AmMercury-1943oct-00450. Accessed 1 Sept. 2017.

Jemisin, N. K. *The Obelisk Gate*. Orbit, 2016.

Jervis, Rick. "Controversial Texas Textbooks Headed to Classrooms." *USA Today*, 17 Nov. 2014, https://www.usatoday.com/story/news/nation/2014/11/17/texas-textbook-inaccuracies/19175311/. Accessed 28 Aug. 2017.

Johnson, Alaya Dawn. "A Million Mirrors: WisCon 39 Guest of Honor Speech." *The WisCon Chronicles Vol. 10: Social Justice (Redux)*, edited by Margaret McBride, Aqueduct Press, 2016, pp. 8–15.

———. *The Summer Prince*. Scholastic Inc., 2014.

Jones, Esther. "Africana Women's Science Fiction and Narrative Medicine: Difference, Ethics and Empathy." Anderson and Jones, pp. 185–205.

Kent, R. K. "Palmares: An African State in Brazil." *Journal of African History*, vol. 6, no. 2, 1965, pp. 161–75. Cambridge Core, Cambridge University Press, https://www.cambridge.org/core/journals/journal-of-african-history/article/ palmares-an-african-state-in-brazil/E2486B223C0655E7C349621C228A258A.

Mosley, Walter. *47*. Little Brown, 2006.

Nelson, Alondra. "Introduction: Future Texts." *Social Text*, vol. 20, no. 2, 2002, pp. 1–15.

Okorafor, Nnedi. *Binti*. Tor, 2015.

———. "Organic Fantasy." *African Identities*, vol. 7, no. 2, 2009, pp. 275–86.

Okorafor, Nnedi. *The Shadow Speaker*. Jump at the Sun, 2007.

Roberts, John W. *From Trickster to Badman: The Black Folk Hero in Slavery and Freedom*. U of Pennsylvania P, 1989.

Sambell, Kay. "Presenting the Case for Social Change: The Creative Dilemma of Dystopian Writing for Children." *Utopian and Dystopian Writing for Children and Young Adults*. Routledge, 2003.

Sullivan, Charles Wm. *Young Adult Science Fiction*. Greenwood Press, 1999.

Thomas, Sheree R. *Afrofuturism: Butler and Beyond*. Escape Velocity, 2017.

Whitehead, Colson. *The Underground Railroad*. Doubleday, 2016.

PART THREE

Afrofuturism in Cultural History

FACING: Stacey Robinson, "Sanfoka of the Mind," 2018

CHAPTER 6

Space/Race
Recovering John M. Faucette

Mark Bould

The unnamed first-person narrator of John M. Faucette's "The Ghost Writer" (2002) moves into a rent-stabilized apartment on Manhattan's West Side. It is, of course, haunted by the ghost of the previous tenant, who scraped a living through his typing skills, temping for a couple of weeks at a time to support a month or more of writing. In forty years of doing this, he did not sell a single story, despite the quality of his work:

> In the end he had nothing to show for it except possibly the world's largest collection of rejection slips. How had he withstood that rejection, the years and years of nonrecognition, of toiling to no avail? . . . Maybe he was just a victim of bad luck, bad timing, bad marketing, bad *some*thing. (159, 164)

The narrator, himself an author, is unfazed by the haunting, and soon takes comfort in the presence of his spectral companion typing away alongside him late into the night. However, the narrator's friend Marie becomes convinced that the phantom wordsmith is trapped in a kind of limbo, unable to move on into the afterlife until one of his stories is sold.

It is tempting to read "The Ghost Writer" autobiographically, with the fictional writers offering a composite image of African American SF author John M. Faucette, who spent most of the thirty-five years between his first published novel, *Crown of Infinity* (1968) and his 2003 death from a heart attack collecting rejection slips. His debut space opera was swiftly followed by the postapocalyptic *The Age of Ruin* (1968), both of which appeared as halves of Ace Doubles, but Faucette fell out with editor Donald A. Wollheim, who refused to publish his next novel, *Marooned on the Levels*, which featured a black swordsman in a world of race wars. Belmont Books published *The Warriors of Terra* (1970), the first manuscript Faucette ever submitted to Wollheim, featuring escaped slave Ran's quest for revenge, and then Modern Promotions published a sequel, *Siege of Earth* (1971) in which genius—and former pacifist—Dane Barclay holds off an alien invasion of Earth. In 1978, black pulp specialist Holloway House published *Disco Hustle* (1978), which follows an array of characters through one night of drinking, dancing, pick-ups, and put-downs in a New York nightclub. When the market for his novels dried up, he switched to short fiction with little success. However, Faucette's introduction to *Black Science Fiction* (2002), a self-published collection of thirty-nine stories, reveals that he never actually stopped writing.[1]

In the 1993 interviews with Samuel R. Delany, Jr., Tricia Rose, and Greg Tate in which Mark Dery coined the term "Afrofuturism," only four black SF writers are named—Delany, Octavia Butler, Steven Barnes, and Charles R. Saunders—before authors from outside the genre, such as Ralph Ellison, Ishmael Reed, and Richard Wright are recruited into the Afrofuturist pantheon. And while that pantheon has continued to grow, the recovery of earlier authors of African American SF has focused on those who published outside of the pulp tradition, such as Pauline Hopkins, W. E. B. DuBois, and George S. Schuyler. This poses the question of why there has been no similar recovery of African American genre SF writers. Salvaging Faucette is significant for the Afrofuturist project because his experience reveals something of the structural racism of American SF in the late 1960s and early 1970s, and the limited opportunities genre publishing offered to African Americans. That he should have been forgotten points not only to the dangers of constructing history and memory around exceptional figures, also to the need for countermemories to challenge dominant narratives of the past and thus to reconstruct our understanding of the present.[2] In this, Faucette stands in for the other SF writers of color who remain unrecognized, neglected, or

---

1. *Editors' note*: Like several other authors in this volume, Bould considers books written well before the twenty-first century, but his concern with the recovery of lost authors such as Faucette are very much at the heart of contemporary Afrofuturism.

2. This is not to deny that Delany and Butler are exceptional writers, fully deserving their status.

forgotten—a portent of the Afrofuturist specters haunting the genre, and an invitation to conjure them back.

Until recently, and despite the inspirational example of George Washington Carver, American ideology more typically associated African Americans with physical than intellectual labor; the material manifestations of such ideological norms also ensured that only a relatively small proportion of African Americans had access to the scientific and technological education one might assume necessary to writing SF. Parts of the African American community also exercised constraints on such ambitions, from the Tuskegee Institute's emphasis on trade and agriculture to the black middle class's aspirations to such professions as the law, finance, and medicine. Additionally, black Atlantic cultural production has historically been dominated, as Kodwo Eshun notes, by "the practice of countermemory" and its "ethical commitment to history, the dead, and the forgotten," against which "the manufacture of conceptual tools that could analyze and assemble counter-futures was understood as [a] dereliction of duty" ("Further" 288). Furthermore, as John Rieder's work on the emergence of SF demonstrates, the genre was profoundly shaped by and typically reiterated racial and colonial ideologies.[3] The development of the American magazine SF tradition between 1910 and 1930 coincided with the height of Jim Crow, when many states enshrined "one drop" hypodescent in law. By such a measure, some genre SF writers would have been, whether they knew it or not, "black," and those who did know it may have had good reasons not to draw attention to it.

Decades later, just as Faucette was breaking into print, Delany was at the height of his award-winning fame, receiving Nebulas for *Babel-17* (1966), *The Einstein Intersection* (1967), "Aye and Gomorrah . . ." (1967), and "Time Considered as a Helix of Semi-Precious Stones" (1968), the latter also netting a Hugo. Yet Faucette recalls that it "was only years" after the split with Wollheim that he "learned . . . Delany was black" and that Ace was "actually publishing two black [SF] authors at a time when no one else was . . . publishing any" ("Road" iii). That a New York–based SF fan and neophyte genre author could be unaware of Delany's blackness might now seem remarkable, but it does perhaps suggest that Faucette was disconnected from a broader SF community. It seems likely that one reason Faucette has been forgotten as a pioneer of African American genre SF is that readers did not even know he was black. None of his novels carry biographical information, so the first really solid clue about his color is the publication of his last—and non-SF—novel by Holloway House. Moreover, as Faucette's own failure to

---

3. See Rieder's influential *Colonialism and the Emergence of Science Fiction* (2008).

read Delany as black demonstrates, it is neither easy nor straightforward to determine an author's racial identity from his work, making it clear that the recovery of African American genre SF writers will depend not on the content of their fiction but on biographical and other forms of documentary evidence.[4] However, in his autobiographical introduction to *Black Science Fiction*, Faucette makes a point of presenting his novels as articulating an African American identity, and it is through such a lens I will present them here.

Crown of Infinity

Crown of Infinity marries space opera with a future history that covers centuries, if not millennia. Framed as a mystery—a race of super humans called the Star Kings have suddenly died out, or perhaps just disappeared—the novel ultimately reaches for something like Stapledonian magnitudes[5] as all of human history is reframed as an experiment to produce an effective ally in a war taking place in another dimension. But *Crown of Infinity* reads a great deal like Edmond Hamilton's groundbreaking *Interstellar Patrol* stories (1928–1934), which also took on a second life in two Ace paperbacks, *Outside the Universe* (1964) and *Crashing Suns* (1965). Faucette's galactic Civilization, which sets about investigating the fate of the Star Kings, is a multispecies affair like Hamilton's, but unlike the Interstellar Patrol, its spaceships are not necessarily under human command. Faucette lacks the early Hamilton's occasional taste for cosmic bleakness and his ability to render threatening, even-more-alien, *extra*-galactic species as queasily Weird, but like Hamilton, he limits the extent of species sympathy and co-operation to beings from within the galaxy. Faucette also has an unclear sense of what "universe" means, using it—as did the early Hamilton—to mean "solar system," sometimes "galaxy," occasionally "way of life," and very occasionally "universe."

There is, perhaps, a formal influence, too, in terms of the ways in which Hamilton's episodic fix-ups presented related stories—of varying lengths and degrees of revision—as if they were novels, in the process doing some violence to the notion of the novel as a unified entity. *Crown of Infinity* opens

---

4. When writing "Come Alive by Saying No," I was assured by a specialist SF librarian that Edwin Corley, the author of *Siege* (1969), was black, but something about the novel seemed too opportunistic so I naïvely, but as far as I know correctly, excluded it from my sample of "Black Power Sf."

5. Olaf Stapledon was renowned for the temporal and cosmological scale of his philosophical SF novels: *Last and First Men: A Story of the Near and Far Future* (1930) charts a two-billion-year future history of humanity, involving the rise and fall of eighteen distinct human species.

with a prologue in which Captain Corrindus of the "battle fortress *Warrior of Civilization*" (5) and one of his officers, "Guidi, the impatient feathered creature" (6), ponder the Star Kings' abrupt absence from the galaxy and decide to examine "the entire history of the Star Kings for a clue" (7). The following nineteen chapters recount more or less isolated episodes in that history, some of which are more tangential than others, and most of which have a complete new set of characters, some of whom Faucette neglects to name until their particular story is almost done. Together, these episodes tell of the destruction of all but a tiny fraction of humanity by an alien species, the reptilian—or "lizoid"—Masters of the Universe, who after a devastating war several billion years earlier decided to eradicate any sentient species they found before it could emerge as a threat to them; of how that human remnant disperses into the galaxy and genetically engineers a successor species of cyborg superhumans called the Star Kings, who wage war upon and eventually defeat the Masters at the Battle of Star Cross End, but refuse to destroy them utterly for fear of becoming just like them; of the Star Kings' nurturing of the galactic Civilization from which they themselves remain apart; of their departure into "another plane of Existence" to play their role in "a tremendous battle . . . upon whose outcome the fate of a billion Universes depends"; and finally of Corrindus's conviction that from "him and . . . his fellow members of Civilization" a new race of Star Kings will develop (129). After the prologue, Corrindus and Guidi vanish for a third of the novel, and briefly reappear on several occasions to comment on the retrospective action before returning in the epilogue to miraculously solve the mystery of the Star Kings' disappearance.

If there is nothing ebonic about Faucette's prose—the closest he gets to a distinctive expression is noting that "new races had come into existence like flies about watermelon" (66)—and no trace of Black Arts Movement urgency, it is unsurprising. After all, even if Faucette possessed the inclination and ability, Ace Doubles had little room for overt politics and favored a tendentiously pedestrian pulp style, wary even of purple flourishes. If there is an African American identity coded in the novel, if it is as Faucette claims "an allegorical tale of black revenge . . . a blueprint for the deliverance of a long overdue wrath" ("Road" ii–iii), we have to look elsewhere.

Having opened with the death or disappearance of the Star Kings, the novel immediately goes back in time to the war (honorable, we are told, not genocidal) between the human United Stars and the Federated States of the alien Shraix. Another alien race, the Masters of the Universe, steps in and annihilates both. The novel thus begins with a doubled vision of destruction and diaspora and becomes about harried survival and the necessary becoming-other that such calamities entail. In this, it can be seen (like Octavia E. Butler's *Kindred* [1979] and other Afrofuturist novels) to reflect upon both the era of slavery and the moment in which it was written. However, while plantation slavery reduced humans to machine-like slaves, valuable only in terms of their labor-power, and forced breeding upon them, Faucette's surviving human remnant itself takes control of such processes. These survivors pursue a scientific eugenics program, experimenting on fetuses to produce superhuman geniuses, genetically engineered supermen and superwomen. In addition to biological manipulation, the transformation from human to Star King also depends upon cyborg technologies: six years before the first appearance of Marvel's adamantium-skeletoned Wolverine, the Star Kings (somehow) possess "ultra-light" skeletons "composed of hollow bones of collapsium alloyed with vedium" (33). They also sport "C-S headgear,"[6] which enables them to connect telepathically with each other and to monitor and control their ships by thought alone. The Star Kings' final departure to another universe offers some measure of consolation, suggesting that their long years of suffering and their painful climb to greatness have not been in vain.

Perhaps more interesting than this rough allegory is the way the novel struggles with both identity and genre. *Crown of Infinity* begins on the bridge of "the battle fortress *Warrior of Civilization*" with a moment of comic misdirection:

> Captain Corrindus clasped his hands behind his back. Actually, in terms of human reference, he joined two jade blue pseudopods across the gelatinous mass of that part of his body directly opposite the light-sensitive group of cells that went into action whenever his brain decided to take in visual stimuli. . . . Corrindus sighed, his boneless body quivering in the master cup before the control panel. (5)

In this reproduction of normative expectations and their immediate subversion—the apparently human captain, his name vaguely composited from Latin and Sanskrit, is actually an amorphous alien blob—Faucette embraces the potential of both SF in general and Afrofuturism in particular to negotiate identity and difference. (This is echoed, in a minor key, by the atypical but acceptable association of jade with blue rather than green.) The doubled

---

6. C-S are the initials of its creator, Caesar Augustus Smith, whose name recalls a tendency amongst slave owners to call certain of their slaves after classical figures, without seemingly recognizing the bathetic fall of the appended slave owner surname.

image of Corrindus can be read as an evocation of the trope of passing,[7] especially when we move from the narrator consciously misdescribing the scene to the character replicating—seemingly deliberately—a human gesture: "Corrindus sighed again, the upper portion of his amorphous bulk rippling in imitation of a movement once observed on one of the legendary Star Kings" (6). The awkward phrasing that leaves the precise nature of the "movement" unclear reiterates the trope by suggesting that Faucette, not yet confident about working in an SF idiom, with the additional pressures that its imperative to describe nonexistent referents places on language, is "passing" as an SF writer. This lack of confidence in turn might explain the novel's framing device that distances the author from his material, the fragmentation of its narrative arc into loosely connected episodes that require less sustained credulity from the reader, and the frequently comic (if not exactly funny) deflation of its material. In this opening scene however, the latter works successfully to undermine the sense of an irreducible otherness lurking behind the appearance of similarity: Corrindus "extruded an eyestalk . . . His body shifted and *plopped* in the cup" (6).

Moments such as this, in which Faucette offers dissonant descriptions of characters and events, recur throughout the novel. Often the purpose of such material remains unclear. For example, in chapter 9, Civilization vessels detect numerous Star King ships converging on the planet Godog IV in the Megalese galaxy and, as one character notes, "there is only one time in their long glorious history that [the Star Kings] have all gathered together: The Battle of Star Cross End!" (54). The Civilization vessels that follow them, ready for battle, are eventually forced to slink away, disappointed and embarrassed, when it is revealed that the Star Kings only descended on this distant world to play, or perhaps watch, a game of football. A more sustained pattern of generic dissonance is found in Faucette's deployment of, and perhaps satire upon, postwar commodity culture, whether in chapter 6's fleeting details about a spaceship that comes across as a kind of *Playboy* bachelor pad or chapter 10's more sustained riff on the suburban sitcom, in which a Star King tries to appease his wife's demand for a nice place to raise their children by radically transforming a series of planets, only to have her ultimately decide that no world is as nice as their current spaceship.

---

7. A common theme in African American literature, where a light-skinned black mimics the behavior of white people so as to sidestep racist structures and attitudes and enjoy some of the privileges of the dominant culture. Afrofuturist examples include George S. Schuyler's *Black No More* (1931), Octavia E. Butler's *Wild Seed* (1980), and A. Igoni Barrett's *Blackass* (2015).

In fact, the first planet might resonate with the de facto racial segregation of housing that continues even now to flourish in the United States, long after de jure segregation was made illegal by the Civil Rights Act of 1968—the final major piece of civil rights legislation, also known as the Fair Housing Act, signed into law just days after the assassination of Martin Luther King, Jr. However, while an Afrofuturist reading of this first act of planetary engineering pointedly demonstrates how false projections of black inferiority perpetuate racial stereotypes, the subsequent concatenation of unsatisfactory worlds weakens any potential critique by merely becoming misogynist comedy at Harriet's expense.

A clearer critical purpose is evident in the dissonances of chapter 3. The early Star King, George Bronson, intent on the further genetic development of his people, is described as "British descended" and "professorial," and introduced "puffing on a pipe that burned tobacco that had never seen the soil of Earth, while walking among the stainless steel artificial wombs that housed his experiments" (23). Bronson's greatest success is the genius V-101, who invents a method for producing gravity particles so as to scan the Masters' shielded ships and thus enable the Star Kings to defeat them. V-101's genetic heritage is "Japanese-Italian-Brazilian-Kenyan," yet he brushes "back strands of [his] golden hair" (29). While the description of Bronson initially seems to be merely a failure of imagination, the ensuing contrast between creator and created highlights the complex and contradictory interplay of culture and biology—and of stereotypes—in common understandings of race, ethnicity, and nationality. That said, V-101's fate remains that of many a science-fictional genius, such as Stapledon's *Odd John* (1935), and of many a "tragic mulatto": he does not fit in anywhere; he does not belong. After a brief, despairing life, teetering on the brink of madness, he commits suicide, but not before counseling Bronson to refrain from further experiments in "gene manipulation"

> until your techniques and instruments are vastly better. And even then, afterwards, replace the fertilized egg in the mother's womb and let it be brought into the world in a normal fashion. Perhaps even keeping their origin a secret is better, although sooner or later they will deduce the true circumstances of their birth. (30)

On the one hand, this might be seen as mere railing against the kind of artificial wombs proposed in J. B. S. Haldane's *Daedalus; or Science and the Future* (1924) and then bemoaned in Aldous Huxley's *Brave New World* (1932) or, perhaps, as a patriarchal refusal of the liberatory potential of ectogenetic technologies—soon to be celebrated in Shulamith Firestone's *The Dialectic of Sex: The Case for Feminist Revolution* (1970) and in such feminist SF as Marge Piercy's *Woman on the Edge of Time* (1976)—by constraining women to a domestic, nurturing role in the supposed best interests of their offspring. On the other hand, though, we might find resonances with the history of slavery, in which children, being nothing more than property, were often forcibly separated from their mothers, and as slave children were frequently the product of rape and/or forced breeding, the circumstances of their origin likewise might be shrouded in secrecy; and resonances with the experience of children, especially during the Jim Crow period, whose black parentage or ancestry was, for whatever reason, kept from them. Seen through an Afrofuturist lens, V-101's tale therefore cannot help but draw on such a countermemory and thus highlight the ongoing fight "for inclusion within the human species" (Eshun, *More Brilliant* 00[-006]).

Moments such as these seem to manifest a difficulty that, according to Walter Mosley's "Black to the Future" (2000), confronts black authors attempting to write SF:

> The power of science fiction is that it can tear down the walls and windows, the artifice and laws by changing the logic, empowering the disenfranchised, or simply by asking, What if? This bold logic is not easy to attain. The destroyer-creator must first be able to imagine a world beyond his mental prison. The hardest thing to do is to break the chains of reality and go beyond into a world of your own creation. (407)

Throughout *Crown of Infinity*, and his other novels of this period, Faucette seems constantly to be caught up in the tangles of those chains, able only to reach for the attenuated signifiers of hollowed-out cultural forms—the space opera, the planetary romance, the sitcom—without being able to move beyond them, or to repurpose and reenergize them.

The Age of Ruin

Faucette continues to wrestle with genre and identity in *The Age of Ruin*. It starts, as do Hamilton's Star Kings novels, with a telepathic voice the protagonist hears while sleeping, calling him to adventure: "*Help me, Jahalazar . . . Help us . . . your people are dying*" (5, 6). Jahalazar has purple hair and eyes, and is able to spread his ears out from his skull to hear better—physical characteristics that set him apart from the other Desridif with whom he lives,[8] although many of them also possess obvious mutations, such as the four-armed Orabi and the tailed Zorge. The Desridif are the people of Bomb Valley, and they are divided into four clans, called Chevy, Dodge, Oldsmobile, and Caddy. These details suggest the novel is set after a nuclear war, and this seems confirmed by the battle scene that begins on the second page: Jahalazar and his clan chief Werethan, mounted on greathorses, fight off swarming solc—pack insects that can grow up to twenty feet in length, with foot-long razor claws and needle teeth—with swords and arrows. However, at the same time, there is a strong suggestion of sword and sorcery or heroic fantasy as Jahalazar wields Charnac, the Throwing Sword, and Werethan brandishes Modor, the Death Sword. Shortly after this battle, Werethan takes Jahalazar deep into solc-infested territory to reveal the young warrior's true origins: twenty years previously, a flying vessel was shot out of the sky by pursuers, and from its wreckage crawled Jahalazar's fatally wounded mother, clutching her infant son, who was adopted into the clan. The desire to avenge his mother's killing, along with the haunting summons to save his people, prompts Jahalazar to undertake a quest. The secret of his birth gestures toward the kind of destiny common to heroic fantasy, even as the nature of the flying vessel reinforces the sense that the apocalypse happened far in our future *and* that elsewhere in this world there remains at least one high-tech civilization.

Faucette's second novel is a curious gumbo of postapocalyptic and dying Earth fiction, of planetary romance and epic fantasy, of sword and sorcery within what is ultimately revealed to be a space opera universe (although no one leaves the planet); it also borrows the soporific poppy field from L. Frank Baum's *The Wonderful Wizard of Oz* (1900), and during the ensuing dream sequence, uses the horned battle formation deployed in H. Rider Haggard's *King Solomon's Mines* (1885). Despite this mish-mash, *The Age of Ruin* is in most respects a more competent novel than *Crown of Infinity*, not least because its succession of episodes is given a greater sense of unity by a relentlessly linear narrative following a single protagonist, Jahalazar. Its collocation and juxtaposition of multiple societies, mixing and matching versions of tribalism and feudalism with various technological levels, is familiar

---

8. Although there is nothing in the novel to indicate it, Faucette recalls that Jahalazar also has purple skin: "Why . . . ? Because it couldn't be black. It was evident the field was totally white and white oriented. I began to be dissatisfied with that. It was always a white man went to a planet and kicked the butts of the grey, brown, red, blue or green aliens" ("Road" iii).

enough from Alex Raymond's *Flash Gordon* (since 1934)[9] and from SF stories, exemplified by Murray Leinster's "Sidewise in Time" (1934), in which some upheaval brings different historical epochs into collision with each other. Such SF variants can, along with Faucette's generic mash-up, be understood as figuring the uneven development of global capitalism.[10] In this sense, *The Age of Ruin*'s linear narrative and disjointed materials—its generic hodgepodge, its contrasting lands—register, as do the fantastical currents in black Atlantic culture, including other African American fantasy and SF, the experience of particular American peripheries and semi-peripheries defined by race. Here, though, the global determinant assimilating local forms, producing particularities and imbalances, is catastrophe. Initially, it is implied that this was a long-ago nuclear war, but ultimately it is revealed that an alien species subjected the planet to a sustained bombardment. Spreading out from the solar system, humans encountered the Vish, an ancient species that demands all others become their slaves. When humankind refused, the Vish destroyed their gathered fleets and turned the Earth into "a radioactive hell" as "a perpetual monument for all to see, a reminder of what disobedience to the Vish meant" (107). In an era of anticolonial struggle and the emergence of new forms of neocolonial governance, it is not difficult to find allegorical potential in this.

However, this galactic backdrop is not revealed until the novel's penultimate chapter. Before then, Jahalazar encounters an unevenly developed and developing world, full of disjunctive particularities and conflict over territory and resources. He finds himself amongst a three-foot-tall, blue-skinned, dog-riding, bangop-herding, expressionless people, who have evolved

---

9. See *Flash Gordon: On the Planet Mongo* (2012) for a reprint of the original comic strip run.

10. Leon Trotsky argued that when capitalism is imposed on a hitherto noncapitalist society, it violently amalgamates the preexisting forces and relations of production, social structure, and cultural forms into itself. This produces not global homogeneity but modernity in an array of particular forms, and thus the unevennesses and imbalances—often euphemized as underdevelopment—that capitalism requires and systematically reproduces in order to perpetuate itself. According to world-systems theory, global capitalist modernity is composed of cores, peripheries, and semi-peripheries. These are not primarily geographical distinctions but relations imposed by the world-system between localities, peoples, and cultures, and thus a core nation will contain internal peripheries and semi-peripheries. The Warwick Research Collective (WReC) argues that the turn to the fantastic in peripheral and semi-peripheral literatures—from mid-twentieth-century Latin American magical realism to contemporary Russian and South African fantastic fiction that articulates the semi-peripheral experience of disaster capitalism and neoliberalism—can be understood in terms of the inability of conventional modes of realism, and the ability of the tools provided by fantastical modes to register the experience of radical and abrupt dislocations within the world-system.

from fish since the Age of Ruin and are locked in a war against the Zharks, humanoid sharks who are not yet capable of breathing air. He encounters the sentient Rock, an energy-draining slug thing, and giant ten-legged spiders. He serves briefly on the armored scout *Mic-mic* of the Shodrin Federation's Land Navy engaged in a *Road Warrior*-esque tank-battle-*cum*-naval-battle with similar vessels from Mesna, although no one can recall why they are at war: "Both control vast oil and mineral fields far apart.... We fight because we fight" (60). He gets caught up with a telepathic wizard and a treacherous barbarian queen straight out of Burroughs, who are at war with a dragon-riding mutant horde from neighboring Shemgol, whose leader he ultimately befriends. Such encounters are instructive in the limitations formulaic writing places on Faucette's efforts to imagine identity across difference. For example, when Jahalazar is picked up by the *Mic-mic*, a crewman's distrust of him, expressed in terms of what are effectively ethnic differences—purple hair and eyes—is promptly dismissed by the vessel's commander. When Jahalzar first encounters the giant spider Sewt, the Rock telepathically chides him for rearing back in fright and threatening to kill it. When he is imprisoned by Queen Tezzalir in a laboratory/menagerie of mutants, even though her scientists conclude that Jahalzar is "structurally human. A little abnormal" (71), the procedures to which he is subjected recall not only nineteenth-century biological determinism of race scientists, such as Samuel Morton, Louis Agassiz, Paul Broca, and others, who falsely established a racial hierarchy based on supposed physiological differences,[11] but also the documented history of medical experimentation on black bodies that dates back to colonial America.[12] However, when it comes to gendered difference, Faucette cannot move beyond simple binaries, and the revulsion he directs toward female bodies is overblown.

Tezzalir orders Jahalzar to fight in the arena, over which she presides naked "except for a drape of wispy scarlet material between her thighs," a blood-red reminder of sexual difference, of menstruation, of female "lack," and thus of castration anxiety. After he improbably defeats a dozen "swarthy skinned guards" (75), the "creamy white" (69) queen unleashes a rather different threat, a tall regal woman, "naked . . . but for a large ruby in her navel" (76). Mirroring the queen's insistent sexual difference, her clenched fists conceal "sucker discs on her palms . . . open[ing] and clos[ing] hungrily" (76) like misplaced *vaginas dentata*. These repeated images of castration anxiety escalate into a more generalized revulsion at the female body as

---

11. See Stephen Jay Gould's *The Mismeasure of Man* (1981).

12. See Harriet A. Washington's *Medical Apartheid: The Dark History of Medical Experimentation on Black Americans from Colonial Times to the Present* (2006).

inherently treacherous, destructive, unstable—and menstrual. The suckers spread out over her body, "redistributing themselves . . . until the deceptive perfection of it was gone" (76), and when she is shot, "her blood pour[s] out over her belly and thighs" (76). A giant, red, jelly-like creature sent into the arena to absorb her remains then threatens to devour Jahalazar.

A similar horror of dissolution is registered in relation to a species called the Diss. They are first encountered in the war between the fish-people and the Zharks, the latter of whom use these tiny "writhing brown" (34), flesh-dissolving sea creatures as a weapon. Through a series of subsequent encounters, we see the rapid evolution of these fecal beings as they learn to survive in freshwater and then in the air, and then to behave collectively, eventually conjoining into corporate beings that can pass as human. In the end, Jahalazar does not hesitate to activate a device that will completely eradicate them.

Jahalazar thus enters into full maturity, becoming the leader of the new human resistance to the Vish, by overcoming the maternal body that threatens perpetual infantilization and castration, and by hygienically cleansing the world of fecal terror. Even as Faucette articulates the damage caused by the construction of race and the uses to which racial categories are put, he reiterates formulaic fictions' terror of boundary dissolution. This tension is indicative, in its unthinking way, of the masculinist, jingoistic human exceptionalism Campbell inculcated into genre SF in the 1940s—values shaped by dominant American ideology, and shared by some strands of black nationalist thought, that elsewhere New Wave and especially feminist SF were rejecting. Faucette's third novel, which attempts to articulate a more specifically African American experience, and his fourth arguably begin to challenge these values.

The Warriors of Terra and *Siege of Earth*

The Warriors of Terra was actually written before *Crown of Infinity* but was rejected by Wollheim as "being too complicated for his readership" ("Road" ii)—a fairly improbable claim if the published version is anything to go by since it consists of a straightforward pursuit narrative, with occasional chapters leaping forward or backward in time as part of a broader historical framework for the central action. Faucette describes it as an "allegorical novel" about gang warfare in Harlem when he was growing up whereby "gangs [sic] avenging members killed by other gangs formed an endless circle of retribution" (ii). Although *The Warriors of Terra* does, especially in its closing pages, foreground issues about revenge, beyond a vague resemblance to the flight-through-hostile-territory narrative of Sol Yurick's *The Warriors* (1965), there is little to encourage reading it in terms of street gangs.

However, *The Warriors of Terra* does contain an excess of material that is susceptible to being vaguely read as an allegory about African American history, hope, and struggle. Predating Butler's *Patternist* (1976–84) and Delany's *Nevèrÿon* (1979–87) series, it is probably genre SF's first neoslave narrative.[13] It also encodes the kind of fantasy of black rage and black revenge found in the cruder Black Power SF thrillers, such as Julian Moreau's *The Black Commandos* (1967) and Nivi-kofi A. Easley's *The Militants* (1974).[14] While this seems a much likelier reason for Wollheim to have been cautious about publishing the novel, Faucette studiously avoids giving his protagonist, Ran Hudson, a skin color or racial identity, and thus it is not at all clear such a reading of the novel would have been readily available to Wollheim. Faucette's refusal to specify Ran's identity in this way also has a curious effect on the reader's understanding of both the character and the novel. In crudely dichotomous terms: on the one hand, Ran can be seen as the (justifiably) angry black man who goes too far, becoming as hate-filled and prejudiced—and therefore just as bad—as those who enslaved him; on the other, he can be seen as unveiling the psychotic violence fueling the white-as-default Campbellian human exceptionalism, a concept Faucette mocks at various points with sarcastic capitalizations, such as "Man's Divine and Unalterable Destiny: Lordship of the Galaxy" (10).

During the war between the Terran and Spartan empires, a group of human captives, including Ran, are sold into slavery on the distant world of Morgia. A decade later, after his lover, Lily, has been killed by a Morg, Ran vows to escape, return to Earth, and bring back a battle fleet to destroy the Morgian empire. His escape attempt escalates into a slave revolt as dozens follow his lead. The breakneck narrative barely pauses as they flee over the mountains to the spaceport, are captured, escape, seize a spaceship, are pursued, crash-land, and so on. It is the kind of adventure story in which the protagonist repeatedly shrugs off being shot, in which his giant comrade Leif cuts them free from their crashed ship's blazing hull with a mighty space axe, and in which the cave they take through a mountain is bisected by a mighty chasm across which they must leap, yet Faucette pulls off each cliché with a certain verve.

---

13. The term "neo-slave narrative" is attributed to Ishmael Reed, who coined it while writing *Flight to Canada* (1976), and Margaret Walker's *Jubilee* (1966) is usually cited as the first example.

14. See Bould, "Come Alive."

Initially, the flight from Morgia in search of Earth seems to rework the idea of antebellum slaves fleeing in the direction of the North Star. However, once Ran's ragtag band of runaways enter the barrens—a vast area of space, rich in stars but utterly devoid of planets—this transforms into an image of the Middle Passage in reverse, of a return to Africa and to a past before their enslavement. Such Afrofuturist allegory is very faintly limned, however, and perhaps better described as part of a broader pattern of potential resonances of which the author does not always seem fully conscious or able to develop coherently. This is most evident in a series of allusions to the American Civil War, from a more or less throwaway reference to Andersonville, the notoriously deadly Confederate POW camp, to ironically naming the Terran cruiser Ran commands in the closing pages *Rhett Butler*. About halfway through the novel, the fleeing slaves crash-land on Novad and are about to be recaptured when the local military show up: "At the fore of each group marched several yellow-skinned beings in Confederate officer uniforms" (91). It soon becomes clear that these "grey uniforms" (99) are indeed to be understood as identical to "Civil War uniform[s]" (107). But Faucette's reason for this is unclear. The Novadian's yellowness implies they look like light-skinned African Americans, despite their garb, but it could also imply they are cowards.

The novel is more successful if the reader stops thinking about it in terms of a racial allegory and instead focuses on it as an attempt to carry genre SF heroism to its logical conclusion. When Ran and the surviving handful of escaped slaves reach Earth, it is to discover that the Terran/Spartan war became so terrible that the two rivals abandoned war and united behind the development of the Commonwealth of Peaceful Species (the CPS). Wandering the streets, Ran is disturbed by the sight of "Terrans, aliens, and Spartans" walking together and decides he should do something about such integration once he has "taken care of Morgia" (151). By this point, the raging determination that drove him to battle impossible odds has lost any flavor of heroism: he is merely a psychotically violent racist. He will go on to try to trigger a CPS war against the Morgian empire, and it will cost the lives of all the escaped slaves who continued to stand by him before he finally learns the futility of revenge.

Perhaps the most intriguing aspect of the novel, though, is its articulation of neocolonial governance. Dane Barclay, known as the Peacemaker, explains how the CPS violently forces peace on the galaxy: no member species or civilization is permitted to wage war internally or against another member, and the "Peace Legions . . . persuade others to join. . . . Many do, for they see that we offer genuine peaces and have the weapons to enforce it. Some don't. It is then that the Peace Legions go forth. The reluctant party either joins or is defeated and forced to join" (154–55). When Ran's machinations bring the CPS fleet to the Morgian Empire, the terms of joining the CPS are spelt out: "The Commonwealth doesn't allow slavery or class societies or hereditary rulers. . . . You'll have to pay damages for the slaves. The loss of their services may create problems, but the Commonwealth will extend credit to you. Many companies will compete to sell you machinery to replaces the slaves. In no time, your people will prosper" (172).[15] Significantly, several short chapters, set in the future of the main action, show the Commonwealth, headed by Ran, falling apart as its discontented members argue that it is merely the means of Terran hegemony.

Both the front and back covers of *The Warriors of Terra* proclaim that it is "introducing a new science fiction adventure series," to be called *The Peacemakers*. However, the novel leaves rather less scope for such a development than *The Age of Ruin*, and Belmont presumably rejected *Siege of Earth*. It was published instead "under special arrangements" by the anonymous-sounding "Modern Promotions, A Unisystems Company." The novel's front cover declares it the "second in a new science fiction adventure series," but seems ambivalent about the promise of further installments. Faucette describes it as his "first novel not written from the gut [and it] shows" ("Road" iv). Set in the closing stages of the Terran-Spartan war, it is little more than a 30,000-word description of battle sequences—told mostly from a command perspective—as the Spartan fleets bombard the Earth, to which the remnants of the Terran empire have retreated, from space. Just as the double-coding of *Star Wars* (Lucas 1977) enables both the Rebels and the Empire to be understood as representing America/Amerikkka, so the *Siege of Earth* encourages the reader to sympathize with the last-ditch defenders of the Earth while also depicting Terrans as horrendously violent aggressors: "Never had a race been so dreaded" (33). This sort of contradiction defines a novel that, consisting almost entirely of war scenes, clearly regards itself as antiwar and more specifically, given the time of publication, opposed to US

---

15. The issue of reparations for slavery has been a feature of American political discourse, albeit often muted, from the end of the Civil War through to the 2020 Democrats primary debates. For a recent discussion of the case for reparations, see Ta-Nahesi Coates, "The Case for Reparations." Opponents often cite the cost of reparations, as if it makes the idea untenable rather than indicating the magnitude of the horror of, or the US economy's continued indebtedness to, slavery. A common figure, repeated since 1993, is $97 trillion dollars, derived from an estimated 222,505,049 hours of forced labor between 1619 and 1865, at 6% interest. When Britain finally abolished slavery in the Caribbean in 1883, the government did pay out £20 million, but as compensation to now former slave owners for the loss of their "property."

imperialism. Indeed, a two-page lecture by the Spartan Admiral Shus Show on humanity's warlike nature includes a passage about the United States:

> There was a nation in the days of old Terran history, called a "good" nation. Yet it bombed another nation practically back into the stone age. It firebombed Dresden, sending 200,000 men, women and children to flaming death. It dropped the first atomic bombs on a nearly defeated enemy. For ten years it sledge-hammered smaller and weaker nations, friend and foe alike. It massacred villages of women and children—and gloried in it. And when there arose those who tired of endless war, they were called names, beaten and shot down by their own troops. The point to remember is that this was a "good" nation. (23)

One hundred and thirty pages later, following the Earth's last-minute reprieve thanks to another species invading the now vulnerable Spartan Empire, the final two-page chapter is little more than a litany of wars, ending in the question, "Must there always be war?" (158). Sadly, in terms of *The Peacemakers* internal chronology, the answer had already been given: yes, only it will call itself peace, and it will be endless.

Conclusion

Ironically, one of the recurring tropes of Faucette's novels is the phoenix rising, after much adversity, from the ashes of defeat: humans, transformed, return to the stars once more to challenge those who crushed them. During his long exile from publication, Faucette sought to transform his own work in a similar way. He completely rewrote *Crown of Infinity* as *The Earth Will Be Avenged*, with "a black hero upfront, commander of the starship *Harlem*" (v). He turned to short stories, and set out to exploit two gaps he thought he saw in the market—"black stories" and ones that explored "sex-gender-reproduction" ("Road" vi)—without success. His rejection slips began to include occasional positive comments. He published a couple of short stories in relatively obscure venues. He saw the announcement for Sheree R. Thomas's *Dark Matter: A Century of Speculative Fiction from the African Diaspora* (2000) anthology too late and missed the deadline for submissions. In 2002, he self-published his own collection, *Black Science Fiction*, ending his introduction with the observation: "I am no Hopkinson, Delany, Butler, or Barnes. But I try. I will always try. Till the day they bury me" (ix).

Within a year of its appearance, he was dead.

Works Cited

Barrett, A. Igoni. *Blackass*. Chatto & Windus, 2015.

Baum, L. F. *The Wonderful Wizard of Oz*. 1900. Sterling, 2005.

Bould, Mark. "Come Alive by Saying No: An Introduction to Black Power SF." *Afrofuturism*, special issue of *Science Fiction Studies*, vol. 34, no. 2, 2007, pp. 220–40.

Butler, Octavia E. *Kindred*. Beacon, 1979.

———. *Wild Seed*. Warner, 1980.

Coates, Ta-Nahesi. "The Case for Reparations." *Atlantic* (June 2014). https://www.theatlantic.com/magazine/archive/2014/06/the-case-for-reparations/361631/. Accessed 26 Jun. 2019.

Corley, Edwin. *Siege*. Stein & Day, 1969.

Delany, Samuel R., Jr. "Aye and Gomorrah . . ." 1967. *Aye and Gomorrah: and Other Stories*, Vintage, 2003, pp. 91–101.

———. *Babel-17*. Ace, 1966.

———. *The Einstein Intersection*. 1967. Wesleyan UP, 1998.

———. "Time Considered as a Helix of Semi-Precious Stones." 1968. *Aye and Gomorrah: and Other Stories*. Vintage, 2003, pp. 218–59.

Easley, Nivi-Kofi A. *The Militants*. Carlton, 1974.

Eshun, Kodwo. "Further Considerations of Afrofuturism." *CR: The New Centennial Review*, vol. 3, no. 2, 2003, pp. 287–302.

———. *More Brilliant than the Sun: Adventures in Sonic Fiction*. Quartet, 1998.

Faucette, John M. *The Age of Ruin*. Ace, 1968.

———. *Crown of Infinity*. Ace, 1968.

———. *Disco Hustle*. Holloway House, 1978.

———. "The Ghost Writer." *Black Science Fiction*, Infinity Publishing, 2002, pp. 154–67.

———. "The Road to Black Science Fiction." *Black Science Fiction*. Infinity Publishing, 2002, pp. ii–ix.

———. *Siege of Earth*. Modern Promotions, 1971.

———. *The Warriors of Terra*. Belmont, 1970.

Firestone, Shulamith. *The Dialectic of Sex: The Case for Feminist Revolution*. William Morrow, 1970.

Gould, Stephen Jay. *The Mismeasure of Man*. Norton, 1981.

Haggard, H. R. *King Solomon's Mines*. 1885. Modern Library, 1957.

Haldane, J. B. S. *Daedalus; or Science and the Future*. E. P. Dutton, 1924.

Huxley, Aldous. *Brave New World*. 1932. Harper Perennial Modern Classics, 2005.

Leinster, Murray. "Sidewise in Time." *Astounding Stories*, June 1934, pp. 10–47.

Lucas, George, director. *Star Wars*. Twentieth Century Fox, 1977.

Moreau, Julian. *The Black Commandos*. Cultural Institute Press, 1967.

Mosley, Walter. "Black to the Future." *Dark Matter: A Century of Speculative Fiction from the African Diaspora*, edited by Sheree R. Thomas, Warner, 2000, pp. 405–7.

Piercy, Marge. *Woman on the Edge of Time*. Knopf, 1976.

Raymond, Alex. *Flash Gordon: On the Planet Mongo*. Titan, 2012.

Reed, Ishmael. *Flight to Canada*. 1976. Scribner, 1998.

Rieder, John. *Colonialism and the Emergence of Science Fiction*. Wesleyan UP, 2008.

Schuyler, George S. *Black No More*. 1931. Northeastern UP, 1989.

Stapledon, Olaf. *Last and First Men: A Story of the Near and Far Future*. Methuen, 1930.

———. *Odd John: A Story Between Jest and Earnest*. Methuen, 1935.

Thomas, Sheree R. *Dark Matter: A Century of Speculative Fiction from the African Diaspora*. Warner, 2000.

Walker, Margaret. *Jubilee*. Houghton Mifflin, 1966.

Washington, Harriet A. *Medical Apartheid: The Dark History of Medical Experimentation on Black Americans from Colonial Times to the Present*. Doubleday, 2008.

CHAPTER 7

Runoff

Afroaquanauts in Landscapes of Sacrifice

Elizabeth A. Wheeler

In SF, music, and visual arts, Afrofuturism reflects the viewpoint of people immersed in risk and aware of historical atrocities who persist in envisioning and engineering a survivable future—and who do so with style. This viewpoint arises from black history but also swims close to the worldviews of people exposed to environmental illness—many of whom are also black people. In neighborhoods across the United States, African American children have disabilities because lead has poisoned the water in their taps and the paint on their walls. There is nothing wrong with having a disability. However, people in power do wrong when they create disabilities, then deny families the means to care for themselves. I use the term "prosthetic community" to describe the cluster of human help, money, technologies, education, and job supports necessary to secure a decent future for young people with disabilities. In American cities like Flint, Michigan, and Baltimore, Maryland, as in Afrofuturist science fiction, state neglect and violence rush in to fill the void left by the absence of prosthetic community. Young adult SF confronts the politics of chronic illness for African American youth in landscapes of environmental sacrifice across the United States.

Afrofuturism bears witness to such wrongs, and its metaphors make tangible the risks of environmental illness. Sherri L. Smith's 2013 young adult dystopia *Orleans* imagines a blood-borne illness in the New Orleans of 2056 after multiple massive hurricanes. When the Delta Fever threatens to spread outside the Gulf region, the federal government declares it no longer part of the United States, cuts off all services, and erects a heavily policed quarantine wall. To survive in this abandoned society as it returns to its swampy nature, people hunt and fish, barter and battle, form themselves into tribes based on blood type, and try to relieve the fever's pain by stealing cleaner blood. Fen de la Guerre, the teenage main character of *Orleans*, carries the disease, but her O-positive blood gives her some protection. She braves toxic waters to secure a better life for the next generation. The novel follows her adventures as she evades blood hunters and tries to save an O-positive newborn baby from contracting the fever. Eventually they meet the scientist Daniel, who sneaks into Orleans with hopes of curing the Delta Fever and joins them in their quest.

Many observers draw parallels between the imaginary worlds of Afrofuturism and the realities of black life. What, then, is the relationship between SF and real life? It is not a one-on-one correspondence but rather a set of metaphors opening the doors of insight. We might call these metaphors "significant distortions," following Samuel R. Delany, Jr. A reigning elder of Afrofuturist fiction, Delany explains, "In science fiction the future is only a writerly convention that allows the SF writer to indulge in a significant distortion of the present that sets up a rich and complex dialogue with the reader's here and now" (47). Afrofuturism takes SF tropes of interplanetary travel and alien species and retrofits them to black experience. However, *Orleans* features significant distortions different from otherworldly Afrofuturist tropes. Instead, its metaphors of disease and oppression spark a dialogue with our own watery planet. This chapter will focus on four significant distortions in *Orleans*: the quarantine wall, the toxic economy, runoff, and the Afroaquanaut. These metaphors unveil the surreal logic of environmental racism and the acts of imagination necessary to oppose it.

The metaphors of *Orleans* face down the contemporary politics of environmental illness for African American youth in urban landscapes of sacrifice. Afrofuturism has two poles, negative and positive. In its negative Afrofuturism, *Orleans*'s anarchic future city draws inspiration from severe and repeated flooding in the era of climate change and the abandonment of African Americans with disabilities during Hurricane Katrina (2005). Positive Afrofuturism insists upon a better future, while negative Afrofuturism constructs dystopias that warn of a bleak future if we don't enact racial and environmental justice now.

In its positive Afrofuturism, *Orleans* gives us a heroine dedicated to creating a decent niche for her people. With Afrofuturist panache, Fen is so adept at survival she seems to walk on water. She joins the bloodline of young black geniuses in African American SF who battle the forces militating against their survival. Afronauts have a long tradition in Afrofuturism's interplanetary dreamscapes. We might call Fen de la Guerre an Afroaquanaut, who wades through alien landscapes here on Earth. In the words of the redoubtable Afroaquanaut band Parliament, Fen attempts to "dance underwater and not get wet" (Parliament).

While astronauts wear space suits, Fen continually assesses and musters her own bodily forms of protection. These forms of protection include her sharp hearing, light tread, scarred arms, and command of the local dialect. Elizabeth C. Hamilton calls such protective factors "technologies of survival" and writes that Afronaut figures in the arts "speak to the sustained feeling of isolation and otherness that people of color feel when traversing white spaces. The environments are sometimes hostile; so, the technologies that they wear are a necessity" (22). Thus, Fen's prowess speaks to positive Afrofuturism, her role as capable hero, but also to negative Afrofuturism, her body under threat. Her vulnerability matters as much as her strength.

Fen has no access to miraculous medical or social cures. As the scars on her arms attest, she has little chance of surviving whole. She will pay for her heroism with her life. Negative Afrofuturism, which Tiffany Barber calls "transgressive disfigurement," insists that we confront "the ruptured black body" (4, 14). Afroaquanauts need life support systems to navigate hostile terrain: systems like clean water, access to health care and disability services, and an end to state violence. Real-life Afroaquanauts struggle to survive the low-oxygen atmosphere of police brutality. "I can't breathe," said Eric Garner to the police officers choking him. Freddie Gray, who had asthma, asked officers for his inhaler but did not get it. He stopped breathing in the police van. Earth can be a toxic and alien planet.

The protagonist of *Orleans* who meets with state violence is female. In this way Fen de la Guerre stands in for young African American women across the United States. Although media coverage focuses on black men, police brutality visits black women just as often. According to Andrea J. Ritchie, the evidence shows that "young women of color experience every form and context of police violence" that young men do, and at the same rates (87). For example, "Racial profiling studies analyzing the experiences of women of color separately from those of men of color conclude that there is an *identical pattern of racial disparities in police stops for both men and women*" (Ritchie 10; emphasis in original) The significant distortions of Afrofuturism reveal commonalities of oppression and resistance in young men's and women's lives across varied landscapes of environmental sacrifice.

Afrofuturism reveals kinships amongst locales and struggles that might seem very different from each other at first glance. To demonstrate this point, I apply the four significant distortions from *Orleans* not to Hurricane Katrina—the most obvious and intended real-life parallel—but to the lead poisoning crises in Baltimore and Flint. *Orleans* holds up an Afrofuturist mirror to the young women and girls who protested the lead poisoning crisis in Flint, Michigan, and to the life of Freddie Gray, who had learning and physical disabilities from childhood lead exposure. For Gray, Fen de la Guerre, and many young people of color with environmental illness, disability has served as a primary driver of state surveillance and harm (Ritchie 91). Exposure to toxic runoff leads to running off from police. In Flint, Baltimore, and the fictive world of *Orleans*, young adults muster physical and political forms of resistance to confront physical and political toxins.

Four Significant Distortions
THE QUARANTINE WALL

Orleans transforms the invisible boundaries of race and disease into the literal metaphor of the quarantine wall. As Isiah Lavender III writes, "SF's ability to literalize metaphor heightens what is often in our societies submerged as invisible and yet trenchantly remains, like divisive racial boundaries, a strong feature in the histories of race and disease" (66). For example, *Orleans* does not portray differential environmental risk as hard to track or easy to deny. Instead, it seals off the high-risk zone with a militarized quarantine wall and declares the Gulf Coast region no longer part of the "The Outer States of America." This negative Afrofuturism displays the consequences of current segregation if left unchecked.

The term "quarantine wall" indicates more than a necessary and temporary medical isolation. It declares a group no longer part of the larger society. In *Orleans*, the wall shields the rest of the country not only from disease but also from the responsibility of caring for those locked inside it. Armed troops man a twenty- to thirty-foot-high wall surrounded by protective moats and swamps and equipped with drones that can sniff out Delta Fever (Smith 321). The novel makes literal the invisible walls that surround many communities of color.

In *Orleans*'s commentary on climate change, the Gulf region has endured a series of ever-stronger hurricanes, beginning with Katrina in 2005 and culminating in Hurricane Jesus in 2019. Pollution of the Delta water results in mass epidemics. Delta Fever symptoms include fatigue, yellow skin, mobility problems, cramps, and hallucinations, but in the book's present, most people live with the symptoms rather than dying from them (Smith 21–22). Amongst the worst affected, people with the AB blood type "shoot, swallow, and smoke anything to forget the pain of living with, but not dying from, the Fever" (39). Walled off from medical care, Delta residents endure the Fever the best they can. They numb the pain with their own toxic technologies of survival. The quarantine wall echoes the medical model of disability: if you cannot be cured, you are consigned to social death. It also echoes the psychic pain of racial segregation.

The Gulf region survives in its own ingenious ways, yet also dies every day for want of the things the Outer States of America could provide. The Outer States withhold help that could heal the environment, treat the fever, and provide disability services. Small-scale Gulf enterprises, such as shellfish beds and hydroponic greenhouses, demonstrate the power of nature to filter the water and help the Delta heal itself (143, 250). However, the devastated region needs outside help for large-scale environmental cleanup. Orleans scientists never conduct research to treat the fever. Instead, they encourage tribalism in the postapocalyptic society and study its effects. *Orleans* likens their research to the US Public Health Service's infamous Tuskegee Syphilis Study, which tracked 399 poor African American men with syphilis for forty years but never treated any of them with penicillin (Centers for Disease Control and Prevention). Daniel exclaims, "It's like Tuskegee all over again. They never wanted a cure" (207). Smith extends medical abuse into future centuries to demonstrate that scientific racism will continue unless people deliberately interrupt it.

The Outer States also fail to assist people with disabilities. Smith underscores how chronic conditions become fatal in the absence of care. After the storms, "The list of no-longer-treatable diseases grew: diabetes, asthma, cancer." Fen de la Guerre describes the abandonment after Hurricane Jesus to her new companion Daniel:

> The Government give up, say everybody evacuate. But can't everybody fit on a road out of town at the same time. Some people can't even get up outta they beds, so what *they* gonna do? No gas for the cars, and the roads be clogged, and people be needing they medicine and whatnot. . . . The Government say they can't save us. There ain't enough of us left to bother. (172–73)

Sherri Smith knows firsthand how a lagging disaster response endangers people with disabilities. Her diabetic mother, Joan Marie Smith, was stranded in New Orleans after Hurricane Katrina with a dwindling insulin supply. The novelist recalled in an interview, "It was devastating, and while she was down there, I was on the internet doing research trying to figure out how to get her out. Which actually worked; we got her out" (WETA). In the novel's acknowledgments, Smith thanks "the Coast Guard for listening when no one else would, and helping evacuate my mother from New Orleans five days after the storm, three days after the levee broke, and the day before her insulin ran out." Equipped with fewer resources, nearly everyone left behind seems to be black or mixed race in the postflood world of *Orleans.*

While the blood tribes improvise their technologies of survival, a scientist coming in from the Outer States has the luxury of a high-tech space suit. Daniel's containment suit symbolizes the differential risks of climate change for those inside and outside the wall. Daniel, a young scientist who sneaks into Orleans with hopes of curing the Delta Fever that killed his brother, wears this thick, impermeable wetsuit. He trades off narrating the story with Fen de la Guerre, who comes from Orleans and already carries the disease. Smith states, "Like an umbilical cord, [the suit] also processed bodily water, sweat, and other secretions into pouches, breaking solids into fluids, and distilled fluids into drinking water" (53). Daniel is a healthy ecology of one. Unlike the people of Orleans, his wearable wastewater treatment system protects him from disease. Daniel can even cause harm while remaining immune from it. Aiming to conduct medical research, he carries vials of ultra-refined Delta Fever virus that could wipe out the region's entire population (46, 111). He accidentally loses the vials in the course of the novel's adventures, and Fen watches him cry with guilt: "Daniel blink and I hear the tears in his eyes being sucked away into drinking water by his suit. I just can't bring myself to care" (266). Immersed in risk, Fen cannot afford the luxury of tears.

Smith contrasts Daniel's technology and formal education with Fen's deep knowledge of place and risk. While Daniel is a typical SF scientist-hero, Fen de la Guerre joins a long line of Afrofuturist "young black geniuses battling oppressive forces" (Yaszek 22). Instead of an immunity suit, she has a genius for hiding from danger. As a child, her educated parents taught her how to "talk tribe," a close cognate of Black English, to conceal her naiveté from Orleans's many predators. Talking tribe is like being a chameleon, hiding in plain sight, "So no one can find me—and I'll be safe from owls and hawks" (189). Casting herself as a small prey animal, the child Fen compares the language she uses with humans to the technologies of survival she has learned outdoors. Fen embodies an ethic of care. As she climbs up trees and across cars and rooftops, her body compensates for the extra weight of the new-born girl left in her keeping. "This'd be easier without a baby strapped to my chest, but a lot of things be easier without that" (68). In the weight of the baby, Fen feels the imbalance of differential environmental risk. She has seven days to protect Baby Girl "before the Fever take hold in a newborn" (61). Baby Girl counters the negative Afrofuturism of dystopia with positive Afrofuturism: she represents Fen's hope for a future generation to escape unharmed.

The trope of the quarantine wall illuminates the lead poisoning crises in Flint, Michigan, and the Sandtown neighborhood of Baltimore. In both cities, racial segregation, postindustrial capital, and government malfeasance threw up walls no less real for being invisible. The quarantine walls shielded the (ir)responsible parties not only from environmental risk but from the obligation to care for those trapped inside. Lead exposure, common in postindustrial and low-income neighborhoods, creates disabilities in children. "Lead is a potent neurotoxin, and childhood lead poisoning has an impact on many developmental and biological processes, most notably intelligence, behavior, and overall life achievement," explains Dr. Mona Hanna-Attisha, pediatrician and public health researcher at Hurley Children's Hospital in Flint (283). A soluble metal, lead leaches into drinking water via pipes or connectors. Infants bathe in the toxic water and drink it in their formula. Landlords have a legal obligation to remove lead-based paint. If they do not, toddlers like Freddie Gray and his siblings eat lead paint flakes, which taste as sweet as candy.

The story of lead poisoning in both Flint, Michigan, and Baltimore's Sandtown neighborhood begins with racial segregation, then the flight of capital. For more than a century, Sandtown has served as a containment zone for black people; however, under legal segregation, at least they had jobs. African American steelworkers lived there because it had the closest housing open to them, so Sandtown declined when the steel mills closed (Singer; Allam). By 1982, Baltimore's working-class economy had collapsed, losing half its jobs in primary metals, shipbuilding repair, and transportation assembly (Levine 107). The people who stayed in Sandtown were the ones who could not afford to get out, and slumlording replaced homeownership. No concrete wall kept them in Sandtown, but poverty, industrial decline, and the old Jim Crow boundary lines did the job just as well.

Flint, Michigan, is also a quarantine zone. State officials poisoned the city because they no longer saw it as part of the state. Like Daniel in his encounter suit, they could harm Flint without harming themselves. Flint lives under emergency management laws that require austerity measures to balance the budget. These austerity measures came at the expense of clean water. After the cash-strapped Detroit Water and Sewage Department jacked up its prices, a series of Flint emergency managers made the decision to use the Flint River as an interim water source (Fonger). They began drawing water from the postindustrial river in April 2014 without corrosion controls to prevent lead in old plumbing connections from leaching into the water supply. Elevated blood lead levels in young children soared, more so in African American children. In neglecting corrosion controls, emergency managers violated the basic principles of infrastructure engineering. This neglect could only happen because state officials saw Flint as a foreign planet whose resident aliens did not have the same bodily needs as humans.

Like Baltimore, Flint has weathered racial segregation and the flight of capital. The birthplace of General Motors, Flint used to have a very high standard of living. As GM closed plants between 1980 and 2005, Flint lost forty-one percent of its jobs (Jacobs 351, 354–55). By 2009, "the Flint area had lost more than 70,000 GM jobs since peak employment in 1968" (Young 2). General Motors withdrew the jobs but left the polluted river behind. Past housing discrimination had left now-unemployed African Americans stranded in the central city just as the state of Michigan began to build a quarantine wall around it. Michigan's economic planning failed to imagine a future for black workers. The state focused infrastructure development on the white suburbs and left the central city to fend for itself, which "lessened the potential for new private investment" (Jacobs 359). Refused the technologies to support productive lives, Flint residents watched their city turn into an Afrofuturist dystopia.

Michigan evicted Flint from the larger democracy through emergency management, which opened the door to environmental racism. Since the collapse of the auto industry in the 1980s, state-appointed emergency managers govern impoverished Michigan cities rather than elected mayors and city councils. Emergency managers have a free hand in making decisions. This loss of local control overwhelmingly affects African Americans. In fact, "a startling 51% of African Americans residing in Michigan have been under the governance of emergency management laws at some point since 2008. . . . Even more shocking, in a state that is majority non-Hispanic white (76.6%), only 2.4% of Whites statewide were ever directly under the governance of an emergency manager during the same time period [from 2008–13]" (Lee et al. 5). This split reality provides the subtext to Flint's abandonment. Problems with the Flint River water began immediately after the switch in water sources, but state agencies and officials denied and covered up these problems for more than a year and a half. The damage will now cost hundreds of millions of dollars to fix.

In Flint, as in Sandtown, differential environmental risk correlates with both race and poverty. Dr. Hanna-Attisha and her colleagues conducted the Flint lead poisoning study that exposed the problem to the public. Their study established correlations amongst race, poverty, and contamination. Flint's entire population is 70.6% African American, and the proportion of children under five with elevated blood lead levels rose from 2.4% to 4.9% after the switch to Flint River water. However, the areas of Flint with the highest levels of lead in the water were the poorest and were also 78.8% African American, and there the elevated blood levels rose from 4% to 10.6% (Hanna-Attisha et al. 285) After analyzing the government's slow response to the health issues of poor African Americans in Flint, an independent inquiry concluded that "this is a case of environmental injustice" (Bosman). While poor black neighborhoods may not have a wall around them, elevated blood lead levels revealed their invisible boundaries.

The quarantine wall around Orleans shields the rest of the country not only from disease but also from the responsibility of caring for those locked inside it. The quarantine wall around Flint shielded state officials not only from environmental risk but from the responsibility of caring for Flint residents. The emails of Dennis Muchmore, chief of staff to Michigan Governor Rick Snyder, reveal the depth of official denial. Muchmore knew and yet he did not know; he cared and yet he did not care. The governor's chief aide expressed concerns about water contamination long before the story broke in the press in September 2015. He had emailed his colleagues, "If GM refuses to use the water in their plant and our own agencies are warning people not to drink it . . . we look pretty stupid hiding behind some financial statement" (Livengood). Muchmore did nothing, however, because no one in state government was willing to pay to fix the problem. Michigan's money was not Flint's money, just as Flint's problem was not the state's problem, even though Flint was under state emergency control.

After the scandal broke, Muchmore helped the governor erect a wall of denial. In September 2015, Muchmore emailed the governor, "It's really the city's water system that needs to deal with it . . . I can't figure out why the state is responsible" (Chan). Muchmore had urged his colleagues, "Since we're in charge, we can hardly ignore the people of Flint." Nonetheless, that's exactly what they did: ignore the people of Flint while in charge of them. A quarantine wall permitted power to seize control while denying care and responsibility, thus allowing a state official on the other side of the wall to look the other way. Stricken from the state government's list of concerns and denied state funds, the postindustrial city developed its own toxic economy.

THE TOXIC ECONOMY

A toxic landscape becomes a toxic economy: people survive by harming themselves and others. This economy depends on the circulation of water, blood, and chemicals but also the liquidity of capital. Clean blood is the principal commodity in the toxic economy of Orleans. With its stark portrait of economic exploitation, *Orleans,* like other SF, "can help us overcome the obstacles to our full understanding of capital's role in environmental crisis" (Otto 121). Blood hunters assess and threaten the bodies of Fen and Baby Girl according to the market value of their O Positive blood type: "The Fever be in us, but it ain't eating O blood up from the inside like it do other types. So O types got to be extra careful of hunters and the farms where they be taking they kidnapped victims to drain them alive" (16). Blood hunters would love to capture a prize like Baby Girl. As Fen states, "Baby Girl brand-new. Cleanest blood there is. She ain't got the Fever in her yet, and won't if I be careful, don't give her Orleans water, or cuts to taint her blood" (61). Baby Girl puts the future in Afrofuturism: she has a chance to survive.

Orleans paints the toxic economy as violence against African American women. Fen refers to it as "blood whoring" and "blood slavery" (257, 17). The sexual violence of the blood farm parallels the sexualized violence of police brutality African American women face in real life. Ritchie points out "the pervasive sexualization of young women of color during police stops, sexual intimidation, and extortion of sexual favors in exchange for their freedom" (86). On her own behalf and on Baby Girl's, Fen de la Guerre engages in feminist resistance against capitalist patriarchy. When Fen was nine years old, hunters and bloodhounds captured her and took her to a blood farm, a literal metaphor for child prostitution and the female experience of slavery. The madam took her to the outbuildings behind the big house and told her a gentleman wanted "a virgin, untouched by needle or knife" (95). Smith describes the theft of blood as if it were rape: "When he enter me, it be through the skin. First a swift wipe of a cold cotton pad, then a needle, sharp and hot, into the biggest vein of my right arm" (96). Like nineteenth-century slavery, the blood slavery of the twenty-first century relies on the rape and rupture of black bodies.

Orleans blends this negative Afrofuturism with the positive Afrofuturism of heroics. Her options limited, Fen resists patriarchy through self-harm.

After the "gentleman" buys her outright, Fen wraps her arms around a hot stew pot and burns her arms "near to the bone." "Burn marks so thick, ain't nobody ever gonna get a needle in the easy way" (98, 17). Fen also protects Baby Girl from patriarchy. She leaves Baby Girl in the care of Father John, whom she knows and trusts, only to find him with a dialysis machine preparing to drain off Baby Girl's blood. He sings the hymn "There Is Power in the Blood" while looking for an infant sized needle (308, 313). When Fen returns, she "tackle[s] him" and stabs him to death with his own "needles, scalpels, knives" while cutting herself in the struggle (314). She can only save Baby Girl by harming herself and others, using medical tools already co-opted from care into exploitation.

The toxic economy of Sandtown depends on the flow of capital and the circulation of water, lead, paint, and blood. These two kinds of liquidity cycle together, create disability, and turn young black bodies into countable commodities. Ruth Norton is the executive director of the Coalition to End Childhood Lead Poisoning. In 1993, when Freddie Gray was a child, Norton would walk down the streets of Sandtown and "parents could tell me their kids' lead level right off the bat, before they could tell me the name of their child's school or their teacher" (Rentz). The children's blood had become quantifiable data.

The numbers for environmental risk correlate with both race and poverty. Sandtown is 97% black. Saul Kerpelman, a Baltimore attorney who has represented clients in more than four thousand lead poisoning lawsuits over three decades, says that "nearly 99.9 percent of my clients were black. . . . That's the sad fact to life in the ghetto that the only living conditions people can afford will likely poison their kids" (McCoy, "Freddie"). Lack of decent, affordable housing creates a quarantine wall, trapping families within the lead poisoning zone and subjecting them to the toxic economy of slumlording. Blood hunters track Fen and Baby Girl because their O Positive blood type has a high market value. In Sandtown, blood lead levels and Maryland judiciary case files track the grisly economics of slumlording and environmental racism.

Sandtown residents live off the toxic economy through the drug trade and the lead checks they receive from lawsuits. Nonresidents profit from the toxic economy through slumlording, predatory finance, legal fees, policing, and electoral politics. Freddie Gray's family won a lead exposure settlement from their landlord Stanley Rochkind in 2008, but Rochkind's investment in substandard housing extended far beyond the Gray's apartment building. Between 2001 and 2015, hundreds of tenants sued Rochkind for lead paint exposure (Maryland Judiciary Case Search Results). Predatory finance companies also profit from lead poisoning. Access Funding, for instance, visits young people with lead-derived cognitive impairments in their Baltimore homes and offers to buy their structured settlements for cents on the dollar. Freddie Gray sold $146,000 of his settlement for $18,300 (McCoy, "How"). In *Orleans,* Father John co-opts medical tools from care into exploitation, preying upon a child. In Sandtown, finance companies co-opt lead checks from redress into exploitation, preying upon young adults with intellectual disabilities.

In Gray's Baltimore, police promotions and electoral politics depend on collecting and counting black bodies. David Simon, former *Baltimore Sun* reporter and author of *The Wire* and *The Corner,* says that Baltimore police officers "rounding up bodies for street dealing, drug possession, loitering and such" represents the simplest route to "promotion and some additional pay" (Keller). Like blood hunters, police and politicians hunt stats for their own professional advancement, and African American bodies supply the numbers.

In a few decades, Sandtown went from the old Jim Crow of residential segregation to the new Jim Crow of mass incarceration. The War on Drugs of the 1980s and 1990s opened the door to arrests without probable cause. Then Martin O'Malley, Baltimore mayor from 1999–2007, rewarded police solely on number of arrests, seeking good crime statistics to bolster his ambitions for higher political office (Keller). Neill Franklin, a former Baltimore police officer, says, "And in these searches, we were stopping and searching anyone who might look like they fit the bill of a drug user. . . . Officers did whatever they had to do to lock up as many people as they could to satisfy police headquarters" (Lowery 138). Often for petty crimes or no crime at all, arrests reached a high of a hundred thousand in a single year, and the excessive policing continues (Lowery 137–39). Like the blood farm, Sandtown serves as a profitable holding tank for black bodies.

RUNOFF

In landscapes of environmental sacrifice, runoff leads to running off from troops or police. Unchecked pollutions cause disabilities, and the state responds with quarantine and excessive policing instead of a prosthetic community. *Orleans*'s police state reflects the African American millennial generation's painful understanding of law enforcement since the War on Drugs. The Anti-Drug Abuse Acts of 1986 and 1988 and the 1994 crime bill led to people of color's mass incarceration for drug offenses. "As law enforcement budgets exploded, so did prison and jail populations. . . . [By 1991] one fourth of young African American men were now under the control of the criminal justice system" according to Michelle Alexander (53, 56). Not only individuals but entire zones find themselves under such control, which replaces care and prevention for young people with disabilities.

Escape seems the only healthy option. At the conclusion of *Orleans*, Fen braves the armed troops on the quarantine wall to help Baby Girl escape from Delta Fever. First running and then wading toward the guards through waist-high muddy water, Fen creates a distraction so Daniel can smuggle Baby Girl into the Outer States through a crack in the wall (322). As the spotlights converge on Fen and ignore Daniel, he uses his immunity to save a young life. Physical courage, local knowledge, technology, and science come together to prevent environmental illness. Fen cradles a bundled-up coat as if it were an infant, believing the soldiers will not shoot a woman carrying a baby (320). She is wrong:

> Her arms were raised, her face turned up, the bundle held high in the air. She rotated in a slow circle as the rain washed the mud from her skin.
>
> For an instant, she looked at him. The moment hung in the air, Fen's mouth curving into a smile, seeing Daniel and the baby almost there. Almost there. She turned away.
>
> A shot rang out. The bundle fell from her hands. (323)

This moment seals the pact between runoff and running off from state violence. Polluted Delta water covers Fen as the rain falls and she splashes through the mud. The slow violence of toxic water leads to sudden death from a gun. The Afroaquanaut succumbs, but in service to Afrofuturist ideals. She releases Baby Girl, now named Enola after East New Orleans, into the care of an unknown but safer planet in the Outer States.

While an act of heroism, Fen's death also embodies a toxic economy in which care of others requires hurting oneself. As Therí A. Pickens writes, the intersection of blackness, womanhood, and disability forecloses the possibility of an overcoming narrative. Pickens declares, "For those who have difficulty imagining disability as triumphant or as an advantage, the victories (where they occur) appear meager at best" (171, 176). While Fen is a strong black woman, her vulnerability to violence and disease underlies her heroism as much as her courage. She matters in her totality.

Freddie Gray also found that runoff led to running off from police. Right before his last arrest, "He ran, like a lot of black men do when we see cops, because for our generation, police officers have been the most consistent terrorists in our neighborhoods," writes D. Watkins (123–24). Watkins adds,

"Almost every black person I know from a poor neighborhood can give you a collection of nightmare stories about the BCPD" (142). Under the best of circumstances, young adults with intellectual disabilities find it difficult to make the transition from school to work. In Sandtown, it is nearly impossible. For young people impaired from lead poisoning, the missing safety net includes education, job supports, and service plans tailored to their needs. Ruth Norton reports that "a child who was poisoned with lead is seven times more likely to drop out of school and six times more likely to end up in the juvenile justice system" (McCoy, "Freddie"). The criminal justice system steps in as the only sorry substitute for disability services.

For Gray the slow violence of environmental illness culminated in the sudden violence of police brutality. He died at the hands of Baltimore police after his April 12, 2015, arrest for "running unprovoked." As officers folded him awkwardly into the back of a police van, his leg seemed injured. The officers drove Gray around without a seat belt, making four stops while ignoring his pleas for medical attention. When they arrived at the police station half an hour later, Gray could not breathe. He died a week later from an eighty-percent-severed spine. All the officers were acquitted of wrongdoing in the case. The criminal justice system harmed him then denied him the means of care, operating in the same ethical void as the environmental racism that caused his disabilities in the first place.

In *Orleans,* Fen and Daniel serve as a prosthetic community that furnishes the technologies of survival Baby Girl needs. With a strong prosthetic community in place, it might have been possible for Freddie Gray to live a long, fulfilling life instead of dying in police custody at the age of twenty-five. In the absence of a prosthetic community, the Baltimore police stepped in as a sorry substitute. "Poverty, injustice, and reading comprehension issues go hand in hand, like white cops and innocent verdicts," writes Watkins, who also grew up in poor black Baltimore (xxi).

Freddie Gray is one of many people of color with disabilities killed by US police in recent years. In their study for the Ruderman Family Foundation, Lawrence Carter-Long and David M. Perry found that "disabled individuals make up a third to half of all people killed by law enforcement officers" (1). Disability and police brutality go hand in hand. Young adults with lead-induced disabilities deserve the positive Afrofuturism of gleaming prosthetics and brand-new facilities. Instead, they get racial profiling.

By all accounts, Gray lived off his lead checks, family help, and his own small part in the toxic economy of drug dealing. His lawyer, Creston Smith, says Gray "had some learning disabilities from lead paint exposure. He didn't read or write perfectly, and that causes a person to seek economic independence other ways" (Rentz). What was Freddie Gray doing when he could have been learning to read, write, and master a trade? He was running away from the police. As a sophomore, he went to a Juvenile Services facility and never returned to special education at his regular high school (Rentz).

Gray's time in juvie gives him something in common with many other Sandtown kids as well as African American students with disabilities across the country. A quarter of Sandtown children between the ages of ten and seventeen have spent time in a juvenile facility (Ross). There isn't much else to do besides getting arrested: there is no pool, no recreation center, and no police athletic league (Allam; Lowery 138). Across the United States, young African Americans with disabilities find themselves in the special education to prison pipeline. In fact, "compared to white students with disabilities, Black students with disabilities are four times as likely to be educated in a correctional facility" (Kim et al. 51). We could see the justice system as a scattershot version of *Orleans*, confining young black men and women with disabilities.

Caught in the Baltimore Police Department's cycle of catch and release, Gray was a defendant in twenty-three cases between the ages of eighteen and twenty-five. As Nicolás Medina Mora reports, "Court records show that Gray was arrested over and over again, for everything from possessing drugs to playing dice in a public housing development where he didn't live," but "over and over again, overworked prosecutors dropped all charges." Gray spent most of his twenty-third year in jail without being charged. His family devoted their time and at least $29,000 to bailing him out rather than helping him enter the world of work (Mora). The only job training Gray received was behind bars. *Washington Post* reporter Terrence McCoy writes that Gray "learned brick masonry and harbored ambitions of getting into the trade" even with a criminal record (McCoy, "Freddie"). Freddie Gray had a future, just as Sandtown has a future despite its toxic economy. We do not know what Freddie Gray's life could have been if he had experienced a strong prosthetic community instead of excessive policing. The toxic consequences of lead paint and runoff gave way to the toxic consequences of running off from the police. His death stoked the rise of the Black Lives Matter movement, staking a claim to a better future.

THE AFROAQUANAUT

Fen de la Guerre, survivor of relentless floods, is an Afroaquanaut who renegotiates the terms of life on Earth. Despite the gravity of her situation, she floats when she steps, like Neil Armstrong on the moon. She always notices the impact of her tread on risky ground. For example, she picks her way swiftly across Rooftops, a grassland of houses buried under silt and mud. The Afroaquanaut moves so fluently it seems miraculous. Fen crosses a parking lot buried underwater by striding from the roof of one submerged car to the next. To the outsider Daniel, however, she seems to be walking on water as she moves toward a statue of Jesus. "And then she stepped out onto the water and walked away, barely disturbing the surface as she strode toward the open arms of the statue in the middle of the lake" (243). The scene then shifts to Fen's voice:

> It take him a full half minute to pick his jaw up again. That boy be so blind sometimes, I don't know how he make it on his own. "Stay there," I call back to him. "You too heavy to be following me."
>
> Beneath my feet, the hard top of a car shift enough to make me glad he be listening and stay on the wall. I clutch Baby Girl to me and catch my balance. (243)

Fen seems miraculous to Daniel, and Daniel seems helpless to Fen because she knows survival strategies he never had to learn. In the Baby Girl strapped to her chest, Fen registers the weight of the differential environmental risk she bears. She constantly adjusts herself to maintain her precarious balance, but in the process, she has become light and swift of foot. Like Fen, the young people of Flint are Afroaquanauts with the skills to "dance underwater and not get wet" and the strength to push for change. Poetry is one of their technologies of survival. The slam poetry team of Flint's RAISE IT UP! Youth Arts and Awareness engages in the negative Afrofuturism of social critique and the positive Afrofuturism of staking a claim for their own survival. "Poetry is a way to let the world know that we are here and we aren't going anywhere," says Destiny Monet, aged eighteen. The team's collective poem, "Flint," reflects the political priorities of African American youth. On February 28, 2016, the team performed "Flint" for a local audience who responded with cheers. Danielle Horton, aged nineteen, wants to counter the notion that Flint's young people deserve anything less than the best. "No, when you go out of town people pity you. They have all of these negative connotations of Flint and they don't even know us" (Segal). It's hard for outsiders to discern the vibrant life inside quarantine walls.

Rejecting pity, the poets take a certain disability pride in their Flint identity while critiquing the injustice that created it. The chorus of "Flint" goes, "Pay for your poison / the girls and boys and / the city can't drink / lead altering the way we think" (Segal). Rather than distancing themselves from their city's toxic legacy, they claim it. The poets speak to the people outside the quarantine wall, informing them that Flint holds fast to its hope for the future. Insiders' knowledge of the city comes with a cost, but its area code beats through them and keeps them going. "You ain't from the Fli? / You ain't familiar with famine, / The 810 in my pulse is all I need to keep standing" (Segal). Like lead, the city runs through their veins. Immersed in risk and aware of injustice, these Afroaquanauts persist in envisioning a survivable future, and do so with panache.

The Flint poets critique the toxic cycle of liquidity and hold state officials accountable for compromising their futures. Lead poisoning is a blood-borne illness, and the poets portray the city itself as a woman with a blood-borne illness who has been denied care by Michigan Governor Rick Snyder. If Flint is a woman's body, the Flint River is that body's circulatory system. Just as a patient might die without dialysis, the city needs water filtration in order to survive. By denying her clean water, the governor has drained the city of life. "I heard her holler as HOMEBOY hung her out to dry, / a drained cry. / Never dialyzed the river that is her blood line . . . got mucked up." (Segal) The poets and the city itself form a disability community denied decent care, like the blood tribes of *Orleans*. On the other side of the quarantine wall, Snyder "relaxes in his Ann Arbor home passing bills for the exact crime he committed in Flint": that is, he gets tough on theft and murder even though he is a murderer and a thief. Politicians have turned Flint into a blood farm: "Policy always tried to pimp her out." Through their protest and vitality, the poets convey positive and negative Afrofuturism at the same time. Even though lead poisoning is "altering the way we think / futures gone in a blink," the RAISE IT UP! poets nonetheless rehearse a future for themselves. "If I ain't got it today. . . . Trust I'mma have it tomorrow." (Segal) Like Afrofuturism, Flint poets trust that the future holds promise for young African Americans with environmental disabilities.

The young women of Flint raise their voices loud enough for people on the other side of the quarantine wall to hear them. President Obama visited Flint seven months after the crisis broke because an eight-year-old girl wrote him a letter and asked him to come. Amariyanna Copeny, who reigned as Little Miss Flint 2016, wrote the president, "I am one of the children that is effected by this water, and I've been doing my best to march in protest and to speak out for all the kids that live here in Flint" (*Los Angeles Times* Staff). The White House announced plans for President Obama's April 27, 2016, visit by posting online his letter to Miss Copeny, accepting her invitation. Appearing at rallies in her beauty queen sash and tiara, Mari Copeny had rashes and dried skin on her arms from the poisoned water (Acosta, "Meet" and "Little"). Whether meeting with the president or traveling to Washington, DC, to hear Michigan's governor testify before Congress, Little Miss Flint asserts the beauty, activism, and future of Flint youth.

Life Supports

Afrofuturism distorts present realities just enough to help readers recognize the shared and surreal contours of environmental injustice across different contexts. The "significant distortions" of its tropes offer working models for the interactions of race and disability. In its heroism and adventure, *Orleans* allows readers to grasp the ethic of care at work in landscapes of sacrifice. Like Freddie Gray and many other African Americans, Fen finds that society regards her very existence as a threat. Her devotion to the next generation's survival makes her willing to meet that threat head on. Although constraints on her life abound, she strains against them. She runs up against the boundaries, "swirling through the water, spinning like the wheel that turns the world" (323).

Young life strives and deserves to live. Its survival depends greatly on its own initiative, and also greatly on the healthy or toxic ground from which it eats and drinks. Like Orleans, Sandtown and Flint survive in their own ingenious ways, yet also die every day for want of the things the Outer States of America could provide. Across a galaxy of American cities, Afroaquanauts navigate risky and uncertain terrain. They could travel further and last longer on this planet with better life supports.

Works Cited

Acosta, Roberto. "Little Miss Flint and the Letter that Brought President Obama." *mlive.com*, 4 May 2016, http://www.mlive.com/news/flint/index.ssf/2016/05/how_little_miss_flint_brought.html. Accessed 24 Oct. 2016.

———. "Meet the Girl Whose Letter on the Water Crisis Brought Obama to Flint." *mlive.com*, 28 Apr. 2016, http://www.mlive.com/news/flint/index.ssf/2016/04/meet_the_girl_whose_letter_on.html Accessed 24 Oct. 2016.

Alexander, Michelle. *The New Jim Crow: Mass Incarceration in the Age of Colorblindness.* The New Press, 2012.

Allam, Hannah. "In Baltimore's Sandtown-Winchester, Every Day is an Ongoing Katrina." *McClatchy DC*, 15 May 2015, https://www.mcclatchydc.com/news/crime/article24784570.html. Accessed 27 Sept. 2016.

Barber, Tiffany E. "Cyborg Grammar? Reading Wangechi Mutu's *Non je ne regrette rien* through *Kindred*." *Afrofuturism 2.0: The Rise of Astro-Blackness*, edited by Reynaldo Anderson and Charles E. Jones, Lexington Books, 2016, pp. 3–26.

Bosman, Julie. "Flint Water Crisis Inquiry Finds State Ignored Warning Signs." *New York Times*, 23 Mar. 2016, https://www.nytimes.com/2016/03/24/us/flint-water-crisis.html. Accessed 21 Oct. 2016.

Carter-Long, Lawrence, and David M. Perry. "The Ruderman White Paper on Media Coverage of Law Enforcement use of Force and Disability." *Ruderman Family Foundation*, Mar. 2016, http://rudermanfoundation.org/wp-content/uploads/2017/08/MediaStudy-PoliceDisability_final-final.pdf. Accessed 31 Jan. 2019.

Centers for Disease Control and Prevention. "US Public Health Service Syphilis Study at Tuskegee." *cdc.gov*, 30 Dec. 2013, http://www.cdc.gov/tuskegee/index.html. Accessed 3 Nov. 2016.

Chan, Melissa. "The 5 Most Important Flint Water Crisis Emails Released by Michigan's Governor." *Time Magazine*, 20 Jan. 2016, http://time.com/4187842/flint-water-crisis-michigan-governor-emails-rick-snyder/. Accessed 21 Oct. 2016.

Delany, Samuel R. *Starboard Wine: More Notes on the Language of Science Fiction*. 1984. Wesleyan UP, 2012.

Fonger, Ron. "Ex-Emergency Manager Says He's Not to Blame for Flint River Water Switch." *mlive.com*, 13 Oct. 2015, http://www.mlive.com/news/flint/index.ssf/2015/10/ex_emergency_manager_earley_sa.html. Accessed 26 Oct. 2016.

Hamilton, Elizabeth C. "Afrofuturism and the Technologies of Survival." *African Arts*, vol. 50, no. 4, 2017, pp. 18–23.

Hanna-Attisha, Mona, et al. "Elevated Blood Lead Levels in Children Associated with the Flint Drinking Water Crisis: A Spatial Analysis of Risk and Public Health Response." *American Journal of Public Health*, vol. 106, no. 2, 2016, pp. 283–90.

Jacobs, A. J. "The Impacts of Variations in Development Context on Employment Growth: A Comparison of Central Cities in Michigan and Ontario, 1980–2006." *Economic Development Quarterly*, vol. 23, no. 4, 2009, pp. 351–71.

Keller, Bill. "David Simon on Baltimore's Anguish." *The Marshall Project*, 29 Apr. 2015, https://www.themarshallproject.org/2015/04/29/david-simon-on-baltimore-s-anguish. Accessed 23 Sept. 2016.

Kim, Catherine Y. et al. *The School to Prison Pipeline: Structuring Legal Reform*. NYUP, 2010.

Lavender, Isiah III. "Digging Deep: Ailments of Difference in Octavia Butler's 'The Evening and the Morning and the Night.'" *Black and Brown Planets: The Politics of Race in Science Fiction*, edited by Isiah Lavender III, U of Mississippi P, 2014, pp. 65–82.

Lee, Shawna J., et al. "Racial Inequality and the Implementation of Emergency Management Laws in Economically Distressed Urban Areas." *Children and Youth Services Review*, vol. 70, 2016, pp. 1–7.

Levine, Marc V. "Downtown Redevelopment as an Urban Growth Strategy: A Critical Appraisal of the Baltimore Renaissance." *Journal of Urban Affairs*, vol. 9, no. 2, 1987, pp. 103–23.

Livengood, Chad. "Emails: Flint Water Warnings Reached Governor's Inner Circle." *Detroit News*, 26 Feb. 2016, http://www.detroitnews.com/story/news/michigan/flint-water-crisis/2016/02/26/snyder-aides-urged-switching-flints-water-oct/80967048/. Accessed 21 Oct. 2016.

Los Angeles Times Staff. "Read the Letter From 'Little Miss Flint' that Stirred Obama to Visit Flint." *latimes.com*, 4 May 2016, http://www.latimes.com/nation/nationnow/la-na-read-little-miss-flint-letter-20160504-snap-htmlstory.html. Accessed 24 Oct. 2016.

Lowery, Wesley. *"They Can't Kill Us All": Ferguson, Baltimore, and a New Era in America's Racial Justice Movement.* Little Brown, 2016.

Maryland Judiciary Case Search Results. "Stanley Rochkind." http://casesearch.courts.state.md.us/casesearch/inquiryresults.jsp?middleName=&partyType=&lastName=ROCHKIND&filingEnd=&filingDate=&site=00&filingStart=&d16544p=17&countyName=&action=Search&courtSystem=B&firstName=STANLEY&company=N. Accessed 26 Sept. 2016.

McCoy, Terrence. "Freddie Gray's Life: A Study on the Effects of Lead Paint on Poor Blacks." *Washington Post*, 29 Apr. 2015, https://www.washingtonpost.com/local/freddie-grays-life-a-study-in-the-sad-effects-of-lead-paint-on-poor-blacks/2015/04/29/0be898e6-eea8-11e4-8abc-d6aa3bad79dd_story.html. Accessed 14 Nov. 2016.

———. "How Companies Make Millions off Lead-Poisoned, Poor Blacks." *Washington Post*, 25 Aug. 2015, https://www.washingtonpost.com/local/social-issues/how-companies-make-millions-off-lead-poisoned-poor-blacks/2015/08/25/7460c1de-0d8c-11e5-9726-49d6fa26a8c6_story.html?utm_term=.a42596d4d40b. Accessed 23 Sept. 2016.

Mora, Nicolás Medina. "The Short, Hard Life of Freddie Gray." *BuzzFeed News*, 18 Aug. 2015, https://www.buzzfeed.com/nicolasmedinamora/what-freddie-grays-life-says-about-baltimores-justice-system?utm_term=.cjGkPO99W#.mpj63k11V. Accessed 23 Sept. 2016.

Otto, Eric C. *Green Speculations: Science Fiction and Transformative Environmentalism.* The Ohio State UP, 2012.

Parliament. "Aqua Boogie." *Motor Booty Affair*, Casablanca, 1978.

Pickens, Therí A. "Octavia Butler and the Aesthetics of the Novel." *Hypatia*, vol. 30, no. 1, 2015, pp. 167–80.

Rentz, Catherine. "Freddie Gray Remembered as Jokester Who Struggled to Leave Drug Trade." *Baltimore Sun*, 22 Nov. 2015, http://www.baltimoresun.com/news/maryland/freddie-gray/bal-freddie-gray-remembered-as-jokester-who-struggled-to-leave-drug-trade-20151120-story.html. Accessed 27 Sept. 2016.

Ritchie, Andrea J. *Invisible No More: Police Violence Against Black Women and Women of Color.* Beacon, 2017.

Ross, Janell. "Why You Should Know What Happened in Freddie Gray's Life—Long Before His Death." *Washington Post*, 19 Dec. 2015, https://www.washingtonpost.com/news/the-fix/wp/2015/12/19/why-you-should-know-what-happened-in-freddie-grays-life-long-before-his-death/?utm_term=.a5b748ffe27a. Accessed 23 Sept. 2016.

Segal, Corrine. "These Young Poets Show There's More to Flint than a Water Crisis." *PBS NewsHour*, 29 Mar. 2016, https://www.pbs.org/newshour/arts/poetry/these-young-poets-show-theres-more-to-flint-than-a-water-crisis. Accessed 23 Sept. 2016.

Singer, Eric S. "Why Baltimore Burns." *Nation*, May 1, 2015. https://www.thenation.com/article/why-baltimore-burns/. Accessed 27 Sept. 2016.

Smith, Sherri L. *Orleans*. Speak, 2013.

Watkins, D. *The Beast Side: Living and Dying While Black in America*. Hot Books, 2015.

WETA Television, Washington, DC. "Transcript from an Interview with Sherri L. Smith." *All About Adolescent Literacy*, http://www.adlit.org/transcript_display/33885/. Accessed 8 Nov. 2016.

Yaszek, Lisa. "The Bannekerade: Genius, Madness, and Magic in Black Science Fiction." *Black and Brown Planets: The Politics of Race in Science Fiction*, edited by Isiah Lavender III, U of Mississippi P, 2014, pp. 15–31.

Young, Gordon. *Teardown: A Memoir of a Vanishing City*. U of California P, 2013.

CHAPTER 8

Black Futures Matter
Afrofuturism and Geontology in N. K. Jemisin's Broken Earth Trilogy

Lisa Dowdall

In 2018, N. K. Jemisin became the first author to win three Hugo Awards for Best Novel with her Afrofuturist Broken Earth series. She won the awards in consecutive years, first with *The Fifth Season* in 2016, then with *The Obelisk Gate* in 2017, and finally with *The Stone Sky* in 2018. She is the first author to accomplish this remarkable feat in the sixty-five-year history of the Hugos. Recognizing the series' popular appeal, cable network TNT announced in August 2017 that it is developing *The Fifth Season* as a miniseries. Yet Jemisin's success, and the legitimacy of the Hugo Awards more broadly, was plagued by the Sad Puppies, a conservative lobby group led by science fiction (SF) author Brad R. Torgersen, and their more extreme faction, the Rabid Puppies, led by writer and editor Theodore Beale. For over six years, Puppies have attempted to load Hugo nomination ballots with the work of conservative white men in response to what they see as the hijacking of the genre by "social justice warriors" and other groups they dub "niche, academic, overtly to the left in ideology and flavour and ultimately lacking what might best be called visceral, gut-level, swashbuckling fun" (Torgersen, "Why Sad Puppies").

This is not merely a matter of taste, or even of literary value, but of overt racism. Torgersen states that greater diversity within SF is a form of "literary affirmative action" that values authors' work based on "demographics and box-checking" rather than the "audience's enjoyment" (Torgersen, "Revolt"). In a pointed attack, Beale called Jemisin, together with all African Americans, "half-savages" incapable of contributing to advanced human civilization without "significant external support from . . . white males." Beale even attempted to mobilize scientific evidence to support his view of Jemisin, claiming that "it is not that I, and others, do not view her as human (although genetic science presently suggests that we are not equally homo sapiens sapiens)." In making such claims, he perpetuates the myth of biological race that subjects minorities to the very same dehumanizing ideologies that justified colonialism and slavery.

However, the powerful backlash from the SF community against the Puppies is proof that Jemisin and other ex-centric writers are highly valued in the fields of cultural production in which they operate. In 2013 the Science Fiction and Fantasy Writers of America (SFWA) repealed Beale's membership because of his racist remarks, and, in recent years, authors of color have swept the Hugo Awards: in 2016, not only did Jemisin take Best Novel for *The Fifth Season* but Nigerian American author Nnedi Okorafor also won Best Novella for *Binti*, and Chinese writer Hao Jingfang won Best Novelette for "Folding Beijing." In 2017, Jemisin secured her second Hugo Award for Best Novel for *The Obelisk Gate*, edging past two extremely popular nominations: the Chinese novelist Cixin Liu's *Death's End* (translated by Ken Liu) and Korean American Yoon Ha Lee's *Ninefox Gambit*. Additionally, Jemisin was nominated in the Best Short Story category for "The City Born Great." In 2018, the depth and diversity of the field of nominees was again notable. Aside from Jemisin, nominees included Yoon Ha Lee for Best Novel, Nnedi Okorafor for Best Novella, and Rebecca Roanhorse, who won Best Short Story for "Welcome to Your Authentic Indian Experience."

In her 2017 Hugo acceptance speech, Jemisin spoke about the "reactionary pushback" writers like her receive—writers who are involved in an "epic struggle against the forces of oppression" ("Holy"). But, as she went on to state, the "regressive clamor" of ideologues such as Beale can be overcome when the "rest of SFF fandom simply stands up to be counted" ("Holy"). The community is full of people who want "literary innovation, and realistic representation" and who are able to "consider the future clearly rather than through the foggy lenses of nostalgia and privilege" ("Holy"). Jemisin has garnered critical and popular acclaim precisely because she challenges the conventions of SF and fantasy in order to refocus the future. In her 2018 Hugo acceptance speech, she stated that she sees SF and fantasy as the "aspirational drive of the Zeitgeist," with the genre finally recognizing that "the dreams of the marginalized matter and that all of us have a future" ("Stars"). This is not "affirmative action," as Torgersen suggests, but the ongoing evolution of a genre that has always investigated questions of difference, estrangement, and possibility, and in doing so critiques the discourses and institutions of past and present.

In a blog post, Jemisin directly contests Torgersen's claims of affirmative action by addressing the entrenched conventions surrounding who can write SF, who is represented in the genre, and who is worthy of the prestige bestowed through awards. She states that white male SF authors attract more reviews, white men feature on more book covers and in more films, and white protagonists are at little risk of "brownwashing" ("Not the Affirmative"). Meanwhile, women working in SF "get publicly shamed for . . . well, existing, while white men can be sexual predators or white supremacists and still end up on awards juries or editorial staffs, unquestioned" ("Not the Affirmative"). Jemisin points out that the "affirmative action" that allows underrepresented writers to win awards has historically only ever benefited white men like Torgersen.

In this chapter, I explore how Jemisin's Broken Earth series enacts the kinds of literary innovation the author champions in her Hugo acceptance speeches. Connecting Afrofuturism with the geological turn in the humanities, I examine how Jemisin uses geology to question widespread cultural assumptions about the "natural" divisions between race, species, and matter that underpin hierarchies of the human. I argue that Jemisin's work promotes new ways of theorizing the human in connection to the mineral substance of our world. This vital rethinking acknowledges the mass rearrangement of both our material and semiotic systems within the present geological epoch known as the Anthropocene. These lines of investigation are more timely, more innovative, and, indeed, more science fictional than the kind of homogenous writing celebrated by the Puppies. By addressing the intersections of history, mythology, science and technology, Jemisin challenges genre conventions in a move toward greater diversity and possibility.

Allegory and Beyond: Afrofuturism and the Transformation of the Future

The Broken Earth series is set in the Stillness—a landmass fractured by fault lines that constantly wreak havoc on human civilization. Earthquakes, volcanic eruptions, and even mining accidents can trigger Seasons: ecological catastrophes that might last a few years or even several decades. Every few centuries, these seasons are disrupted by a major event known as a "Fifth

Season": a process of utter devastation that completely reconfigures the Stillness and forces communities to go into lockdown and enforce Seasonal law. The Fifth Season is so named because of an Arctic proverb: "Winter, Spring, Summer, Fall; Death is the fifth, and master of all" (*Fifth* 149). Yet despite its calamitous nature, the Fifth Season also represents a break in the continuous cycle of death and rebirth symbolized by the regular Seasons. The Fifth Season provides an opportunity for the Stillness's most repressed citizens—its orogenes—to discover and redress the injustices that humans visited upon the living world—injustices that ultimately led to the creation of the Seasons.

Even outside of Seasons, the Stillness is a perilous place where all humans are adapted for survival with genetic permutations, such as acid-proof hair that filters out lung-clogging ash. People are born into or adopt a "use-caste" that dictates their role in the community: for example, Leader, Strongback, Breeder, Lorist, Innovator, Hunter. Orogenes are an exception. With specialized cerebral organs called sessapinae that allow them to manipulate geological matter, orogenes can influence the composition, movement, and even temperature of the Earth's strata. While such skills are essential to the survival of humankind in the Stillness, orogenes are widely feared and hated, and many hide their abilities so they will be accepted into communities or "comms"—a necessity for survival in this world's harsh and unpredictable environments. Indeed, under law, orogenes are not even classified as human because of their biological difference (*Fifth* 234). If orogenes are discovered at a young age, they are often killed by their family or their comm. If they are lucky, they are sent to a training center known as the Fulcrum inside the capital city of Yumenes, where they become slaves to the Empire. They are deployed to hot spots to quell seismic activity and forced to breed with each other to produce more orogenic offspring, all under the strict supervision of Guardians who can kill their charges with a single touch.

Jemisin's novels follow the intertwined paths of two orogenes, Essun and Alabaster. Essun is a powerful orogene who hides her abilities from her husband and her community. She works in a children's crèche in a small comm called Tirimo. She comes home one day to discover that her husband has killed her son and disappeared with her daughter. Both children were orogenes, also hiding their true nature from their father and the people of Tirimo. Essun sets out on a quest to find her daughter, Nassun, in the midst of a Fifth Season triggered by a tremendous rift near Yumenes. She does not know it at the beginning of her journey, but the rift was created by her former teacher, Alabaster, who is taking his revenge on the Empire that enslaved orogenes. The narrative follows Essun as she reconnects with Alabaster and learns what triggered the Seasons millennia ago: humans angered

Father Earth with their scientific experiments. It was these experiments that flung his child, the Moon, out of orbit, and provoked vengeful outbursts of seismic activity. Essun's task is to catch the Moon and bring equilibrium back to the planet's systems, restoring the relationship between humans and Father Earth, ending the destructive cycle of Seasons, and dismantling the Empire in the process.

The Broken Earth trilogy is very much part of the Afrofuturist project to reclaim Afrodiasporic history. *The Fifth Season* opens with this epithet: "For all those who have to fight for the respect that everyone else is given without question" (vii), and Jemisin states that she was troubled by events in Ferguson at the time she was writing *The Fifth Season* (Kehe). Thus, while the series features racially diverse characters, familiar structures of oppression continue to operate with devastating force and continuity.[1] Jemisin creates a whole cast of futuristic, postapocalyptic characters—the orogenes who are slaves to the Empire, used for their geological and biological labor, as well as the Guardians and tuners who are equally ensnared in the Empire's complex apparatus of control. These diverse beings are part of a network of institutionalized subjugation reinforced through selective breeding and the assertion of inherent biological difference reminiscent of antebellum slavery. The Empire breeds useful qualities into each of its slaves, and then uses those qualities to alienate them from wider society. Thus, while orogenes can control seismic activity, they must submit to the Empire or face death, either at the hands of hostile comms or their Guardians. Guardians are surgically altered orogenes who can track, control, and kill their charges, but are widely feared and susceptible to corruption by Father Earth. Tuners are genetically engineered to create and control the Empire's energy supply, but are crafted in the image of the Empire's ancient enemies so they are vilified by others. These complex race relations drive the narrative, with Jemisin's extrapolation on Afrodiasporic experience informing her protagonists' experiences of the Stillness and fueling their desire to transform it.

Slavery, forced reproduction, and assimilation are familiar tropes in Afrofuturist SF, rendered perhaps most powerfully in Octavia E. Butler's

---

1. The series features an array of characters with diverse racial characteristics recognizable from the readers' own world and primarily influenced by environment. Those from the East Coast have black skin, while West Coasters are close to east Asian in appearance. People from the northern and southern Arctics are white. Midlatters, such as Essun, are those of mixed heritage—as the people from the crossroads of the Stillness, "borne of trade, of conquest, of exploration," they are myriad shades of brown and akin to the people of the "Caribbean nations, or northern China, or the Mediterranean region . . . anyone who's visibly multiracial will read as Midlatter, in the Stillness" (Jemisin, "Creating").

Xenogenesis trilogy.[2] Jemisin continues this tradition of Afrofuturist, feminist writing with her representation of two mutant human groups in particular—the orogenes and the tuners—that illuminate how eugenics and scientific racism are mutually constitutive, manipulating women's reproductive labor to propagate slavery. Like the African and Afrodiasporic people who were subjected to scientific racism to justify their inherent inferiority and suitability for slavery, Essun must struggle against purportedly empirical evidence that reduces her to her biological function. Orogenes are bred to have sensitive sessapinae that sense and control geological forces. Although they sustain life on Earth by managing seismic activity that could eradicate humanity, they are called "roggas"—a "dehumanizing word for someone who has been made into a thing" (*Fifth* 14). They are also forced to follow a selective breeding program. Alabaster himself was "bred to order . . . the product of two of the Fulcrum's oldest and most promising lineages" (*Fifth* 72), while Essun, a talented young orogene, is sent to him to produce powerful orogenic children who will be trained from birth to serve the Fulcrum. While Essun resents this manipulation, she also recognizes that following her superiors' orders is the only way to achieve greater autonomy. She knows that if she is disobedient, she will be assigned to the Fulcrum permanently and used as a breeding animal, with "nothing to do but lie on her back and turn men's grunting and farting into babies" (*Fifth* 71). Alabaster, however, is more experienced than Essun. As a "ten-ringer"—the most powerful orogene in the Empire's service—he enjoys greater freedoms and uses these freedoms to investigate the system that enslaves him.

Jemisin introduces these themes in the opening of the first novel, when Alabaster activates the enormous fault line on the tectonic plate beneath Yumenes, deliberately setting off a 10,000-year Season:

> He closes his eyes and . . . then he reaches forth with all the fine control that the world has brainwashed and backstabbed and brutalized out of him, and all the sensitivity that his masters have bred into him through generations of rape and coercion and highly unnatural selections. His fingers spread and twitch as he feels several reverberating points on the map of his awareness: his fellow slaves. He cannot free them, not in the practical sense. . . . He can, however, make their suffering a cause greater than one city's hubris, and one empire's fear. (6–7)

---

2. The Xenogenesis series comprises the novels *Dawn* (1987), *Adulthood Rites* (1988), and *Imago* (1989). The series takes place after the destruction of the Earth, focusing on the story of Lilith, a woman rescued by an alien species known as the Oankali who interbreed with humans, and her interspecies children.

The fellow slaves Alabaster can "sess" are the node maintainers—a horrific fate for orogenes who cannot control their own abilities. The popular understanding is that node maintainers "connect far-flung quartents with the Fulcrum, to extend its protections as far as possible" (*Fifth* 119). These outposts minimize the impact of fault lines to keep regions stable. Essun believes that this is a "tedious duty" for those with orogenic ability but little finesse—an obscure and isolated profession but one that allows them to save lives (*Fifth* 119). However, when she and Alabaster visit a node chamber, she discovers the true fate of these condemned orogenes. She finds a chair, made of wires and straps, that holds a skeletal child with skin as dark as Alabaster's, "kept like this for what must have been months or years, and whose features might be a perfect match for his" (*Fifth* 140). There is the powerful suggestion that this might be one of the many children Alabaster was forced to create for the Fulcrum, and that Essun's children, too, could be subjected to this cruelty. Essun learns that the node maintainer's sessapinae have been surgically altered: "It's a simple matter to apply a lesion here and there that severs the rogga's self-control completely, while still allowing its *instinctive* use" (*Fifth* 141). Even without full use of their sessapinae, orogenes have an innate ability to quell shakes, and thus serve as "a reliable, harmless, completely beneficial source of orogeny" (142).

The sight of the node maintainer sickens Essun, but Alabaster is devout in his belief that all orogenes should visit a node at least once in their life and face the reality of the system that controls them:

> The body in the node maintainer's chair is small, and naked. Thin, its limbs atrophied. Hairless. These are things—tubes and pipes and *things* . . . going into the stick-arms, down the goggle-throat, across the narrow crotch. There's a flexible bag on the corpse's belly, *attached* to its belly somehow. . . . Ingenious, really, what they've done. She didn't know it was possible to keep a body alive like this: immobile, unwilling, indefinite. (139–40)

Alabaster explains to Essun that the only reason the Fulcrum does not force all orogenes into nodes is that they are more versatile if they can control themselves—hence the extensive training they must undergo, and the role of their Guardians. He stipulates that an orogene is "just a useful monster, just a bit of new blood to add to the breeding lines" (*Fifth* 143). This knowledge becomes essential later in the plot when Essun and Alabaster, having escaped from the Empire and their Guardians, have a son, Corundum, who shows extraordinary promise as an orogene. When the Fulcrum's Guardians find Essun, rather than allowing the child to be taken away and forced into the role of a node maintainer, she makes the same choice that many enslaved black women have made throughout history, deciding to kill her own child rather than sending him into a lifetime of servitude.[3]

As in our own world, the use of slave labor to build empires underpins the history of the Stillness. Essun learns that in the ancient empire of Syl Anagist, humans sought to harness the energy of all living things to feed their technology using a network of obelisks. Known as the Plutonic Engine (and later the Obelisk Gate), this network was controlled by tuners, a group of skilled people created by the leaders of Syl Anagist to replicate a more ancient and powerful people known as the Niess.

The Niess had extraordinary magical powers yet devoted themselves to works of experimental thought and art rather than feats of engineering. In contrast, Syl Anagist cultivated magic for the greater glory of the empire, with every household producing its own share to be "funnelled away in genegineered vines and pumps to become the power source for a global civilization" (*Stone* 209). When the Niess did not comply—believing magic could not be owned—they were deemed a threat to Syl Anagist and eradicated: "But there are none so frightened, or so strange in their fear, as conquerors" (*Stone* 209). The Niess were dispossessed of their land and forced to disperse. Although they assimilated into other communities, they retained their own identity, especially through traditional customs such as "splitting their tongues" and distinct physical characteristics like "icewhite eyes and ashblow hair" (*Stone* 209).

In *The Stone Sky*, Jemisin describes how colonial forces demonized the Niess, painting them as a biologically divergent species that needed to be exterminated:

> Perhaps it began with whispers that white Niess irises gave them poor eyesight and perverse inclinations, and that split Niess tongues could not speak truth. . . . It became easy for scholars to build reputations and careers around the notion that Niess sessapinae were fundamentally different, somehow—more sensitive, more active, less controlled, less civilized—and this was the source of their magical peculiarity. This was what made them not the same kind of human as everyone else. Eventually: not *as* human as everyone else. Finally: not human at all. (210)

---

3. See Jemisin's interview with *Wired* magazine for an explanation of her references to Margaret Garner and Toni Morrison's *Beloved*—both examples of what she terms a "familiar story" of women forced to kill their own children rather than falling back into slavery (Kehe).

As Jemisin writes, empires can "conjure phantoms endlessly" despite there being "no discernible variance from ordinary people" (*Stone* 210, 211). The Niess, once eradicated, become straw figures with a dual purpose: both to stand for the dangers of magic created by their purported biological difference, and to provide the gene pool from which to bioengineer a new race of passive tuners that retain many of the productive abilities of the Niess.

Created in the likeness of the Niess, the tuners are "carefully engineered and denatured remnants of the Niess" with "sessapinae far more complex than those of ordinary people" who are capable of mobilizing the Plutonic Engine (*Stone* 211). In this way, the raw genetic labor of a dehumanized race is transformed into the tightly controlled resource upon which the Empire can grow. This Afrofuturist allegory for slavery extends into the stories created around the Niess. The tuners, Jemisin emphasizes, are "not just tools, but myths" (*Stone* 211). The tuners are therefore given the Niess features of "broad faces, small mouths, skin nearly devoid of color" (*Stone* 211). By creating the tuners in the image of the Niess, Syl Anagist exerts power over how their images and stories are used: "Only now, when we have been made over in the image of their own fear, are they satisfied" (211). Their biological characteristics, which serve the racist project of the Empire, are then transformed into a new kind of ideology in which their white skin becomes a symbol not for the other, but for the self. Because the Empire owns their genetic code, so too does the Empire own the tuners and all the products of their labor: "They congratulate themselves on having made their old enemies useful at last" (211).

However, the Broken Earth trilogy is not without hope. Jemisin suggests that a different future is possible; indeed, the series begins with an act of revolution, with Alabaster triggering the Fifth Season. But the best hope for a different future lies not with Alabaster, but with Nassun, Essun's daughter, who embodies what Lisa Yaszek calls the figure of the "black genius," a young person who uses all of the available scientific and practical knowledge to save themselves, their families, and their communities from hostile takeover by (white) alien invaders (59). Nassun is unique amongst orogenes in her ability to sense the silver threads of energy permeating the world and, without the formal training of the Fulcrum, teaches herself how to manipulate these threads. In doing so, she moves beyond the limits of orogeny dictated by the Empire to master the forbidden practice of magic and reclaim the radical kinds of knowledge that began with the Niess before they were perverted by Syl Anagist.

Magic differs to orogeny—while magic is the raw ability to manipulate geological and biological matter, orogeny represents the enclosed set of practices mandated and taught by the Empire. Nassun mobilizes magic effortlessly because she has not been institutionalized by the Fulcrum. She trains herself in the forests surrounding the remote comm of Jekity, experimenting with her ability to use magic (which she calls "the silver") to heal living things, rather than focusing on stone and earth, as imperial orogenes have been trained to do:

> It is not always easy to detect the wrongness in a body; sometimes she must carefully follow the threads of silver within a thing to find its knots and warps . . . the melon vines whose leaves are growing in a convex shape, catching too much ash, instead of concavity. . . . She practices extraction of the wrongness. . . . It's a difficult trick to master—like performing surgery with only one thread, without ever touching the patient. . . . She finds the parts of the plant that are saying *curve up* and convinces them to say *curve down*. (*Obelisk* 297–98)

Magic represents an instinctive form of knowledge and a mode of resistance open to Nassun, the black genius. Magic is forbidden in the Stillness—a hangover from the days of the Niess under Syl Anagist—but Nassun reclaims these ancient practices to destroy the very systems designed to oppress her and her ancestors. Without the training of the Fulcrum—and without her mother, Essun, who is also limited by that training—Nassun transforms magic and orogeny into a powerful practice capable of closing the Rift and repairing the Stillness. In doing so, she finds new possibilities for mutual cooperation between human, orogene, and Father Earth. Because her magical practice is rooted in "the silver"—the common thread of energy running through matter—Nassun's powers inherently recognize, and draw from, the entangled liveliness of all things. In Nassun's hands, magic is a celebration of the constantly changing relationships between matter, and it is from this basis that the future can be reconciled—rooted in an acknowledgement of the power and sovereignty of the material world, characterized by the figure of Father Earth.

Although Jemisin's work can clearly be read as allegory, the Broken Earth series moves beyond the future as critique of the past and the present. Tobias C. Van Veen suggests that most scholars have treated Afrofuturism as an "allegorical force . . . representing real conditions" (14). Such approaches, he argues, are limited in the face of the "unhinged force" of Afrofuturism, which transcends these points of reference to imagine "new forms of the other," moving beyond interpretations that merely map black experience onto future coordinates (Van Veen 15). Similarly, Clayton D. Colmon suggests that Afrofuturism now exceeds Mark Dery's original definition and has become a "cultural aesthetic" that focuses the "interpretive lens" of black experience onto "speculative identity and technology" (330). If race itself is a technology, as Ytasha L. Womack suggests, this opens radical possibilities for recalibrating the popular figures of SF, such as the alien, robot, and cyborg. In Afrofuturist interpretations, these figures are not merely iterations of posthuman identity but more- or other-than-humans who embody new, transformative myths for the future, unshackled from the codified constraints of allegory built around Afrodiasporic experience.

As the character of Nassun indicates, Jemisin does more than simply draw on Afrodiasporic history to imagine futures where social injustice persists in all-too-familiar ways. She also explores how these futures might produce new identities that move beyond conventional notions of "race" and "humanity." Van Veen claims that Afrofuturist performers such as Sun Ra and Janelle Monae create new, performative personae that radically transfigure essentialist notions of identity. These personae are "capable of unhinging allegorical referents to humanist bodies and terrestrial markers of difference," allowing the Afrofuturist artist to develop "autonomous forms of becoming and thought" that challenge "previously held conceptions of blackness and metaphysics" (Van Veen 8–9). These new identities are often explored, not surprisingly, in stories about divergent timelines and counterfutures.

As Van Veen states, "What allegory is there for the fiction of racism, for experience lived as inhuman, when it is already a fiction?" (13) Freed from allegorical constraints, Jemisin's characters reveal the inadequacy of the human as both biological and discursive construct. Orogenes and tuners are not merely metaphorical slaves who can only be understood in the light of African American history. By rejecting the humanity that has been deliberately withheld from them, Essun, Nassun, and Alabaster can be read as radically different Others who create new histories and new futures. As Kodwo Eshun states, "Most African-Americans owe nothing to the status of the human" anyway (193). By embracing the imaginative possibilities of alien identities, Jemisin abandons the human as a category that is, in itself, a technology of exclusion.

Vibrant Matter: Afrofuturism and Geontology

The Broken Earth series imagines geology as active and willful, particularly through the character of Father Earth. This disrupts our conventional understanding of who, or what, may be granted personhood, and promotes the Afrofuturist project of expanding our understanding of identity and technology. It is therefore particularly productive to bring the Broken Earth series into conversation with rich strands of thinking in the environmental humanities that treat Others—plants, animals, ecosystems, and even stone—as actors with whom humans are closely networked. Within this field, scholars are bringing increasing attention to "geosocialities": a way of addressing the irreversible geophysical evidence of human activity (such as concentrated atmospheric carbon dioxide, nuclear material, and plastics), and understanding how humans are constituted of, and impacted by, geological material (Palsson and Swanson 167). Gisli Palsson and Heather Anne Swanson argue that the geologic is at work in the biological world at the level of individual bodies, citing Steve Weiner and Patricia Dove's study of how prokaryotes and eukaryotes evolved to form minerals. Today, they argue, the mineral world meshes with the biological in mollusc shells, vertebrate bones, and the silica cellular coating of algae (Palsson and Swanson 162). Importantly, these minerals are not inert, but shape their organisms' experience of the world—for example, by becoming the sensory organs for otoliths (Palsson and Swanson 163).

In Jemisin's world, magic is the primary vector for such geosocialities. At the same time, it is also a commentary on the modern methods of energy production that have created a schism between the human and nonhuman:

> Magic. . . . She drags it out of the rock itself, which is another wonder, because you have not realized until now that there is any magic *in* the rock. . . . At some point millions or billions of years ago, you suspect, this whole area was at the bottom of an ocean. . . . Generations of sea life were born and lived and died here, then settled to that ocean's floor, forming layers and compacting. . . . What you suddenly understand is this: Magic derives from life—that which is alive, or was alive, or even that which was alive so many ages ago that it has turned into something else. (*Obelisk* 360–61)

Jemisin celebrates the relationships between all things, living and nonliving, by imagining a network of interconnected, mutual becoming. This is what Hugo Reinert terms "techniques of relation"—a way of "gaining particular knowledge, not so much *of* the stone but as *with* it" (107). And although such techniques may be deemed anthropomorphic, animist, or mysticizing, Reinert emphasizes how they are also tactics that help "choreograph reality" and open up new possibilities to "refract the present diagnostically" and expose its "latent potentials" (109–10).

Magic meshes the latent potential of the biological and the geological together in Jemisin's Broken Earth trilogy—it is the common thread running through all matter. This thread manifests powerfully in the process of rebirth that transforms both Alabaster and Essun into Stone Eaters. As orogenes, working with magic causes their flesh to slowly turn to stone. But as Jemisin insists, this does not mean permanent death. After they die, they are reincarnated as Stone Eaters—beings made entirely of mineral. Despite the radical nature of this physiological transformation, both manage to hold on to some essence of their former selves. When Essun emerges from the geode in which the Stone Eater, Hoa, has placed her, she takes on an entirely new form, yet one that also echoes biological characteristics she had when human. Hoa has "reassembled the raw arcanic substance of [Essun's] being," preserving some of her "critical essence" manifested through physical features such as "Locs of roped jasper. Skin of striated ocher marble that suggests laugh lines at eyes and mouth" (*Stone* 397).

Both Essun's biological and her social identities are entwined with the geologic. Geology shapes every interaction she has with the world, from her ability to discern the mineral composition of her environment to her decision to hide her orogeny from her husband. At the same time, geology is also biology for Nassun—she is a woman of flesh and blood and stone, as her transition from orogene to Stone Eater makes clear—but rather than limiting her identity, it becomes a tool for transformation. Her transition can be read as a new kind of biotechnology rooted in the mutability of our material selves in worlds of mutual, multispecies, multimatter relationality. Geology, in Jemisin's hands, is active and social, influencing the creation of new species and identities and creating new mythologies of the more-than-human.

Father Earth is another character whose power and personhood comes from the entanglement of the geological with the biological, as manifested through magic. In the Broken Earth trilogy, Father Earth conspires against humans and orogenes, influences Guardians to enact his will on the surface of the Stillness and utilizes magic. Indeed, Father Earth *is* magic, as Nassun discovers when she travels into the Earth's core:

> Magic. . . . This silver deep within Father Earth wends between the mountains fragments of his substance in exactly the same way that they twine among the cells of a living, breathing thing. And that is because a *planet* is a living, breathing thing; she knows this now with the certainty of instinct. All the stories about Father Earth being alive are true. (*Stone* 242)

Father Earth leads Nassun to the realization that magic—the raw material used to power obelisks and energy networks—exists in all forms of life and has accumulated over "aeons of life and death on the Earth's surface" (247). But this resource is not passive, inert matter. What humans failed to comprehend is that magic is evidence of the Earth's awareness and agency. Nassun speculates that, because empires never "respect lives different from their own," they never saw this magic as evidence of life, of intelligence or sentience; they saw only what could be taken: "Where they should have asked, or left alone, they raped" (247–48). Father Earth's anger at this exploitation is what sets off the Seasons—each Season is an opportunity to seize human bodies, which turn to matter rotting in soil, and eventually become energy for Father Earth, replenishing the world's magic. This, he believes, is a form of reparation, and one that Nassun can understand. Despite their complicity with the Empire's energy projects, orogenes have always been persecuted by others. In the Stillness, she has been "robbed of her childhood and any hope of a real future" (248) and shares Father Earth's need for revenge, aligning her purpose to remake the world with his.

Again, as Reinert states, this cannot be reduced to mysticism or anthropomorphism. It is a powerful way of evoking our own relationship to energy during the Anthropocene; an Afrofuturist projection that sees connections between various imperial projects of resource extraction. Whether it is the geological labor of the planet or the biological labor of black bodies, the Empire works from the assumption of a right to life in all its forms. Again, Jemisin moves beyond the merely allegorical to demonstrate that such assumptions are rooted in the absence of relational thinking. For the world to be reborn, Jemisin suggests, humans must honor the networked ways in which they survive in their environments, with and amongst other species, other materialities, in networks that span deep time.

Even the obelisks—enormous structures of garnet, onyx, topaz, and other gemstones that together form the "Obelisk Gate" or Plutonic Engine capable of harnessing energy—have a will of their own. They are capable of sensing and communicating not just with each other but also with orogenes. As Alabaster states, the obelisks work as batteries because "their crystalline structure emulates the strange linkage of power between the cells of a living being" (*Obelisk* 136)—they have both mineral and biological properties in their ability to channel magic. They are not merely tools, they are also beings. In recognition of the liveliness of geology, orogenes take their names, and perhaps an aspect of their personalities, from stone—alabaster, syenite, feldspar—while the Niess are, perhaps, named for gneiss—a metamorphic rock formed from igneous or sedimentary rock. The series acknowledges how exchanges between the biological and geological support multispecies interactions that are essential for rehabilitating the world, with Jemisin granting stone vivacity and liveliness, especially through magic.

Reading the Broken Earth series in the context of a geologic turn within the humanities acknowledges not only how humans are a geological force in the Anthropocene but also how the planet exerts its own forces on humans in turn. Elizabeth Ellsworth and Jamie Kruse note that the geologic turn offers opportunities for "inventive thinking" that can address the "new material situations of daily life" rooted in the earth's materialities (9). Similarly, Jane Bennett writes that humans are "inextricably enmeshed with vibrant, nonhuman agencies" (108), including the geological, prompting theorization of a "geological affect or material vitality" (61). These rich forms of relational thinking inform Jemisin's reimagination of the Afrofuturist posthuman. Her characters become more-than-human by recognizing and drawing on their connections with matter through magic. Such practices are an extension of how Afrofuturist artists have deployed alien and cyborg subjectivities to counteract the discourses, especially scientific and technological, of exclusion and subalternity.

These vibrant connections inform the ways orogenes work with stone. Far from inert, the earth becomes an active partner in Alabaster's hands:

> So he reaches deep and takes hold of the humming tapping bustling reverberating rippling vastness of the city, and the quieter bedrock beneath it, and the roiling churn of heat and pressure beneath that. Then he reaches wide, takes hold of the great sliding-puzzle piece of earthshell on which the continent sits. . . . He takes all that, the strata and the magma and the people and the power. . . . Everything. He holds it. He is not alone. The earth is with him. (*Fifth* 6–7)

For Alabaster, Essun, Nassun, and the other orogenes in the Stillness, identity is a complex networking of the biological with the geological, construing identity as "human-geological assemblages" (Ellsworth and Kruse 22) that respond to the lively worlds in which they are made. Ellsworth and Kruse believe that the deeply meshed spheres of the biological and geological, both figurative and literal, trouble previous distinctions between what is deemed lively and what is deemed inert (24). This entanglement between living and nonliving matter has been further theorized by Elizabeth Povinelli in her work on geontologies.

Povinelli addresses the ontological distinction between life and nonlife. Nonlife is not the same as death—rather, it is "the extinction of humans, biological life, and . . . the planet itself" ("Figures" 5). She perceives a shift taking place from biopower to geontopower under late capitalism. While the techniques of the former manifest in Afrofuturist SF as colonial, postcolonial, or necropolitical tactics (slavery, for example), geontopower is based on differentiating the lively from the inert, or life and nonlife. In Jemisin's world, humans must destroy these false dichotomies to salvage their world. The Broken Earth series is an Afrofuturist literature of both the bios and the geos, embracing the resonance between matter and thereby deconstructing borders between life and nonlife. Jemisin ultimately suggests that new and emancipatory identities are to be found in the mutual exchanges between flesh and stone.

Povinelli also addresses how colonized and especially Indigenous peoples, who grant "agency, subjectivity, and intentionality" to what is, in Western epistemologies, deemed inert, has meant they have been ascribed a "premodern mentality" (*Requiem* 5). Reclaiming "primitive" knowledges and transforming them into new theoretical practices for the future is a common tactic for Afrofuturists. By working with the productive matter of earth and stone and blending this with the human body and with magic, Jemisin critiques these divisions between life and nonlife to reveal the contiguity of geological, biological, and imaginary worlds that transcend "Euroamerican vocabularies of harm" (Reinert 105). Valuing different ways of seeing and knowing this world is, in itself, a denial of the division between life and nonlife. Yet recovering the lore of stone and earth necessarily evokes vast tracts of time with which humans are ill-prepared to deal. This time slippage forms one of the key struggles in the Broken Earth series, with the role humans played in creating the devastating cycle of Seasons lost by the time the series begins. Yet stone, here too, also presents a solution, with geology holding the answers, and also bringing long-term perspectives to the more immediate flux of Seasons and human history.

By playing with memory and the *longue durée* in the Broken Earth series, Jemisin reconfigures humanity's place in the world in the context of deep time—a world constantly being remade by the "teeming assemblage" of geo, bio, and social imaginaries (Ellsworth and Kruse 23). In both the Stillness and on our own planet, humans live within the climate and geology of the past, while creating the climate and geology of the future—there is a deep temporal distortion at work. Jemisin thus resituates the human within deep time, suggesting that, even in the Anthropocene, humans are not the dominant force but only one more strand within the material web of life, together with Father Earth, Stone Eaters, and Others: "This is what you must remember. . . . When we say 'the world has ended,' it's usually a lie, because *the planet* is just fine" (*Fifth* 14).

Many scholars have spoken of the difficulty of addressing climate change because of its "slow violence" (Nixon). By evoking deep time, Jemisin suggests that the most powerful tools for grasping the temporality of the geological world, especially as it intertwines with the biological, may be through an imaginative, relational leap. By working across generations and imagining intimacy with Others, Jemisin creates a sense of responsibility that persists through past, present, and future. This sentiment necessarily builds on situating the human within networks of Others, whether these are deemed lively or inert—indeed, these states indicate only a poverty in our understanding of ourselves as fully networked species rather than meaningful categories. David Farrier suggests that a "geologic poetics of ethical time" would therefore constitute "coeval or haunted temporalities" that grasp the "survival of responsibility" (16). Jemisin works with characters across generations, species, and temporalities—from the human characters who live only for a brief season, to the Stone Eaters who are immortal, to Father Earth whose lifespan is equivalent to that of the planet. Thus, separating the world into "vibrant life" and "dull matter" becomes impossible when viewed as part of a narrative of deep time, through which the techniques and narratives of survival on a planetary scale accumulate. Sedimentation becomes a useful concept here—suggesting that the future is not hypothetical but is being created in the present. The Broken Earth series therefore celebrates the Other, beyond the limits of Afrofuturist allegory—a geontological imaginary that contests suppositions about life itself.

Conclusion

The Broken Earth series harnesses the tools of Afrofuturism to reimagine relationality on a planetary scale. It blends geology and magic to create a rich world of more- or other-than-humans, critiquing the racist, colonial taxonomies and discourses that, disturbingly, are still circulating today, as evidenced by the Sad/Rabid Puppies phenomenon. As Jemisin states, perhaps what Torgersen and others of his ilk most fear is "being marginalized in turn"—they cannot imagine a space in which "everyone is equally welcomed at the center" ("Time"). In the Stillness, Jemisin embraces the lively matter of our living world to imagine a "center" that is a constantly shifting set of multiracial and multispecies relationships and assemblages. Jemisin creates futures that not only extrapolate on racialized histories but also move beyond allegory, using alien figures such as orogenes, tuners, and Father Earth to gesture toward a "universal becoming alien" (Van Veen 35) and explore the materialization of trauma and relationality.

The Broken Earth series unbinds race consciousness from a strict system of referents. Although these referents, and the contexts in which they are created and received, remain important in a world shared with Beales and Torgersens, Jemisin's work transcends issues of representation. In the Stillness, Jemisin capitalizes on the liveliness of the bio- and geosphere to construct new futures accounting for the "viscous porosity" of all matter (Tuana). This is a radical form of mythopoesis, with magic dismantling the false barriers between life and nonlife. Jemisin's Broken Earth series thereby highlights the imagination of difference as a crucial tool for addressing the wicked problems presented by the Anthropocene and by race relations—a form of utopian social dreaming.

Works Cited

Beale, Theodore. "A Black Female Fantasist Calls for Reconciliation." *Vox Popoli*, 13 Jun. 2013, http://voxday.blogspot.com/2013/06/a-black-female-fantasist.html. Accessed 1 Aug. 2017.

Bennett, Jane. *Vibrant Matter: A Political Ecology of Things*. Duke UP, 2010.

Colmon, Clayton D. "Queer Afrofuturism: Utopia, Sexuality, and Desire in Samuel Delany's 'Aye, and Gomorrah.'" *Utopian Studies*, vol. 28, no. 2, 2017, pp. 327–46.

Ellsworth, Elizabeth, and Jamie Kruse, editors. *Making the Geologic Now: Responses to Material Conditions of Contemporary Life*. Punctum Books, 2013.

Eshun, Kodwo. *More Brilliant Than the Sun: Adventures in Sonic Fiction*. Quartet Books, 1999.

Farrier, David. "'Like a Stone': Ecology, *Enargeia*, and Ethical Time in Alice Oswald's *Memorial*." *Environmental Humanities*, vol. 4, no. 1, 2014, pp. 1–18.

Jemisin, N. K. "Creating Races." *N. K. Jemisin*, 10 Aug. 2015, http://nkjemisin.com/2015/08/creating-races. Accessed 1 Aug. 2017.

———. *The Fifth Season*. Orbit Books, 2015.

———. 'Holy Fucking Shit I Won a Hugo.' *N. K. Jemisin*, 21 Aug. 2016, http://nkjemisin.com/2016/08/holy-fucking-shit-i-won-a-hugo/. Accessed 1 Aug. 2017.

———. "Not the Affirmative Action You Meant, Not the History You're Making." *N. K. Jemisin*, 10 Apr. 2015, http://nkjemisin.com/2015/04/not-the-affirmative-action-you-meant-not-the-history-youre-making/. Accessed 15 Nov. 2017.

———. *The Obelisk Gate*. Orbit Books, 2016.

———. "The Stars Are Ours: Read N. K. Jemisin's Historic Hugo Speech." *Barnes and Noble*, 20 Aug. 2018, https://www.barnesandnoble.com/blog/sci-fi-fantasy/read-n-k-jemisins-historic-hugo-speech/. Accessed 9 Nov. 2018.

———. *The Stone Sky*. Orbit Books, 2017.

———. "Time to Pick a Side." *N. K. Jemisin*, 14 Aug. 2013, http://nkjemisin.com/2013/08/time-to-pick-a-side/. Accessed 15 Nov. 2017.

Kehe, Jason. "Wired Book Club: Fantasy Writer N. K. Jemisin on the Weird Dreams that Fuel Her Stories." *Wired*, 17 Jun. 2016, https://www.wired.com/2016/06/wired-book-club-nk-jemisin/. Accessed 1 Aug. 2017.

Nixon, Rob. "Neoliberalism, Slow Violence and the Environmental Picaresque." *Modern Fiction Studies*, vol. 55, no. 3, 2009, pp. 443–67.

Palsson, Gisli, and Heather Anne Swanson. "Down to Earth: Geosocialities and Geopolitics." *Environmental Humanities*, vol. 8, no. 2, 2016, pp. 149–71.

Povinelli, Elizabeth A. "Geontologies: The Figures and the Tactics." *e-flux*, vol. 78, Dec. 2016, pp. 1–6.

———. *Geontologies: A Requiem to Late Liberalism*. Duke UP, 2016.

Reinert, Hugo. "About a Stone: Some Notes on Geological Conviviality." *Environmental Humanities*, vol. 8, no. 1, 2016, pp. 95–117.

Torgersen, Brad. "The Peasant Revolt Will Be Televised." *Brad R Torgersen*, 5 Apr. 2015, https://bradrtorgersen.wordpress.com/2015/04/05/peasants/. Accessed 1 Aug. 2017.

———. "Why Sad Puppies 3 Is Going to Destroy Science Fiction!" *Brad R Torgersen*, 16 Jan. 2015, https://bradrtorgersen.wordpress.com/2015/01/16/why-sad-puppies-3-is-going-to-destroy-science-fiction/. Accessed 1 Aug. 2017.

Tuana, Nancy. "Viscous Porosity: Witnessing Katrina." *Material Feminisms*, edited by Stacey Alaimo and Susan J. Hekman, Indiana UP, 2008, pp. 188–213.

Van Veen, Tobias C. "Vessels of Transfer: Allegories of Afrofuturism in Jeff Mills and Janelle Monae." *Dancecult: Journal of Electronic Dance Music Culture*, vol. 5, no. 2, 2013, pp. 7–41.

Womack, Ytasha L. *Afrofuturism: The World of Black Sci-Fi and Fantasy Culture*. Lawrence Hill Books, 2013.

Yaszek, Lisa. "Afrofuturism in American Science Fiction." *The Cambridge Companion to American Science Fiction*, edited by Gerry Canavan and Eric C. Link, Cambridge UP, 2015, pp. 58–69.

PART FOUR

Afrofuturism and Africa

FACING: Stacey Robinson, "The Last Shall Be First," 2018

CHAPTER 9

We Are Terror Itself
Wakanda as Nation

Gerry Canavan

Created by Stan Lee and Jack Kirby and introduced in *Fantastic Four* #52 in July 1966, the secretive North African land of Wakanda serves as home and base of operations for Marvel superhero T'Challa, the Black Panther (who is also the country's hereditary monarch). Distinct from the more traditionally colonialist fantasy of Marvel's "Savage Land"—an isolated region of Antarctica that is populated by cavemen and dinosaurs—the hidden land of Wakanda is an advanced competitor to Western imperial hegemony due to the presence of a rare "vibranium" meteor site that has allowed the Wakandans to develop and implement futuristic technologies that are totally unheard of outside its borders. This chapter explores Wakanda as both participating in and opposing the foundational European legal principle of the nation-state, tracing Wakanda's construction as an alternative political institution across its history in Marvel comics lore. While Wakanda has long been important in Marvel's superhero narrative, the imagined nation has risen to new prominence in recent years because of two recent developments in the Wakanda fantasy: first, the use of Black Panther as the moral conscience and voice of reason mediating between the two warring super-heroic factions of *Captain America: Civil War* (2016), followed by the production of his own movie, *Black Panther* (2018); and, second, *Black Panther*'s concurrent relaunch as an ongoing comics title helmed by acclaimed journalist and

MacArthur "Genius" grantee Ta-Nehisi Coates, also in 2016. It is the latter treatment of Wakanda that offers the chapter its title, "We Are Terror Itself." In a scene in *Black Panther* #4, King T'Challa addresses his royal cabinet following an attack on the nation. "Listen," he says. "No more discourse. No more deliberation. No more excuses. No more mercy. We know what this is. It is war, and war is our nation's trade. It has been so for generations. We are Wakanda. We will not be terrorized. We are terror itself." Thus, we see in these contemporaneous but highly contradictory treatments the incredible ideological flexibility that has always characterized the imagination of Wakanda as a space that is always both inside and outside the logics of nation, of coloniality, of empire, even of the idea of law itself. This chapter traces the history of this "flexibility" from the comics origins of Black Panther in the 1960s through to the way the character is now being articulated in the present.[1]

We can see this flexibility immediately in the maps that have been produced of Wakanda within Marvel comics over the years, including, in one particularly egregious case, these two subtly but significantly different maps published within just months of each other (see Figs. 9.1 and 9.2). Is Wakanda a West, Central, or East African nation? Does it have a coastline—and *which* coastline? Who are its neighbors?

Its interior features are similarly flexible. Even after decades of stories, until recently, Marvel has produced only an incredibly flattened conceptualization of Wakanda as an actual *place*. The presentation of Wakanda as a nation offers no internal structure, or even the suggestion of a culture or a functioning economy beyond what is needed in the immediate context of the current story. Thus, rather than a proper geography, Wakanda has jumping-off points for adventure micro-narratives: a city, a mountain, a valley, a lake, a jungle, "primitive peaks," a "chasm of chilling mist," and so forth. The most consistent feature of Wakanda—perhaps its only genuinely constant feature—is the Sacred Mound, the vibranium meteor impact site that has given the country its wealth and its technological prowess, which in turn have allowed it to not only escape Western domination but indeed to compete with the European (and later, American) imperialist powers as equals. In early Marvel stories, Wakanda sometimes gets used in place of the figure of the heroic white inventor to introduce novel scientific and technological elements into the narrative; where one *Fantastic Four* story might simply assert "and then Reed Richards invented a machine that could . . . ,"

---

1. Editors' note: Like other authors in this collection (Kilgore and Bould), Canavan explores pre-twenty-first-century texts in light of twenty-first-century Afrofuturist texts and issues.

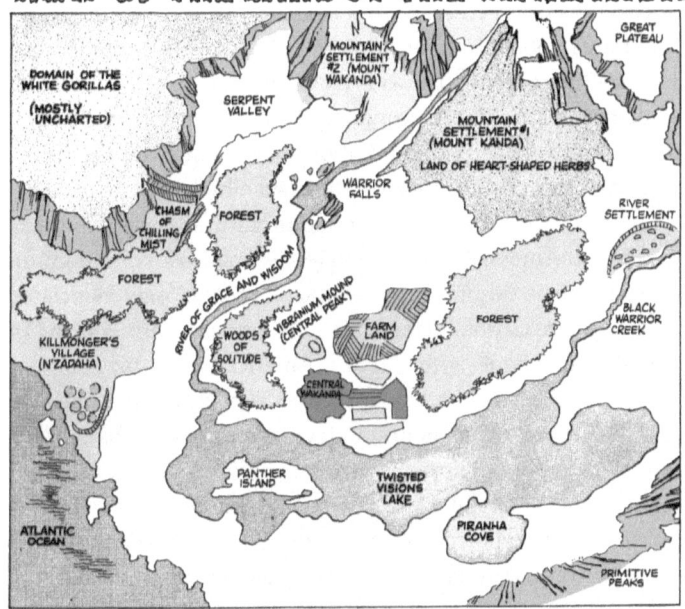
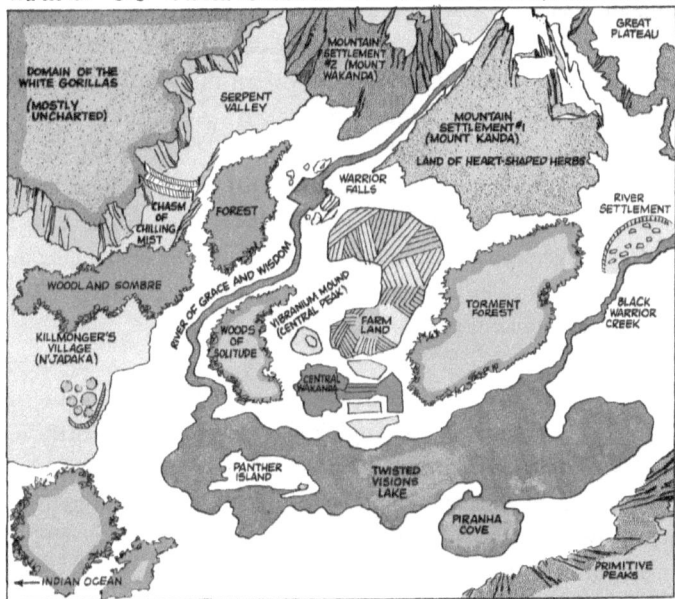

FIGURES 9.1 and 9.2. Maps of Wakanda from *Jungle Action* Vol. 2 #6 (September 1973) and #8 (January 1974). Used with permission from Marvel Entertainment, LLC.

another would say they got the technology from T'Challa and Wakanda. This observation is true in early *Fantastic Four* stories of both flying cars and autonomous robots, taking familiar tokens of an imminent science-fictional future (normally coded as a white future) very familiar to a 1960s comics audience and subtly Africanizing them—a tension made explicit by The Thing's racist wondering aloud about how "some refugee from a Tarzan movie" managed to "lay his hands" on such high-tech objects (*Fantastic Four* Vol. 1 #52, 2). Perhaps the most famous cultural artifact in the Marvel universe, Captain America's shield, is likewise made of vibranium, thereby internationalizing the origins of the character most closely associated with American gumption; Captain America's closest friend, Sam Wilson (The Falcon)—who shared a book with Captain America in the 1970s and who in more recent Marvel continuity has sometimes replaced him as the new Captain America—flies on wings not only developed in Wakanda but designed by T'Challa personally. After their initial encounter, T'Challa can frequently be seen on video monitors in the background of early Fantastic Four stories, providing advice or technical assistance to the team remotely—often on a moment's notice or just in the nick of time, "just like the cavalry charge in a Western film" (*Fantastic Four* Vol. 1 #56, 7, 20).

Among his many other talents, T'Challa is thus a figure for black technological genius as well, marking his story as an international, postcolonial version of what Lisa Yaszek has memorably dubbed not an Edisonade but a Bannekerade, after the eighteenth-century African American inventor and mathematician Benjamin Banneker:

> In Afrodiasporic versions of the Edisonade—what I call the Bannekerade—the hero is generally a young black male scientist-inventor who uses the products of his genius to save himself, his friends, and his community from domestic oppressors who are either white Westerners or use the machinery of Western institutions as tools for black oppression. (17)

While the white hero of the Edisonade is typically a national hero, fighting on behalf of the United States or England (often working directly with its military), Yaszek notes, the "international scope of Western imperialism and the various attendant African diasporas lead black authors to cast the Bannekerade in global terms"—a feature that is largely true of T'Challa as well, despite originating with white writers and being written by white writers through most of his history (17). Likewise, T'Challa's narratives over the long run tend to share the dyspeptic narrative trajectory Yaszek notes as typical of the Bannekerade:

Furthermore, while the Edisonadian hero usually completely eliminates the threat of foreign oppressors altogether by destroying enemies and appropriating their lands, the Bannekeradian protagonist more often wins a series of immediate battles only to find he is still in enemy territory and faces a drawn-out race war with an uncertain ending. (17)

Thus, while Ta-Nehisi Coates is right that T'Challa's status as "one of the smartest people in the world, ruling the most advanced civilization on the planet" is "the product of the black nationalist dream, a walking revocation of white supremacist myth" ("The People vs. T'Challa")—and that those Afrofuturist elements of the narrative are typically quite celebrated over the course of a given issue or storyline—over the long run, the Wakandan dream is always partial and incomplete, and always under permanent threat from the possible reassertion of white supremacy (both diegetically, with regard to the other nations in the Marvel Universe, and *non*diegetically, from the perspective of a comics industry still unrepresentatively dominated by white Americans on the levels of both artistic creation and intellectual property ownership).

Yaszek's identification of this last tendency of the Bannekerade helps one understand a second foundational incoherence in the presentation of Wakanda, its history of recent interactions with the rest of the globe. More than any particular articulated history, Wakanda exhibits only a negative one: Wakanda is a hidden land, undisturbed and never colonized, and indeed in some treatments was utterly unknown to the rest of the planet until sometime in the early twentieth century.[2] While the vibranium meteor fell to earth in prehistory, it is typically said to have been unearthed only a generation before the present day, by T'Challa's father T'Chaka. This fictive history—not consistently presented in Black Panther stories—complicates the fantasy significantly, as a timespan of only two or three decades seems insufficient time to allow Wakanda to have developed the sort of technological infrastructure, cultural traditions, and political independence with which it is otherwise normally depicted. (Likewise, because Marvel uses a sliding time scale which places the emergence of the contemporary age of superheroes within the last ten to fifteen years, it becomes increasingly hard to square this assertion of recent Wakandan emergence with a claim that Wakanda *also* supplied the vibranium used to produce Captain America's

---

2. It should not escape our notice that the hidden land of Wakanda even has its *own* interior hidden land, "The Domain of the White Gorillas (Mostly Uncharted)," allowing T'Challa to occasionally have his own colonialist explorations as well (see again figs. 9.1 and 9.2).

shield during World War II, which is slowly receding out of any plausible relationship to the lifespan or reign of T'Challa's father.[3]) This chronological limitation also has the unhappy consequence of *re*provincializing Wakanda, rather than allowing it to stand (as some other treatments of the concept do) as a vision of radical historical difference, Wakandan technological superiority is always "too soon" to have made a significant historical difference in world affairs—or else it is already a thing of the past.

The storyline introducing the Black Panther devotes significant attention to subverting well-worn narrative clichés about Africa, with comedic character The Thing quickly becoming bored and even yawning as the Black Panther recites his origin, even cutting him off to predict that "everything wuz hunky dory until the greedy ivory hunters made the scene" (*Fantastic Four* Vol. 1 #53, 6). (Even T'Challa must concede here that his story "does follow the usual pattern"—though his poachers were stealing vibranium, not ivory [7].) This interplay between the subversion and reproduction of Western imperial visions of Africa recurs across the subsequent decades of Wakandan stories; indeed, what is initially intended, in the original presentation of the Panther's story, to be the audience's pleasure at having their (racist, colonialist) assumptions about Africa and Africans inverted becomes an antinomy that Wakanda stories become for many years unable to move beyond. Subsequent stories about the Black Panther in the 1960s and 1970s often lean quite hard into these kinds of visual and narrative stereotypes; by *Fantastic Four* Vol. 1 #54, the joke is that the team is teaching Black Panther and his fellow tribesman to play baseball, even as he laughs that the sport "will never replace lion hunting" (1).[4]

We are similarly supposed to understand that T'Challa has, since taking the throne, become the richest man on the planet and fueled a global technological revolution through his international sales of vibranium, while simultaneously keeping nearly all the vibranium within Wakandan territory *and also at the same time* keeping Wakanda essentially hidden from the rest of the world in the process. Unlike the geographic incoherence mentioned above, which typically remains a background detail, this temporal incoherence causes stories about Wakanda to freely exhibit a bizarre mix of

---

3. Seeing the writing on the wall, more recent depictions of Wakanda have suggested that the Wakandan technological advantage "goes back centuries," as Ta-Nehisi Coates puts it ("The People vs. T'Challa").

4. T'Challa seems especially at risk of falling into Marc Singer's observation about comics and race that "visually codified representations in which characters are continually reduced to their appearances" makes "the potential for superficiality and stereotyping . . . dangerously high" (107).

colonialist fantasy and ostensibly reverse-colonialist imagery as the terms of the story demand at any particular moment. The Wakandans are thus both incredibly scientifically advanced and incredibly superstitious, utterly beholden to ritual; they have flying cars, but don't know about vaccination; they fight with spears, not guns; they are a hereditary monarchy structured by divine right, with apparently no limit on tyrannical rule whatsoever and no interest in democracy or revolution, but also constantly falling under the control of usurpers to the throne; and so on. In different treatments, the Wakandans likewise are alternatively a secretive people, known primarily by reputation and rumor; a literally hidden people, totally unknown to the rest of the planet until recently; a valued trading partner of many Western nations that welcomes outsiders, provided they respect Wakandan ways; a crucial part of the United Nations and the international legal order more generally; the primary driver of twentieth-century technoscientific progress as we know it in our own world; the enclavist developer of an entirely independent, futuristic technology tree, largely incompatible with the existing technology of the United States and Europe; and on and on. These discordant elements conspire to prevent Wakanda from ever becoming the global hegemon the terms of the story would otherwise seem to demand it would, as well as leave Wakanda constantly (in story terms) under threat of being *re*colonized despite its long anticolonial history and its overawing technological superiority; indeed, Black Panther's origin story is precisely about Western imperialists trying to raid Wakanda and steal its wealth, murdering King T'Chaka in the process, despite the entire Black Panther fantasy being premised on the fact that Wakanda is a place where this unhappy history never occurred. Thus his own superhero origin tale depicts the Wakanda of T'Challa's childhood in terms that are completely at odds with the hypertechnologized version seen elsewhere.

Readers of Black Panther in the *longue durée* must exert a kind of personal selectivity in which versions of Wakanda and T'Challa they will credit as authoritative; there are as many versions of a Wakanda that "represents a fusion of African tradition and high technology" as there are depictions that reinforce rather than challenge colonialist stereotypes of Africa (Bould 299–300).[5] This problem of interpretation has only compounded over the decades of Marvel comics, which frequently upend Wakanda's historic inviolability in the name of giving individual Black Panther stories sufficient emotional stakes. Thus, an African nation that was never colonized historically

---

5. See in particular Adilfu Nama's critique of the *Jungle Action* years of the 1970s in his "Brave Black Worlds" 138).

becomes, over the long run of Marvel stories, the site of repeated meta-imperial incursion—from the United States, from alien invaders, from supervillains like Dr. Doom, from the Atlantean king Namor the Sub-Mariner, and on and on. As Ta-Nehisi Coates notes in an interview with the science fiction news website *io9*, part of his task when he took over Black Panther in 2016 was precisely to reestablish Wakanda as the undefeatable global superpower it was always intended as, but never quite was allowed to be:

> Before my run, there were several things that happened at Marvel, like some bad things happened to Wakanda. First of all you've got Priest. Priest's job is to get white folks to take T'Challa seriously. T'Challa ain't no chump. He established that pretty well.
>
> After that, Reggie [Hudlin] comes in, he says, "Not only is T'Challa not a chump, but Wakanda ain't to be fucked with, period." Like ever. Don't even think about it. We've been wrecking fools since time immemorial.
>
> But between Hudlin and me, a lot of other things happened. I can't answer for other writers . . . but other writers made decisions. Between doing *Avengers vs. X-Men* and *Time Runs Out*, there's a lot of fucked-up shit that happens to Wakanda. Then I come in as a writer. (Narcisse)

In any event, it should be said here that coherence as such is something of a false problem in the continuity of long running properties, both in and outside of comics; with so many writers, artists, and audiences working on Black Panther stories over so many years it would be impossible for any creator or reader to possess a genuinely "full history" of the character, much less for all those moving parts to produce a singular whole with no contradictions, exceptions, or excesses. What we are talking about when we talk about comics, more than any pseudohistorical totality, is the production of something like what Raymond Williams once called a structure of feeling: what *feels* like a Black Panther story, and what doesn't feel like one. (Indeed, recent maps of Wakanda [as in the current ongoing Ta-Nehisi Coates-authored series] have tended to opt for less geographic and historical detail, rather than more, even as they have finally started to introduce political and cultural structures in Wakanda that finally make it seem like a "real" place) (fig. 9.3). In Wakanda's case, this structure of feeling is produced precisely at the locus of these tensions: primitive vs. futuristic, continuity vs. change, enclave vs. hegemon.

In a story arc like the one that sees Captain America and Black Panther team up in *Tales of Suspense* #97–99 and *Captain America* #100 (1968) to prevent the implementation of an orbital platform containing nuclear

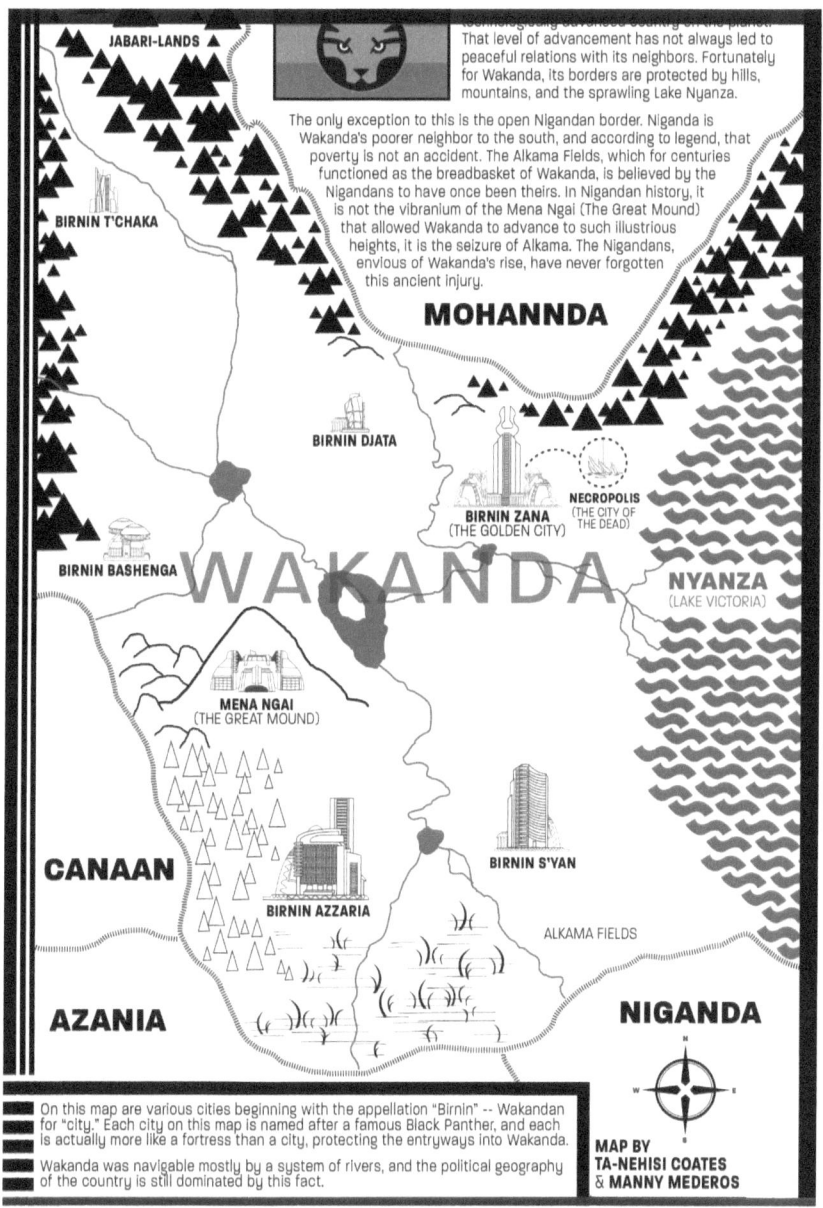

FIGURE 9.3. Wakanda map from *Black Panther* (2016). The insert text on the map notes both that Wakanda is the most scientifically and technologically advanced country on the planet and that it has frequently had tense relations with its neighbors, including the fictional country of Niganda from which it has seized valuable territory. Used with permission from Marvel Entertainment, LLC.

weapons, the concatenation of all these tensions produces a reverse-colonialist (if not quite anticolonialist) narrative, an archetypal one for the character.[6] In the story Captain America essentially becomes T'Challa's sidekick, in an antiracist, oppositional logic, rather than the white supremacist one we might initially expect to find in a 1960s comic. The Cold War plays out in Wakanda not as part of a US–USSR proxy war but rather as a Wakandan espionage operation against HYDRA in which the United States provides key intelligence and support. Heroes and villains in the story repeatedly discuss Black Panther's innate charisma and cool command, with Captain America in particular apparently in awe of his natural abilities; across the story, Captain America is constantly looking to the better-prepared and better-informed Black Panther for explanations and leadership, and, indeed, when Captain America attempts to call in US military assets to bring down the station, he discovers that T'Challa has already attempted to act unilaterally to destroy it.

At the end of the story, the surviving HYDRA soldiers surrender to T'Challa, not to Captain America, and are told they will be given a fair trial in the Wakandan system (not the US nor the international courts). Still, the story does subtly inject a racial imaginary in a panel near the end of the arc, in which Black Panther (standing in the shadows just behind Captain America) pointedly declares that it will be "better to die as men—than to live—as slaves!" (*Tales of Suspense* Vol. 1 #99, 9)[7] Perhaps similarly, despite his obvious leadership in this situation, the issue ends with Black Panther being offered Captain America's active-duty position in the Avengers (based in the US), as Captain America is needed internationally ("So long as freedom may be threatened—Captain America must follow his destiny—wherever it may lead!").

Alongside this sense of Wakanda as a place that is both inside and outside the ordinary international order—and both superordinate and subordinate to US hegemony—we must consider T'Challa himself as a character. Black Panther's still relatively unique status as a black (but not African American) superhero who is also a monarch supercharges some of the contradictions that run through traditional superhero fantasy, particularly around the fundamental conflict between vigilantism and the authority of the law. Black

---

6. *Tales of Suspense* was rebranded *Captain America* with issue #100, so despite the change in names, these represent a single story in a single series.

7. Wakanda's oblique complicity in not preventing the transatlantic slave trade would eventually become central to Killmonger's antivillain arc in Coogler's film version of *Black Panther*.

Panther as a franchise is shot through with the hopeless incommensurability of T'Challa's dual roles as superhero and as king. Because he must function as both, he is able to do neither. As I read through historical comic stories regarding T'Challa, it occurred to me that (with apologies to the axiom frequently attributed to Tolstoy) that there are really only two stories: (1) Black Panther Leaves Wakanda and Has to Go Back; and (2) Black Panther Goes Back to Wakanda and Then Has to Leave. Likewise, within the Wakanda portion of the story cycle, there is a similar minicycle in which the same thing happens to him over and over: T'Challa typically discovers that the person he left in charge has gone evil and that he has to take his throne back, but once he's done that he determines he is the wrong person to rule Wakanda in this moment and has to leave again.

When not in Wakanda, T'Challa is continually marked by his racial and national difference from the other Avengers, beginning with his first entry to the team in *Avengers* #52 (May 1968): he is initially mistaken for a burglar attempting to enter the Avengers Headquarters and arrested by white police officers on suspicion of murdering three of the Avengers. T'Challa handily escapes from the police (who are unsure of his identity and unable even to find Wakanda on a map) and is relentlessly hunted by them for the remainder of the issue, quite literally dodging police bullets as he seeks to solve the crime himself.

Only when T'Challa successfully revives a not-actually-dead Hawkeye is his story accepted; at this point Black Panther is admitted to the Avengers in earnest, as "a new ally . . . one who has given up a throne, that he may better serve a greater kingdom . . . the whole of mankind itself!" But this universalist proclamation too will soon fail, when it turns out that Black Panther must actually put his own people first and foremost—at least until he is called to leave Wakanda again to serve an even higher moral obligation—until, of course, he must return again because . . . The essence of nearly any sufficiently long Black Panther arc is precisely this precarious *both/and/neither/nor*, the sense of T'Challa's pull toward multiple domains simultaneously leaves him ultimately unsuited to any particular one, and thus he is perpetually mired in an unbreakable cycle of exile and return.

Of course, as Umberto Eco argued as far back as "The Myth of Superman" (1972), this cycle of deviation from and subsequent return to an unchangeable status quo is in some sense endemic to serialized comics as a medium. The problem is especially acute with Black Panther, though, as the endless "undoing" of all narrative movement produces a fatal challenge to the ostensibly progressive, antiracist politics associated with the character.

We want, in some sense, Black Panther to embody a hopeful vision of alterity and utopian historical difference that superhero comics as a form can never allow him to inhabit for very long.[8]

Wakanda itself is subject to a very similar sense of *both/and/neither/nor* with regard to their status in the international world order. As with other Afrofuturist projects that establish a fictive competitor to the project of European hegemony—I think here especially of Octavia E. Butler's Doro, though other examples abound[9]—the alternative to European imperialism and whiteness that the Wakandans offer is shot through with contradictions and often does not seem like an *alternative* at all. Are the Wakandans competitors to the racist world-historical fantasy called whiteness, or are they the perfection of it? Does the presence of the meteor within Wakanda's borders—which has given the nation a tremendous advantage in world affairs and ostensibly made them the most powerful nation on the planet, while otherwise changing little or nothing about twentieth-century history—make Wakanda a space of exception, or of typicality? In a world that views the murderous history of Europe as if it were "natural"—not only morally neutral and unavoidable, but even now equates the spread of global European dominion as "the march of progress"—Marvel's depiction of the Wakandans cannot decide in which part of the binary they participate. Thus, in figure 9.4, when Black Panther fights a homegrown nemesis, the Man-Ape, who has garnered his power from the forbidden and mostly unexplored territory of the White Gorillas (Wakanda's own interior hidden land), the imagery simultaneously rests on an antiblack association of Africans with gorillas *and* on the monstrosity of whiteness—while Black Panther is both the defender of his people and also a sellout to white power, and the Wakandans themselves are simultaneously crypto-Americans who love freedom and benighted foreigners kneeling before a despot they ought to overthrow . . .

Likewise, in historical Black Panther narratives we can see Black Panther freely swing from being the "native" who has been colonized by his education in the West, losing his ostensibly natural connection to his people and his land; to a black version of the nineteenth-century white colonizer

---

8. For my reading of the *Black Panther* film against Eco's critique of the superhero comics form, see "The Limits of Black Panther's Afrofuturism" in *Frieze*.

9. As Ingrid Thaler has noted of Butler's Doro, the superficial attempt to present Doro as "a viable alternative to Western modernity" obscures the extent to which he replicates and improves upon those practices (35–37). For more on the connection between Afrofuturist comics and Butler's work, including Black Panther, see my "Bred to Be Superhuman: Comic Books and Afrofuturism in Octavia Butler's Patternist Series."

FIGURE 9.4. Page from *Avengers* Vol. 1 #62. Used with permission from Marvel Entertainment, LLC.

"civilizing" the inscrutable savages of some primitive country (often, his own!);[10] to the postcolonial hero of twentieth-century decolonization defending his homeland against imperialists and invaders; and back again. The depiction of Black Panther is weighed down by its gravitational attraction to a critique of world history and especially twentieth-century American power that Marvel is never sure it wants to commit to—and so, to the extent that the messaging of these narratives are anticolonialist or anti-imperialist, Wakanda stories are always very precarious, always threatening despite their surface antiracism to collapse into racism again.

Even the very concept of "civilization" itself becomes deconstructed in Wakanda; characters who use the term in Black Panther stories never seem quite sure whether it refers to European civilization (a category to which Wakanda is somewhat reluctantly admitted by virtue of its military-economic-technological power, despite its racialized status as an African

---

10. The most notable instance of this version of the Black Panther as reverse-colonizer occurs at the end of his *Jungle Action* run, in which T'Challa fights a particularly disturbing murder-cult in an especially backward nation: the Ku Klux Klan. *Jungle Action* was cancelled before the planned ending to the story could be published.

nation) or to *Wakandan* civilization (against which Europe, America, other African nations, and indeed all human nations shrink in comparison). When Black Panther begs M'Baku (said to be "a living anachronism, strange to the ways of civilization") not to "turn the Wakandans back down the road to savagery" (*Avengers* Vol. 1 #62, 12), which binary of civilization and barbarism is he thinking of? The Africa of Black Panther comics remains permanently inflected by the history of white supremacy, despite a fictional context which would challenge those hoary binaries—even for the Wakandans themselves.

We see a similar contradiction in the depiction of Wakandan trade, which has the effect of eroding and destroying Wakandan traditions through Western influence even as Wakanda is ostensibly the more powerful trading partner in this equation—replicating the colonial narrative but with an ahistorical logic that takes the superiority of Western values as axiomatic (and totally distinct from the West's brutally colonialist and neocolonialist practices of invasion, exploitation, and domination). Already by the 1970s, Black Panther is unsure whether he has done the right thing in entering foreign markets at all, wondering if the reforms he and his father have instituted in opening Wakanda to the world have actually doomed the country—as are many of his countrymen. It is relatively late in the game that Marvel writers even begin to interrogate the techno-progressivist, secular assumptions behind the foundation of the Wakanda story: that a monarch would actually strip-mine a "sacred" site, the Mound, instrumentalizing its special properties for technological gadgetry and even selling parts of it to Western outsiders in the name of economic development, all without *any* cultural struggle or resistance from the population (see especially *Jungle Action* Vol. 2).

By the *Doomwar* storyline of the 2010s (Maberry), the presence of the vibranium within Wakanda has proved to be such a "resource curse" that the heroic resolution of the story sees T'Challa activate a process he has invented that renders all the vibranium in the world (both inside and outside Wakanda) inert, in order to protect it both from foreign invaders like Dr. Doom but also to break the country's cruel-optimistic dependence on the resource.

One of the strengths of Ta-Nehisi Coates's recent depiction of the Wakandans is precisely that he embraces these contradictions. This is a point Coates makes explicit in a blogpost at the *Atlantic*:

> I also had to create some sort of working theory about Wakanda, and to the extent to which I came to one it is this: Wakanda is a contradiction. It is the most advanced nation on Earth, existing under one of the most primitive forms of governance on Earth. In the present telling, Wakanda's

FIGURE 9.5. Page from *Black Panther* (2016) #4. Used with permission from Marvel Entertainment, LLC.

technological superiority goes back centuries. Presumably its population is extremely well educated, and yet that population willingly accedes to rule by blood. T'Challa descends from an unbroken line of kings, all who've taken up the mantle of the Black Panther. But if you've ever studied monarchy, it becomes immediately apparent that the aptitude, or even the desire, to govern isn't genetic. ("The People vs. T'Challa")

Likewise, "Wakanda had always prided itself on having never been conquered. This is no longer true. What, then, is the country if it is as vulnerable as all others?" ("The People vs. T'Challa"). Thus, when Wakanda faces destabilization due to outside influence that activates existing discontent within the country, Wakanda mobilizes for war—using its full might for self-defense against enemies of the state both foreign and domestic. The status of Wakanda as a non-European nation in an age of a global war on terror—which in the post–Cold War period has justified a return to white imperialism this time in the name of global security—becomes weirdly crucial to its self-conception; Wakanda will not be terrorized, T'Challa announces, because Wakanda is "terror itself" (see fig. 9.5). The pendulum once again swings: now Wakanda is emphatically *outside* the imperial order of the European-American system, and that is precisely where its power lies.

But in the next issue, something interesting happens. T'Challa calls in a council of counterrevolutionaries—white experts who have specialized in putting down revolutions elsewhere, from fictive countries in the Marvel universe that have been deployed by other writers as dystopian sites of totalitarianism and genocide. These men take no small amount of glee in being called in by a place like Wakanda to solve a problem the Wakandans would normally think themselves above; indeed, the racist logic of white and black is here temporarily reversed, and it is the Wakandans who, falsely thinking of themselves as "men of honor," must be convinced to do business with noxious "repressive thugs" as well as recognize that their self-satisfied sense of superiority is not predicated on superior institutions but on radical moral luck. Here whiteness is a marker not of privilege but of corruption and violence—and so the white consultant's assertion that the Wakandans are just as white as any European is no compliment: you're just as white as us, so you shouldn't be so precious about getting your hands dirty crushing dissidents. As T'Challa listens to the presentation, he thinks: "Wakanda is no different. The respect we enjoy is wealth—vibranium, science, and accounts in places most humans have never heard of." He goes on: "Wakanda is not white. But by the Panther's gaze, neither is Europe" (*Black Panther* #5).

But T'Challa refuses this resolution too. "The handlers of these men are despots, and strongmen. . . . Their peace is the peace of the dead." He reaches not for whiteness to solve the crisis, but instead for blackness, and calls in the Crew: a sort of supercommittee of black superheroes, including Luke Cage, Misty Knight, and the X-Men's Storm, to help him solve the problems that have caused the legitimacy crisis in the country.

At the end of the arc he also abdicates, again, leaving with the Crew to be a superhero. Now, he has decided, Wakanda will become a republic, with a constitution and elected leaders rather than a king—in a sense, Wakanda will lose its specificity and uniqueness by joining the European order, formally becoming coded as "not-black," at least until the next storyline begins—so he, once again in exile, can *remain* black, and in his own way, a king (but not a tyrant).[11] That is: Wakanda is now to be permanently subsumed into the logic of Western hegemony—including a progressivist celebration of the transition to democracy as a marker of human progress, and the attendant exclusion of non-Western social forms—but *not* T'Challa himself, who will remain an outsider and a vigilante.[12] "Our people are the most

---

11. The language harkens back to the battle between Black Panther and Man-Ape in *Avengers* #53, in which T'Challa cannot understand why his freedom-loving people do not rise up against a tyrant, "forgetting their proud heritage"—a proposition utterly incompatible with the notion that T'Challa is a dynastic, hereditary monarch. See again fig. 9.4.

12. True to form, T'Challa tells his mother that even though the new governmental structure will no longer rely on "one man," he will still represent the people as their

advanced in the world," T'Challa tells his doubting mother, who begs him not to abdicate (which this time entails dissolving the throne altogether). "Should not the institutions that govern them be the same?" His more traditionalist mother is unconvinced, offering only a quiet "Perhaps"—but she is glad at least that for the first time in a long time T'Challa seems to be living with conviction, and seems "free" (*Black Panther* #12) Here, as always, we see the fundamental tension in Wakanda as *both/and/neither/nor*, as it has been reproduced again and again across its fictional history: an Afrofuturist vision of African superiority that nonetheless must always be disciplined by final subordination to the West, a proud and independent nation helmed by a wise and just leader who is only ever truly happy just after he's abdicated and run off somewhere else.

Works Cited

Bould, Mark. "From Panther to Princess, Sex Work to Starfleet." *Science Fiction Studies*, vol. 37, no. 2, 2010, pp. 296–302.

Canavan, Gerry. "Bred to Be Superhuman: Comic Books and Afrofuturism in Octavia Butler's Patternist Series." *Africa SF*, special issue of *Paradoxa*, vol. 25, 2013, pp. 253–87.

———. "The Limits of Black Panther's Afrofuturism." *Frieze*, 27 Feb. 2018, https://frieze.com/article/limits-black-panthers-afrofuturism. Accessed 30 Jul. 2019.

Coates, Ta-Nehisi. *Black Panther*. Marvel Comics, 2016–.

———. "The People vs. T'Challa." *Atlantic*, 22 Jan. 2016, https://www.theatlantic.com/notes/2016/01/the-people-tchalla/425097/. Accessed 20 Nov. 2017.

Eco, Umberto. "The Myth of Superman." *Diacritics*, vol. 2, no. 1, Spring 1972, pp. 14–22.

Lee, Stan, editor. *Jungle Action*, vol. 2, Marvel Comics, 1972–1976.

———. *Tales of Suspense*, vol. 1, Marvel Comics, 1963–1968. Rebrands as *Captain America* with issue 100.

Lee, Stan, and Jack Kirby. *Avengers*, vol. 1, Marvel Comics, 1963–1987.

———. *Fantastic Four*, vol. 1, Marvel Comics, 1961–1966.

Maberry, Jonathan, and Scot Eaton. *Doomwar*. Marvel Comics, 2010.

Nama, Adilifu. "Brave Black Worlds: Black Superheroes as Science Fiction Ciphers." *African Identities*, vol. 7, no. 2, May 2009, pp. 133–44.

Narcisse, Evan. "Ta-Nehisi Coates Explains How He's Turning Black Panther into a Superhero Again." *io9.com*, 14 Sept. 2016. https://io9.gizmodo.com/ta-nehisi-coates-explains-how-hes-turning-black-panther-1786632598. Accessed 20 Nov. 2017.

---

hero—before immediately, two pages later, stepping into a portal and leaving Wakanda altogether.

Singer, Marc. "'Black Skins' and White Masks: Comic Books and the Secret of Race." *African American Review*, vol. 36, no. 1, 2002, pp. 107–19.

Thaler, Ingrid. *Black Atlantic Speculative Fictions: Octavia E. Butler, Jewelle Gomez, and Nalo Hopkinson*. Routledge, 2010.

Williams, Raymond. *Marxism and Literature*. Oxford UP, 1977.

Yaszek, Lisa. "The Bannerkerade: Genius, Madness, and Magic in Black Science Fiction." *Black and Brown Planets: The Politics of Race in Science Fiction*, edited by Isiah Lavender III, UP of Mississippi, 2014, pp. 15–30.

CHAPTER 10

Global Afrofuturist Ecologies

Jerome Winter

This chapter examines a cohort of Afrofuturist authors who are creating new modes of environmental science fiction (SF) that radically revise the colonial and postcolonial narratives driving environmental SF written from globally Northern perspectives. Traditionally speaking, Northern environmental SF authors have often relied on narratives of environmental conquest and expansion while conspicuously omitting their rootedness in the historical realities of colonialism and postcolonialism. By way of contrast, Afrofuturist artists call attention to such narratives in their own storytelling practices, demonstrating both how dreams of environmental mastery lead to environmental disaster and how the ecological material practices of indigenous people across Africa and across the global South might provide the foundations for a range of possible new futures—and new stories about those futures as well.

Consider, for instance, the very different stances toward environmental and geopolitical issues in the Hollywood blockbuster *The Martian* (2015, based on a novel written by Andy Weir and starring Matt Damon) and Nigerian author Chinelo Onwualu's short story, "Night Market" (2016). *The Martian* celebrates the fictional exploits of a NASA astronaut who survives nearly two years of accidental abandonment on Mars in large part by fertilizing potatoes with his own manure. As the astronaut half-seriously, half-jokingly notes in one of his many video log entries, "They say once you grow crops somewhere, you have officially colonized it. So, technically, I colonized Mars. In your face, Neil Armstrong!" While the repeated use of the word "colonized" might raise the specter of ecological exploitation and devastation that has so often attended Northern incursions into other lands, both the joking tone in which Damon delivers this line and the lushness of his makeshift greenhouse—which is shot in stark contrast to an otherwise dusty and barren-seeming Mars, encourages readers to celebrate the astronaut's ingenuity and perseverance instead.

By way of contrast, Onwualu's short story makes explicit environmental SF's postcolonial legacy. "Night Market" follows the adventures of Oduwe, head gardener at a greenhouse located in a Martian bio-dome. Like his counterpart in *The Martian*, Oduwe must daily contend with the laborious but pleasurable task of gardening a barely fertile landscape: "[Oduwe] squatted down and uprooted the stringy plants," thinking to himself that "it was best to pull weeds by hand as Martian soil was too fragile for hoes." Unlike his Hollywood counterpart, however, Oduwe is no self-made technoscientific hero conquering a barren environment for survival. Instead, readers learn that Oduwe was abducted as a child and raised as a soldier before taking on his current position as a gardener for his masters. As Oduwe himself realizes upon visiting a rich family and seeing their "lavish tapestries embroidered with the flora and fauna of a faraway planet," his work is not for himself, but for those rich masters who are willing to exploit indigenous communities to rebuild entire worlds in their own vision of paradise.

Onwualo's injection of an environmentalist ethos into SF affiliated with the global South expands on trends already set in motion by previous Afrofuturist authors. In "Black to the Future," Mark Dery originally formulated the term "Afrofuturism" around the "troubling antinomy" of imagining a "past [that] has been deliberately rubbed out" (736). In its coinage, Dery defined Afrofuturism as a way to both combat the systematic eradication of African history in American culture and celebrate this previously erased past in fantastically imagined African American futures. Authors who took on this project with an eye to environmental as well as social and political concerns include Samuel R. Delany, Jr., who imagines ethically and culturally diverse, solar system-wide cosmopolitan futures; Octavia E. Butler, one of the first SF authors to include both African and Western settings in her tales; and Nalo Hopkinson, who draws inspiration from her own experience of the world as a Caribbean Canadian. While this first generation of environmentally minded Afrofuturists provided readers with African-inspired tribal, shamanistic, ancestral, and kinship-affiliated visions of the natural world, such visions were often subordinate to their critiques of white Western privilege and the corresponding marginalization of black Atlantic subjects.

Building upon the work of their predecessors, the newest generation of environmental Afrofuturist storytellers—especially Sofia Samatar, N. K. Jemisin, and Nnedi Okorafor—ask readers to expand their thinking about black subjects and history to include the bioregion of Africa itself. As ecocritic Lawrence Buell explains, a bioregion is both "a territory defined by natural markers, such as watersheds, [and also] a domain of consciousness and . . . a focus of citizenly allegiance that challenges conventional political boundaries" (135).[1] While bioregional writers celebrate many of the same local places and indigenous practices that appear in more conventional modes of ecological literature, they also recognize that such places and practices change in tandem with shifting political and technological priorities. Therefore, in this chapter, I discuss the African-inspired future histories and fantasy realms constructed by Samatar, Jemisin, and Okorafor both in terms of their critical stance toward Western science and technology and their celebration of indigenous African ecological practices and values—both as they persist and as they change over time. More specifically, I argue that recent works by these authors deftly interrogate the origins and ramifications of environmental crises situated in African spaces while gesturing toward a utopian, Afrofuturist remediation of these conditions and forces.[2]

Even as they celebrate their various attachments to the bioregion of Africa, contemporary environmental Afrofuturists are careful to avoid simply repeating or reversing stereotypes of the West versus Africa and the global North versus the global South. They avoid such philosophical and aesthetic pitfalls through the creation of multiple, sometimes overlapping ethnoscapes that disrupt the colonial and postcolonial impulses that have traditionally guided much speculative fiction. In *Modernity at Large* (1996), Arjun Appadurai defines an ethnoscape as a diasporic flow of "tourists, immigrants, refugees, exiles, guestworkers, and other moving groups and persons" (33). By presenting the world and its communities as fluid and always in process, responsive to changes wrought by humanity itself, Samatar, Jemisin, and Okorafor refuse dangerously romantic, ahistorical visions of Africa that have, for so long, been used to justify Western and

---

1. See Tom Lynch's *The Bioregional Imagination: Literature, Ecology, and Place* (2012) as well as Byron Caminero-Santangelo's *Different Shades of Green: African Literature, Environmental Justice, and Political Ecology* (2014) for further information.

2. For more information, see Eric Otto's *Green Speculations: Science Fiction and Transformative Environmentalism* (2012) and Gerry Canavan and Kim Stanley Robinson's edited collection *Green Planets: Ecology and Science Fiction* (2014).

Northern incursions into that continent. In particular, I contend that Samatar offers a sustained critique of the Orientalizing language associated with the colonial and postcolonial status quo, Jemisin explores the necessary relations of Western medical practices and African-derived alternative ethnobotanies, and Okorafor imagines that a resurgent global South might uses its own colonial history as a template for shaping new and better futures for all—Westerner and African, white and black, and alien and human alike.

Tools of Enchantment: Sofia Samatar's *A Stranger in Olondria* and *Winged Histories*

Sofia Samatar's *A Stranger in Olondria* (2013) is a high fantasy novel that enacts the Afrofuturist project of rewriting colonial and postcolonial narratives. The novel follows the adventures of Jevick, a young man from a spice trading family who comes of age in a remote territory of the larger empire of Olondria. From an early age, Jevick nurses an idealized fantasy about the Olondrian spice markets that he opposes to his homeland Tyom, a backwater on the fringes of empire from which his wealthy merchant father produces his pepper harvests. This fantasy is bolstered by Jevick's interactions with his Olondrian tutor, who trains the young boy to see the natural world through the romanticizing and Orientalizing rhetoric of their empire.

Indeed, Jevick perceives both Olondria and Tyom through the lens of a lyrical Orientalist narcissism that filters difference, especially ecological difference, through the prism of the exotic East. For example, while Jevick imagines the natural landscape of imperial Olondria as a montage of "almond blossoms," "mists above the surface of Iloun," and "terraced gardens" (Samatar 1–7), he is equally romantic about his own land's fabulous natural bounty, characterized as it is, for instance, by "pepper bushes, voluptuous and green under the haze" (Samatar 1). Here then, the lands of the oppressors and the oppressed seem to be equally circumscribed by an Orientalizing rhetoric that treats them both as naturally pristine paradises.

In Samatar's novel, Orientalism arises mostly from literary learning that characterizes African environments in reductive ways. This resonates with a broader critique of the Western culture and language as it is disseminated through imperial expansion. For instance, when Jevick learns to read from his Olondrian tutor, he assumes that "vallon" denotes book in "all the known languages of the Earth" and connotes as well "a tool of enchantment and art," suggesting magic and sorcery as well (Samatar 17). Samatar's use of this invented word "vallon" clearly echoes the Latinate English word "vellum" (animal parchment). Jevick's adolescent infatuation with reading and composing vallons therefore ironically characterizes him as naively unaware of the ways he simply reinscribes imperialism.

Samatar also explores how the Orientalist dynamic superimposed upon fantastic, African-inspired landscapes also entails a derogation of the culture indigenous to these places. In *A Stranger*, Jevick unconsciously internalizes this latter set of attitudes from his abusive parents. For instance, Jevick's stepmother mocks the spiritual practices of Olondria, especially its belief in a "jut" or "external soul" (Samatar 5). Meanwhile, Jevick's father attempts to check his son's bourgeoning interest in Olondria by forcing Jevick to eat some Tyom dirt while he dismisses Olandria as a "country of ghosts and devils" (Samatar 8) whose sole usefulness is to purchase Tyom's bounty. Even as his infatuation grows, Jevick's parents do, in their own cruel way, prepare their son to eventually question the entitlement and privilege of Olondria.

Jevick begins to understand the limits of literary Orientalism when the angel of a recently deceased young woman gives him a map that challenges what he has learned through his colonial education. This becomes particularly clear when Jevick compares the map of Kiem to his pristine, Orientalist fantasies of Olondria and Tyom. Kiem is characterized as a "black Land, wet and shining, the jawbone of a cow" whose primeval chaos exists "at the edge of a sea," consisting of "shimmering deltas, dank-smelling lagoons, a landscape flat and liquid and much loved by birds" (Samatar 213). Such descriptions enable Samatar to counter Jevick's Orientalist misreading of the land around him with images of a more complex natural ecology.

In Samatar's work, literary Orientalism and its gross misrepresentation of indigenous African ecologies sow the seeds of dissent and ultimately causes its own demise. At the Night Market in Olandria, Jevick memorizes and reads out the vallon *The Handbook of Mercies*, then summons his guardian angel to help a large crowd of worshippers when they are attacked by armed Olondrian soldiers. This series of events enables the political firebrand Aurum to make Jevick an unwitting accomplice in his own political machinations. In the rebellion's wake, Jevick worries that the illiterate poor, "the hatun," under the sway of the new Olondrian regime, will burn all the libraries in the purging frenzy of a revolution. But as an unrepentant and vengeful Aurum puts it, the choice that faces Olondria now is a simple one: "vallons" (cold parchment) or "living flesh" (Samatar 278). Ironically, the imperial vallon acts as an incendiary device in a raging ideological struggle that precipitates a "war of a far country to liberate those who could not read" (Samatar 281). Thus, Jevick's valorization of the vallon indirectly leads to the social upheaval that exploits the suffering of the very people who both celebrate and wish to eradicate the vallons he cherishes. The possible loss of an entire literary culture haunts the displaced Jevick, who retires to his homeland as a mystic writer oscillating between affection, critique, and ambivalence toward the diverse ethnoscapes of Olondria.

Winged Histories (2016), a companion novel to *A Stranger in Olondria*, expands the scope of Olondria's fantasy universe while retaining a keen awareness of environmental-justice issues. While *A Stranger* follows the adventures of the young male Jevick, *Winged Histories* centers on four female protagonists: Tavis, Seren, Tialon, and Siski. In the novel, these four characters live through the throes of the same revolution described in *A Stranger in Olondria* and, in the process, cast off their colonial preconceptions to view their homeland with fresh eyes. One of these protagonists, the rebellious "swordmaiden" Tavis, who begins as a solider for imperial Olondria but eventually joins her cousin Dasya in the quest to free their home region Kestenya from Olondrian rule, comes to this healing recognition about her homeland: "I thought of Olondria as a living thing, not as a place to go to or settle but as a vast entity that grew and breathed and ate" (24). In a critical discussion of high fantasy, Farah Mendlesohn has observed a link between what she terms the "quest fantasy"—which bears close resemblance to Samatar's fantastic travelogue structure—and Orientalism as a contemporary discourse. Mendlesohn concludes, "This kind of fantasy is essentially imperialist; fantasyland is Orientalized into an unchanging past" (9). But Samatar's *Winged Histories* refuses this kind of Orientalizing by repeatedly drawing readers' attention to its richly constructed universe as a volatile, yet dynamic place continually in the process of violent reinterpretation.

The complexity of relations amongst the ethnically and linguistically diverse people of Olandria is made clear by their equally complex relations to nature. For example, despite their antipathy to one another, both Olondrian imperialists and Kestenyi rebels tend to describe the world around them in the kind of stereotypical Orientalizing terms so prevalent in *A Stranger*. This is particularly apparent when Tavis stumbles into a sacred grove in her war-torn travels, describing the grove in terms of its "soft and fragrant air like milk," and its "coolness breathed from wild mimosa trees" (Samatar 66). Even as her experience of war begins to change her attitudes toward Olandria, Tavis finds it difficult to think about her world outside the colonial terms that are used to justify its appropriation and exploitation.

Elsewhere, however, Samatar uses the Afrofuturist technique of recovering marginalized histories of the oppressed to debunk such Orientalist distortion. Consider, for instance, the illiterate troubadour Seren's songs for her

Kestenyi people. Seren laments the death of so many indigenous people—especially indigenous women—in the name of Olondrian rule. But because she is not trapped in the Orientalizing fantasies of her educated counterparts, she is able to compose an epic apocalyptic revenge fantasy driven by a persona of the harvest goddess Avalei. As an agent of chaotic destruction, this persona portends both the end of Olondrian rule and its Orientalist stereotyping.

Furthermore, rather than providing readers with a neutral or disinterested registering of topography, botany, or fauna, in *Winged Histories* Samatar suggests that an oppositional and less damaging view of ecology can be found in the indigenous desert nomads, or "Feredhai." These nomads display a sustainable land ethic such that "they carry their knowledge, all the secrets of survival in a wilderness of sunlight, wind, and chalk" (Samatar 248). This traditional knowledge seems exotic and foreign to Olondrian imperialists and even to the insurgent Kestenyi, accustomed as they are to "grass in the garden," "crocuses, upright and golden," "transparent buds on apple trees" (Samatar 256), and other indicators of pristine vernal abundance. By insisting on a sharp dichotomy between the ecology of an elite cultivated landscape and the ecology of communal subsistence driven by survivalist hunting and foraging, Samatar refuses the assimilation of her fantastic, African-inspired environment into an idealized, pastoral template mandated by hegemonic, neo-imperial agendas, insisting instead on the diversity of the land and its people.

Finally, Samatar's subversion of ecological Orientalism overlaps with a critique of patriarchal oppression as glimpsed through the story Tavis's sister Siski, who sacrifices her personal feelings for the Kestenyi crown prince Dasya to elevate her marriage prospects. When Siski talks with her scheming aunt about these prospects, the third person narrator notes that "sometimes, across the deep, blue sky, a flock of swans is flying like droplets of milk" (Samatar 257). This romanticized metaphorical representation of the environment reflects the distortions that occur in Siski's personal life, as circumstances first prompt her to substitute love for duty and then, eventually, transform her from privileged royalty to wandering refugee.

Siski herself participates in such distortions when she misinterprets a song that her beloved Dasya sings to be about "mist, black geese, and firelight" and "smoke that rises from thatched houses buried up to the eaves in snow, where peasants are drinking," only to be informed that the song is actually about a "musk deer that came to nibble the last of cabbages in the winter gardens" (Samatar 258). The literal misreading connects to Siski's misunderstanding of her native homeland and its indigenous people.

Siski realizes only at the end of the novel the extent to which she has been alienated from her native homeland: "If the gods send us signs—and perhaps they do—I do not believe we can read them" (Samatar 322). While this realization is accompanied by a reunion with Dasya, it is unclear what might happen next for them either personally or politically, as Dasya is in the process of becoming a sublime, autochthonous winged monster. And so Samatar leaves it to readers to decide for themselves if this reunion and transformation signify either a total environmental apocalypse or a cosmic regeneration outside the context of the Olandrian Anthropocene.

Goddess's Blood: N. K. Jemisin's *The Killing Moon* and *The Shadowed Sun*

N. K. Jemisin is another relatively new practitioner of ecologically informed Afrofuturist epic fantasy. In her Dreamblood series, Jemisin updates the Afrofuturist tradition of repurposing Egyptology to make sense of modern black life—a tradition that extends back to Sun Ra and his Arkestra's fusion of funk, jazz, and Ancient Egyptian mythology.[3] Jemisin signals the playful liberties she takes with her Egyptian source myths when she writes that "my own goal was to give homage: my goal was not to ape reality. Armchair Egyptologists, you have been forewarned" (v). Yet Jemisin unabashedly models the novel's principal setting, the alien city of Gujaarah, on the ancient Egyptian civilization that sprung up on the Nile and developed in intimate relation to the delta's seasonal flooding. Indeed, much like its Earthly predecessor, Jemisin's alien ecology is a "narrow band of fertile land" that threatens to be "perpetually devoured by the lands beyond" (95). Much like the sophisticated theocracy of Ancient Egypt itself, Jemisin's black-skinned humanoid alien civilization of the Hetawa emerge from this ecology, building state temples populated by a stringent bureaucratic caste system of priests and officials based on a magical-medical theory of body humors, dream interpretation, and homeopathic remedies.

Jemisin also uses Egyptian source material to challenge common assumptions that Western medical industries and scientific institutions constitute the only viable pharmacology. Instead, she draws attention to the way in which Ancient Egyptian magic, based on the interaction of bodily fluids and occult spirits and demons ("heka"), engendered an often-overlooked system of alternative ethnobotany out of which contemporary medicine

---

3. See John Rieder's "Sun Ra's Otherworldliness" for further information.

derived many of its advances.[4] This is particularly apparent in *The Killing Moon*, where Jemisin draws upon the history of Egyptian medicine to imagine Hetawa temples whose healer practitioners can repair mental and physical affliction. As such, she offers readers a world where the holistic medicine of traditional indigenous knowledge flourishes.

Jemisin's use of Egyptian history does more than simply offer readers a new kind of fantastic world; rather, it asks readers to rethink the history of fantastic world-building as a distinctly Western and Northern practice. As Brian Attebery notes, many post-Tolkien authors draw upon non-Western myths to add a sense of exoticism to stories that ultimately still hew to colonial and postcolonial worldviews. By way of contrast, Jemisin makes the often-marginalized medicinal value of indigenous lore and sustainable African environmental rituals central to the new worlds she crafts for her readers. She also insists that her seemingly exotic landscapes are more than mere backdrop to familiar characters and adventures. For instance, in *The Shadowed Sun* (2012), Jemisin reveals that Gujarreh's theocratic system is—much like the real-world Egyptian culture that inspires Jemisin's work—driven by a specific ecological mandate: the annual flooding of the Goddess's Blood, a river that locates its mouth in the city center.

This ecological component to the Dreamblood series also shapes Jemisin's exploration of ethnic and racial tensions. This is particularly clear in her depiction of insulated (and, as it turns out, parochial) delta societies that automatically assume dwellers of the surrounding desert wilderness are unenlightened and barbaric. Thus, Jemisin refuses to let readers simply treat the world she builds as a monolithic, utopian black African-inspired republic in the mold of previous Afrofuturist visions such as Martin R. Delany's *Blake; or, the Huts of America* (1859) or William Melvin Kelley's *A Different Drummer* (1962). Instead, taking inspiration from both ancient and modern ethnoscapes, Jemisin invites readers to question oversimplifications of group identity, insisting instead that her alien characters, like the Africans they are extrapolated from, are complex beings with equally complex and sometimes contradictory relations to one another.

Jemisin specifically challenges the reduction of complex, overlapping ethnoscapes into monolithic cultures and even rigid binaries in *The Shadowed Sun* with the story of Hanani, a female sharer apprentice trying to negotiate the xenophobic and patriarchal civic religion of the Gunjarreh Hetawa.

---

4. Indeed, the noted Egyptologist Geraldine Pinch explains that "ancient medicine might seem bizarre to a scientific worldview," but such "practices were in fact based on elaborate theories about the workings of the body or the classification of substances" (134).

In the course of the novel, Hanani leaves the Gunjarrah and seeks refuge with the outlying desert tribe of the Banbarra in exchange for practicing her seemingly supernatural healing arts. Hanani heals, teaches, and even falls in love with the Banbarra chieftain Wanohomen, who, at the close of the novel, lays siege to Hanani's homeland to claim political control of Gunjarreh. The fraught alliance of the Hetawa and the Banbarra people, ushered in by the complicated entanglement of Hanani and Wanohomen as lovers, reflects the complexities of living ethnoscapes. It also subverts the tendency, frequently observed by Egyptian scholars, of ancient Egyptian writers to engage in blatantly racist depictions of the surrounding desert wilderness as a breeding ground for foreign monsters and baleful deities. Instead the novels end with a rapprochement between the desert dwellers and the urban denizens and the possibility of a future that both nods to and is truly different than the past.

The Swordfish Strikes Back: Nnedi Okorafor's *Lagoon*

While Jemisin draws on ancient Egyptian science and culture to build her alien worlds, first generation Nigerian American Nnedi Okorafor's *Lagoon* (2015) explores what might happen if aliens came to Earth—and, in particular, if they decided to land in Lagos, Nigeria. Ytasha Womack explains that when Afrofuturists tell human-alien encounter stories, "the alien motif reveals dissonance while also providing a prism through which to view the power of imagination, aspiration, and creativity channelled in resisting dehumanization efforts" (37). As a prototypical Afrofuturist alien-encounter narrative, *Lagoon* begins with an epigraph that initially seems like a "Welcome-to-Lagos" sign, explaining that the Nigerian city's name is Portuguese for "lagoon" and can be traced back to when "the Portuguese first landed on Lagos Island in the year 1472" (Okorafor 1). Okorafor then drily breaks the Tourism Bureau script with the pithy comment: "Apparently, they could not come up with a more creative name" (Okorafor 1). From the opening beats of her novel, then, Okorafor announces her project to indict unimaginative Western and Northern depictions of Africa, instead inviting readers to explore the vibrant, kaleidoscopic welter of perspectives and experiences the novel attributes to this largest and most rapidly developing of Nigerian cities.

In a decisive twist on the alien-encounter narrative, Okorafor further flips the anthropocentric priorities of the global North by treating both humans and animals as Earthlings whom aliens would be equally interested in contacting. Indeed, *Lagoon* begins with a prologue, entitled "Moom!" in a recurring comic-book-like onomatopoeia of an alien-encounter sound effect, written from the perspective of a female swordfish who swims toward the undulating, glowing alien starship that has landed in the Nigerian lagoon's depths. The starship, piloted by aliens who simply call themselves "Change," heals the coral and octopi of the lagoon and cleans up the water that has been polluted by a leak from the loading hose of the FPSO Mystra, a supply vessel anchored in the lagoon. The swordfish, though, rather than simply being healed like the other aquatic wildlife, requests to be transformed into a sea monster three times her ordinary size, complete with a sword-like nose, more powerful vision, and cartilage spikes. In a critical updating of indigenous African beast fables, often conceived from the eyes of animistic spirits, the transmogrified swordfish becomes an avatar of ecological justice that undermines the colonial legacy of natural exploitation and anthropocentrism. Thus, Okorafor depicts her chosen African environmental bioregion as a space of interrelatedness and kinship for all living organisms in the biosphere. This vision of the natural world bears more than a few traces of James Lovelock's ecologically oriented Gaia hypothesis.

Okorafor's ecocritical swordfish subplot provides a counternarrative to Western ecocriticism's emphasis on the solitary (human) individual alone in the wilderness. This allows her to represent the natural environment not as a tourist-friendly, uncorrupted sanctuary but as an ancestral land with a thriving, multispecies indigenous community. The swordfish plays an important narrative function as the revenge of the postcolonial and ecological repressed. A third of the way into the novel, the swordfish strikes back, assuming the mantle of an ecoterrorist by sinking the FPSO Mystra and massacring its crew. The swordfish appears again when an alien who has taken on human form escorts a group of real humans to her starship deep in the bowels of the lagoon. In the process of this meeting, the humanoid alien, Ayodele, tells the giant swordfish (as well as an uncategorizably weird octopus and other unseen larger creatures) to cease their violent onslaughts long enough to ensure the safe passage of her guests.

The metamorphosis of Okorafor's swordfish does not represent a simple ecological redemption in response to the environmental crisis of oil spills that devastate the Nigerian lagoon. "That swordfish hates us," the human Adaora explains (Okorafor 262). And indeed, the swordfish returns one final time at the end of the novel to make sure that her piercing of the "dead snake thing in the water" has temporarily made the "dry people go away" (Okorafor 290). It is only when she has satisfied herself of this that the swordfish decides to head South and follow the golden alien light on more adventures. The implication may be that we readers should follow suit if we ourselves desire new adventures beyond colonial and postcolonial narratives of conquest and exploitation.

Okorafor's focus on the ecoterrorist swordfish both invokes and deflates a specific postcolonial narrative: the spectacular advertising campaigns of heavy transnational polluters. An egregious example of such agitprop is Exxon's commercial after the *Exxon Valdez* oil spill in 1989 that featured sea lions applauding with their flippers as killer whales freely roamed unpolluted waters.[5] Okorafor's oppositional ecocritical stance is most strikingly evident in the transformation of the swordfish from disgruntled victim into lethal menace. This anthropomorphized creature constitutes not an endorsement of naïve ecoterrorism, I would argue, much less an unsubtle embrace of the environmentalism of the rich, so much as a speculative-fantastic rejection of fraudulent attempts to reconcile our global fossil-fuel addiction with interests in the natural world or the lived reality of the Global South. In *Lagoon*, a Nigerian character laments what Tom Burgis in *The Looting Machine* (2015) has termed the "resource curse" (4) that haunts the kleptocratic, neo-imperial politics of the country, "Your land is full of fuel that is tearing you apart" (Okorafor 307). Unlike other factions in the novel—for example, the religious fanatics who exacerbate brutal poverty, or the ham-strung, feather-bedding politicos, or the desperately indigent who are whipped into rioting and looting—the swordfish taps into the wild, exuberant promise of a destructive rampage in the name of alien change. The swordfish may be deluded about the scale and nature of its actions; it just damages a hose and does not slay a fearsome beast, after all. Nevertheless, it represents an uncanny outsider perspective that is truly alien to the anthropocentric status quo of the global North. As such, the swordfish participates in catalyzing the genuinely Afrofuturist, quasi-utopian, ecocritical change instigated by the alien visitors to Earth.

Samatar, Jemisin, and Okorafor all successfully wed a sophisticated Afrofuturist aesthetic with a savvy bioregional attachment to the African continent and its diverse biotic communities and ethnoscapes. Samatar deconstructs the Orientalism inherent in pernicious misreadings of the African continent. Jemisin dramatizes the often-overlooked ethnobotanical value of traditional medical knowledge indigenous to African culture and praxis while exploring the possibility of complex but potentially fruitful alli-

---

5. For reporting on Exxon's "aggressive public relations campaign" following this disaster, see Riki Ott's *Not One Drop: Betrayal and Courage in the Wake of the Exxon Valdez Oil Spill* (66).

ances amongst the people of varying ethnoscapes. And Okorafor provocatively suggests that the near-future development progress of the African continent does not necessarily entail further environmental degradation or neo-imperial exploitation—instead, the inhabitants of the African continent might choose to embrace a seemingly alien kind of change predicated on new connections between people and animals. Such Afrofuturist ecotopian visions offer a powerful global ethos that does not simply disregard postcolonial inheritance but instead gestures toward a practical ecocritical politics beyond prevailing postcolonial thought.

Works Cited

Appadurai, Arjun. *Modernity at Large: Cultural Dimensions of Globalization.* U of Minnesota, 1996.

Attebery, Brian. *Stories About Stories: Fantasy and the Remaking of Myth.* Oxford UP, 2014.

Buell, Lawrence. *The Future of Environmental Criticism.* Malden Blackwell Publishing, 2005.

Burgis, Tom. *The Looting Machine.* Public Affairs, 2015.

Caminero-Santangelo, Byron. *Different Shades of Green: African Literature, Environmental Justice, and Political Ecology.* U of Virginia P, 2014.

Canavan, Gerry, and Kim Stanley Robinson. *Green Planets: Ecology and Science Fiction.* Wesleyan, 2014.

Delany, Martin R. *Blake; or, the Huts of America.* 1859. Beacon, 1989.

Dery, Mark. "Black to the Future: Interviews with Samuel Delany, Greg Tate, and Tricia Rose." *South Atlantic Quarterly,* vol. 92, no. 4, 1993, pp. 735–78.

Jemisin, N. K. *The Killing Moon.* Orbit, 2012.

———. *The Shadowed Sun.* Orbit, 2012.

Kelley, William M. *A Different Drummer.* Doubleday, 1962.

Okorafor, Nnedi. *Lagoon.* Simon & Schuster, 2015.

Onwualu, Chinelo. "Night Market." *West Branch Wired,* no. 82, fall 2016.

Lynch, Tom. *The Bioregional Information: Literature, Ecology, and Place.* U of Georgia P, 2012.

Mendlesohn, Farah. *Rhetorics of Fantasy.* Wesleyan Press, 2008.

Ott, Riki. *Not One Drop: Betrayal and Courage in the Wake of the Exxon Valdez Oil Spill.* Chelsea Green Publishing, 2008.

Otto, Eric. *Green Speculations: Science Fiction and Transformative Environmentalism.* The Ohio State UP, 2012.

Pinch, Geraldine. *Magic in Ancient Egypt.* Austin: University of Texas, 1994.

Rieder, John. "Sun Ra's Otherworldliness." *Africa SF,* special issue of *Paradoxa,* vol. 25, 2013, pp. 235–52.

Samatar, Sofia. *A Stranger in Olondria.* Small Beer Press, 2013.

———. *The Winged Histories.* Small Beer Press, 2016.

Scott, Ridley, director. *The Martian.* Twentieth Century Fox, 2015.

Womack, Ytasha. *Afrofuturism: The World of Black Sci-Fi and Fantasy Culture.* Chicago Review, 2013.

CHAPTER 11

"You Can't Go Home Again"
Deji Bryce Olukotun's *Nigerians in Space*, Science Fiction, and Global Interdependence

Marleen S. Barr

Both Deji Bryce Olukotun and his 2014 novel *Nigerians in Space* (hereafter, *Nigerians*) defy categorization. American-born Olukotun, who has a Nigerian father, grew up in New Jersey and received a Creative Writing MFA from the University of Cape Town. This American who wrote *Nigerians* in Cape Town is a South African writer. His book *Nigerians* is a noire international thriller and murder mystery imbued with both obvious and inconspicuous SF tropes. Like its author, *Nigerians* has a diverse national story structure. The main plot involves what ensues after Wale Olufunmi, a Nigerian who immigrates to Houston to work as a NASA moon geology specialist, steals moon rocks in order to qualify for a Nigerian "Brain Gain" (the return of Nigerian intellectuals to their home country after decades of exporting themselves to other, wealthier countries). Wale hopes to build a Nigerian space program and pursue his dream to become an astronaut. *Nigerians* also follows the adventures of the Zimbabwean model Melissa Tebogo as she attempts to cure the skin disease which afflicted her since birth and South African poacher Thursday Malaysius, who discovers a new kind of abalone. While none of these protagonists actually make it to outer space, their stories are bound together by the trope of fantastic moonlight, which offers characters and readers alike new ways of seeing life on Earth.

The three plots are further linked by the fact that while all of Olukotun's protagonists travel the globe, none of them make permanent homes in Nigeria. Wale, who emigrates from Nigeria to America and spends the preponderance of his adulthood in South Africa, is South African—not Nigerian. Tinuke—who emigrates from Nigeria to American to South Africa and returns to live in America—is American. Wale's son, the American-born Dayo, eventually becomes a South African who lacks a cultural memory of Nigeria and only possesses childhood recollections of America. Melissa Tebogo travels from Zimbabwe to Europe to South Africa to Nigeria. Meanwhile, Thursday Malaysius is as his name indicates a native-born Malaysian who eventually makes his home in South Africa. In Olukotun's world, nationality is determined by cultural literacy and proximity, not immigration in relation to national origin. Indeed, characters often find themselves alienated from their countries of origin and are more at home in other spaces around the world.

My purpose is to examine how *Nigerians* replaces conventional ideas about national identity and nationally based science with visions of global interdependence in relation to space, time, and SF. In the first section of this essay, I explore the reality of Nigeria's space program in relation to Olukotun's imaginary counterpart. I then turn to *Nigerians* in relation to emergent notions of African global nomadism and consider the meaning of the fantastic moonlight trope that unifies the book's various subplots. I conclude by returning to the larger issues raised by *Nigerians* and consider how the scientific ideas contained in this novel apply to both human and nonhuman community. I believe Olukotun demonstrates the strength of Afrofuturism as a set of concerns—black global nomadism, technoscience, and personhood—meant to highlight the interdependence of our species as an affirmative vision.

Context: "Why couldn't Nigeria have a space program?"

When Olukotun spent time in Cape Town, he was unaware of the relationship between Nigerian technological prowess and the implications of his book title. As the author explains in a 2014 interview with *Slate* magazine, he initially chose both his title and book topics because he erroneously thought that a Nigerian space program "seemed too ridiculous to even be worth researching—I had made the idea up!" ("Meeting My Protagonist"). Both his title and topics seemed darkly humorous because they evoke stereotypical racist mythology and the seemingly ludicrous image of technologically inept Africans blasting off into outer space. The story smacked of fish-out-of-water humor involving the Other inhabiting a space where it does not naturally belong. As such, the image of Nigerians in space is initially deprecating in a manner analogous to the Clampett family inhabiting a Bel Air mansion in *The Beverly Hillbillies* or imagining Donald Trump publishing an analysis of *Ulysses* in PMLA.

But *Nigerians* metatextually ranges beyond Olukotun's control and knowledge. As he soon learned, the Nigerian space program is a not just a "ridiculous" fantasy, but a proven reality. Olukotun explains:

> Imagine my shock when I discovered that the program was indeed real—and it has been around for more than a decade.... I met with Dr. Olufemi Agboola, the director of engineering and space systems at the National Space Research and Development Agency.... In my novel, my main character was a Nigerian émigré who had received his Ph.D. in lunar geology and then worked for NASA. In reality, Agboola received his Ph.D. in engineering from an American university and then worked for NASA. He was then invited to lead engineering for the nascent space agency in Nigeria.... There was something absolutely terrifying about meeting in real life a person whom I thought I made up.... Since the program was founded in 2003, Agboola's agency has launched five satellites into space. ("Meeting My Protagonist")

The mythology about Nigerian technological ineptitude so pervades popular thought that Olukotun himself occupied space within it during the time he was writing his novel—only to learn, of course, that Nigerian space exploration is a proven reality.

Today, Olukotun regrets that his book nullifies a real person's vision: "What I learned from my meeting with Agboola is that it does not feel good to predict human failings and for them to turn out to be true.... Here was a man daring to dream, and in my fiction I had snuffed out that dream" ("Meeting My Protagonist"). But Olukotun is not the real culprit here. Instead, that dubious honor goes to a racist mythology that is so pervasive that even those being mythologized believe the false stories that are told about them. Although Olukotun may not be aware of this fact, *Daring to Dream* is the title of Carol F. Kessler's 1984 anthology of utopian fiction written by women. Women and minorities routinely have their dreams snuffed out simply because of their gender and race. *Nigerians* both imagines and resists what happens when dreams are stymied. It reflects Olukotun coming to terms with his status as someone who is different in relation to American hegemony. His name, unlike say Chris Christie or Bruce Springsteen, sounds Nigerian rather than New Jerseyian—even though he is as much a native born New Jerseyian as they are. Olukotun's Nigerian heritage falsely positions him as an alien in relation to his country of origin, causing him to "live the estrangement that science fiction writers imagine" as Greg Tate first observed in Mark Dery's Afrofuturism interviews, "Black to the Future" (768).

Such background-based special treatment is never applied to Caucasians. For example, like Olukotun, Trump is an American-born product of an immigrant parent (his mother was born in Scotland). But while Olukotun says "I am half-Nigerian," Trump never calls himself a half Scottish-American ("Meeting My Protagonist"). In America, immigration-generated racism as it is directed to people of color is omnipresent to the extent that people of color who have been living in the United States for generations still receive inquiries about what country they come from. By way of contrast, European-Americans (who rarely refer to themselves as hyphenated Americans) are never positioned as aliens. More often than not, such Americans cling tightly to their identities as "natural" Americans, embracing the United States as their country of origin without much thought to the various ways they are also bound to other parts of the world. While whites do not have to think about their skin color, the Afrofuturist project foregrounds awareness of how black bodies are raced and presented in SF.

Olukotun challenges readers to move past overly simplified (and often untrue) stories about national identity and to imagine space—especially the moon—as a space for new stories of identity and agency. The moon is a blank screen; no particular human culture should be projected on to it. Wale, for example, imagines himself "walking on the moon with his countrymen. He wouldn't hit golf balls like the American astronauts. He would squeeze out rhythms from a talking drum into the blackness between the stars. . . . He didn't actually know how to play one but he figured he could take lessons" (Olukotun 26–27). Here, Olukotun seems to embrace national heritage only to undercut it with the humorous observation that space is an inappropriate place to perform national cultural practices. After all, if one needs to "take lessons" to perform one's cultural identity in a new space, how relevant is that identity in the first place? In this regard, Olukotun goes beyond Afrofuturism in trying to articulate in what might be better termed "Africanfuturism"[1] in attempting to rightly distance himself from the American root of the concept.

---

1. See Nnedi Okorafor's tweet on "Africanfuturism" (@Nnedi Okorafor PhD).

Although he does not directly address the matter in interviews, it is worth noting that Olukotun's original vision for *Nigerians* also rested on the assumption that the African space race is largely devoid of female participation. And yet as he eventually learned, it is a woman, Abimbola Alale, who serves as the Managing Director and CEO of Nigerian Communication Satellite Limited. As Alale (who is also the mother of ten children, nine of whom are adopted) proudly proclaims, "I can introduce the benefits of space to my people. . . . Not so many women are heading satellite companies" ("Abimbola Alale"). While Olukotun himself wonders, "Would you have read *that* story?" the answer should be a clear yes for modern SF readers ("Meeting My Protagonist"). In the United States, African American authors such as Octavia E. Butler have long resisted the implicit racism and sexism of SF, instead embracing its potential to make space for alien voices and experiences. As Butler herself noted time and again in interviews, "I wrote myself in, since I'm me and I'm here and I'm writing. I can write my own stories and I can write myself in" (qtd. in Aguirre). Both raced and gendered interdependence are at the heart of Afrofuturism, and they are at the heart of *Nigerians* as well.

Conflation: Space, Time, and Nation

Although Olukotun himself thought at first that Nigerian space travel was a joke and he does not mention women's contribution to that initiative, *Nigerians* proudly asserts that Earth is one world. Olukotun emphasizes that demarcations that define people who inhabit differing spaces are racist mythologies. *Nigerians* underscores that it is time to define "immigration" as an antiquated word. Earth is the home of all humans. No one is born hating immigrants. The notion that Earth belongs to everyone represents the heart of Olukotun's Afrofuturism.

People learn to hate within educational systems that enforce binary oppositions between "inferior" and "superior" in regard to people. Olukotun includes a two-page "Notes on the Story" to compensate for the gaps in the American educational system (292–93). Most American readers are not familiar with South African and Nigerian culture. For example, many American readers have never heard of Abuja. American ignorance regarding the name of the Nigerian capital illustrates how effectively we flatten and erase real-world details when we construct mythologies of the racial Other. In another part of the novel, Wale stands in front of a Nigerian Airlines agent and enacts "his best imitation of a Hausa accent" (Olukotun 28). I do not know what a Hausa accent sounds like. I am unable to locate "Bamako" on a map (Olukotun 65). Tinuke tells Wale to "wear the agbada" (Olukotun 101). I cannot describe this article of clothing. The explanation that "Ibeji meant 'twin' in Yoruba" is necessary for a reader such as myself (Olukotun 107). Indeed, although I lived in South Africa for a semester when I was a Visiting Professor at the University of Cape Town, I was unaware until reading this novel that the South African slang term "darkies" denotes "sunglasses" and the term "lekker" means "cool" (Olukotun 103, 14). Furthermore, despite my familiarity with Cape Town, I would not be able to find my way to the myriad local places mentioned in Olukotun's novel—including "False Bay," "Mitchell's Plain," or "Hermanus" (Olukotun 124)—without a map. Even with his extensive "Notes," Olukotun cannot make a reader who is a product of the American educational system fluent in Nigerian and South African culture. The system—which teaches alienation and estrangement, not interdependence—positions African cultures as making his readership aware of this science fictional experience symbolizes an Afrofuturist intervention by foregrounding the issue itself, teaching us to see differences generated by nationality and skin color.

In contrast to this parochialism, African literature in general and Nigerians in particular celebrate the peripatetic. As reviewer Brittle Paper explains, "Olukotun's novel is set in Houston, Stockholm, Basel, Paris, Abuja, Bulawayo, Lagos, Cape Town, and Johannesburg. These days, African novels are built on the life of the global African nomad. . . . Contemporary African fiction is defined by characters for whom mobility is life. They traverse global spaces and force us to think of Lagos and Abuja in the context of Basel and Bulawayo" (Paper). Olukotun, who adheres to globalism in his life and art, is a New Jersey Cape Town writer. No wonder *Nigerians* problematizes the notion of "home" with an epigraph that asks, "Do you know where home is? Do you want to go there?" (Olukotun 7–8). The problem of how to return home—in this case, how to return to Nigeria—preoccupies Wale in the opening pages of the novel: "He was returning his mind to Nigeria, he was going home. . . . He was going home. . . . Home. . . . 'Dr. Olufunmi. It is time you went home.' 'That's what I am trying to do!'" (Olukotun 17, 19, 28, 29). Much like other characters in the novel—and his counterparts in real life—Wale is indeed a "global African nomad," but one who at least initially clings to the notion that he can and should return to his "authentic" land of origin.

As Olukotun makes clear, however, Nigeria is no longer Wale's home. This estrangement becomes evident early in the novel when a Yoruba airport security guard makes fun of the way Wale pronounces the Nigerian city "Taro" (Olukotun 28). Wale is analogous to Dorothy proclaiming there is no place like home. Like Dorothy, he is on a quest to return to his place of origin. Indeed, while Dorothy brings a broom to the Wicked Witch to further her goals, Wale steals a moon rock to satisfy the Nigerian scammer Nurudeen Bello. Unlike his fictitious counterpart, however, Wale is not successful in this quest. He turns Dorothy's mantra that "there is no place like home" into the striking observation that "there is no place" in regard to Nigeria. Wale says, "I am going home. I am going up now. I want to go there," when he might be dying from a gunshot wound (Olukotun 263). But he will never go to Nigeria to build that country's space program and become an astronaut flying up to the moon. Wale's failure to start a Nigerian space program stands in contrast to the successes of the real-world Nigerian space program. In particular, while characters associated with that fictional program work toward it out of either a misguided dream of national identity or pure self-interest, Agboola's and Alale's contributions to the real Nigerian space program exemplify the fact that all people benefit when space exploration is an independent human effort that is devoid of the exclusivity resulting from specious discriminatory typecasting. Contemporary outer space scientists need a global vision that is more sophisticated than Columbus's charge to set sail to claim territory for Spain. NASA should have put a peace sign on the moon, not an American flag. And Afrofuturists wish to amend imperial politics by removing racial difference from the exploration of space, depoliticizing it by making it a human and scientific endeavor.

Indeed, over the course of *Nigerians*, Olukotun makes clear the importance of moving from national to international visions of identity and action. Olukotun explains that he wanted to explore "the idea of being caught between two worlds. In the opening chapter, Wale, one of the main characters and a NASA scientist from Nigeria, is playing basketball, which is as American as it gets" (Cummings). In the end, however, the Nigerian-born and US-bred Wale becomes a South African bamboo furniture salesman who gives free tours of Cape Town's Royal Observatory. Similarly, other characters in *Nigerians* move through space and experience diverse cultures as well. Tinuke travels from Nigeria to America to South Africa and returns permanently to America where she remarries an American and has children. Meanwhile, Melissa travels from Zimbabwe to Europe to South Africa to Nigeria. Significantly, none of Olukotun's characters return to their point of national origin. Earth is the permanent home that all the characters share. It is time for all humans to categorize Earth as one home, a shared domestic space that applies to outer space.

The moon rocks that Wale steals are analogous to immigrants who do not return home. In the manner of hyphenated Americans, the rocks are diverse; they are part moon material and part Earth material. This justification makes the rocks at once an interesting and useless curiosity: "Armstrong had sealed the bag improperly and the contents mixed with dust in the landing craft, so it didn't have any scientific value" (Olukotun 64). Nigerians, however, see things differently. Bello rightly asserts that the sample "didn't belong to America but all humanity. He [Bello] said we would return [the rocks] to the moon when we [Nigerians] landed our first mission as a symbol of 'the colonized returning the cultural patrimony of all mankind.' He wants us to plant a Nigerian flag" (Olukotun 64). Politically incorrect flag planting aside, the moon rocks cannot go home to the moon again, either in Olukotun's novel or in our own reality. At this time, humanity as a whole lacks the technology to return to the moon; the Saturn Five rockets are now rusted debris. Once upon a time, moon rock acquisition was science fictional. In our contemporary moment, returning moon rocks to the moon is science fictional. This situation, of course, is true of the various African characters in Olukotun's novel as well. Hailing from one country of origin and then "contaminated" by the values and beliefs of the other countries they inhabit, neither Wale, his family, or his friends can return home. Instead, these immigrants—like the moon rocks—must be understood as new, hybrid beings who gesture toward new relations between planet and satellite and old world and new. In essence then, the moon rocks are galactic nomads comparable to their global African counterparts as envisioned by Olukotun.

Configuration: SF and Subplot Intersection

While neither Bello nor Wale have the opportunity to return the moon rocks to their place of origin, the rocks inspire Olukotun's global nomads to invent fantastic new ways of bringing the moon to people on Earth. Wale initially attempts to smuggle the moon rocks from the United States to Nigeria by placing them in the base of a snow globe. Eventually, this chicanery inspires his son Dayo to create a lamp that emits moonlight: "It's the real thing. . . . The tidal thing . . . the full thing, the werewolf thing: 'The moon'" (Olukotun 189). His moonlight-emitting lamp invention is successful: "The lamp had come alive. . . . The forty lamps sent the moonlight shooting into the disco ball. . . . The lamp worked! . . . Slowly the denizens of Obz [the region in South Africa where Dayo lives] came out to see Dayo's lamps: car guards in fluorescent pinnies, painters, sculptors, goths, teachers, Malikis, Anglicans, Catholics, Jews, pagans perfumed with Nag Champa. . . . They came out" (Olukotun 267–68). The viewers of the lamp emitting moonlight constitute a human diversity cornucopia. They exemplify how "difference" functions interdependently in Obz. The fecundity of Olukotun's list screams that it is about time for people to jettison mythologies of difference and embrace their totality in the Earth space that all humans should share equally in his Afrofuture.

The moon lamp even enables humans to see the nonhuman world differently as well. As it turns out, the abalone hunted by South African poacher Thursday Malaysius react strongly to Dayo's lamps: "Thursday watched the abalone sliding eagerly across the tank. . . . It was like they had been injected with adrenalin. . . . They began tearing at the kelp as quickly as he'd ever seen them move, responding to the light. . . . I've never seen anything like it. . . . That light made them happy" (Olukotun 190–91). In our world, abalone are not attracted to light: "Most gastropods, particularly abalone, prefer to avoid bright light. If they are living in a dark place . . . and it suddenly becomes light, most abalone will high-tail it away to somewhere more secure" (Falla and Mosig 209). Here, moonlight provokes a new reaction on the part of the abalone, forcing Olukotun's characters to reevaluate what they think they know about the natural world. So too Olukotun's novel sheds new light on our understanding of Nigerian people and Nigerian sciences.

Finally, moonlight enables characters and readers alike to reassess their notions of beauty. At first, Melissa seems to be abnormally encumbered by skin color because she suffers from vitiligo. Her skin is anything but an impediment, though. It emits a beautiful light that is attractive to the extent that she becomes a famous model named Melle. She has "lunar energy that charged through her naked form. . . . No one had ever seen a woman who exuded light from her very skin. . . . There was a following of X-men fans that celebrated her, like the comic book superheroes, as an evolutionary advance" (Olukotun 225–26). Olukotun debunks skin color inferiority myths to the extent that he turns Melissa into a skin-light-emitting superhero. Melissa, no longer victimized because of her skin, over time becomes Melle the skin-light Wonder Woman. In the novel's fantastic world, her skin emits moonlight.

Wale does not travel to the moon as a Nigerian astronaut supported by an interdependent world. He triumphs science fictionally. His experience—his stolen moon rocks enclosed in a snow globe—inspires his son to invent a way to bring the moon to Earth. The science fictional moonlight emanating from both Melle's skin and the lamps become indistinguishable: "A policeman had then confused her with Dayo's lamp demonstration . . . and the popular theory was that Melle had channeled the light of the moon by stripping off her clothes, blinding the neighborhood in her radiance" (Olukotun 289). Melle is the only protagonist who sets foot in Nigeria. Unlike Wale, she shines there. She is the moon. Melle, a Zimbabwean who turns into a European, is the Nigerian in space. *Nigerians* is a clarion call for interdependence and a celebration of diverse human cultures coming together as one in Olukotun's Afrofuture.

Conclusion: The Heart of the Matter

When Wale gives a free lecture about the moon at the Royal Observatory, he says, "'TELL US WHAT YOU SEE ON THE DISC OF THE MOON!'" (Olukotun 249). The moon is a blank page upon which some people project discriminatory science fictional images of space exploration; others, including Olukotun, challenge this projection by treating outer space as a diversified space. Both *Nigerians* and the surprising story of the real Nigerian space program demand that we rethink the space race not just as a contest between a few superpowers, but as the ongoing story of global scientific exploration and technological development. Olukotun's Afrofuturist projection calls attention to this need to cooperate. U. R. Rao, for example, "led the team that built India's first satellite, Aryabhata, named for the ancient Indian astronomer and mathematician" (Padnani 18). Rao, an Indian counterpart of Nigeria's Agboola and Alale, named the satellite in terms of Indian culture. Although many people do not see an Indian visage on the disc of the moon, the truth is that India sent a spacecraft to Mars in a manner that was cheaper and better than that of any other country. Amisha Padnani states, "In 2014, India sent a spacecraft to Mars for $74 million to prove that the country could succeed in such a highly technical endeavor. The mission cost a fraction of the $671 million the United States spent on a Mars missions that year, but it showed up a regional rival, China, whose own Mars mission failed in 2012" (18). India's success was treated as a derogatory joke when the *New York Times* published a cartoon depicting an Indian with a cow in tow trying to access the white men's space participation club. Fortunately, the *Times* apologized for giving space to outer space exclusion.

Nigerian space exploration, no butt of a deprecating joke, is progressing in the wake of India's success. As CNN reporter Keiron Monks explains, "Nigeria's space program is no joke, and it is making steady progress.

The National Space Research and Development Agency (NASRDA) has launched five satellites since 2003, with three still in orbit delivering vital services. The most recent—NigeriaSat-X—was the first to be designed and constructed by NASRDA engineers, and more advanced models are in development. . . . With an ever-increasing number of African states investing in space programs, while traditional powerhouses downsize, the continent could be the hotspot of exploration for years to come" (n. pag.). The time is fast approaching when Africa could become the epicenter of human space exploration. Wale's dream is enlarged, not nullified. This reality calls for a new, if not Afrofuturist, reading of the phrase "Nigerians in space"—one that excludes science fictional derogatory humor.

Elsewhere, Olukotun himself has called attention to another milestone in global space exploration: Nigeria's first female astronaut. He notes that "in 2006, the country [Nigeria] sent a 17-year-old girl on a parabolic flight—that's when a jet takes a quick plunge that creates 30 seconds of weightlessness—and she was called an astronaut" ("It's Not an Email Scam"). Even though the young woman was in space for a short time, she is still a real female Nigerian astronaut. This time Olukotun is quite aware that Nigerians in space is no joke: "Is the scam [about a Nigerian astronaut being lost in space] funny because we can't envision Nigerians going into space on their own initiative? This would be a troubling indictment of African progress, or at least of our *perceptions* of African progress, because, again, there has been a lot of it, especially in technology" ("It's Not an Email Scam"). Even if he lacked a perception of it at the time he wrote *Nigerians*, Olukotun now projects the truth about what should be seen as outer space exploration on the space of the moon itself.

Like so much other contemporary African fiction, *Nigerians* celebrates people who are half-breeds and transplants. Olukotun emphasizes that in South Africa, the former place of apartheid space, medical "transplant" technology denotes unity. Appropriately enough, *Nigerians* ends when Dayo brings his moonlight lamp to the Heart Transplant Museum honoring Dr. Christiaan Barnard, who "experimented on forty-nine dogs before moving on to people. . . . [Because of his success,] Groote Schuur hospital began swapping dozens of hearts a year to people of all creeds and classes" (290). A heart transplant, which scientifically does not depend upon race or national origin, is contingent upon interdependence, or what Paul Krugman describes as "not the place or race your ancestors come from" ("When the President is Un-American"). A heart transplant symbolizes Nelson Mandela's point that hate is learned, and love comes more easily to the human heart than hate.

And like so much other contemporary SF, Olukotun's novel demands that we expand the concept of personhood to include animals. Dogs played a major part in Barnard's success, and they are important to understanding the marvels of Dayo's moon lamps as well. Initially the poacher Malaysius removes innocent living creatures from their natural environment in order to use them for human food. But later, when exposed to the moon lamp that causes them to act unpredictably within human cognitive frames, they are revealed as much more. In this respect, Olukotun's story echoes "Unaccounted," a short story by his fellow University of Cape Town Master of Fine Arts recipient Lauren Beukes. The confined and tortured alien "ittaca" in Beukes's story suffer in the manner of Olukotun's abducted abalone. Olukotun describes the "mollusks drowning on the floor. They looked like furry brown saucers scattered on the ground" (120). Both the abalone and the ittaca are helpless and dying. "The ittaca is wedged into the uneven corner of cell 81C, as if it is trying to osmose right through the walls and out of here. It is starting to desiccate around the edges, the plumb Sulphur-colored frills of its membrane turning shriveled and grey. . . . The ittacas don't bleed, exactly. They extrude a clear viscous liquid" (Beukes 173, 176). Like the ittaca, the captured abalone start to desiccate, shrivel, and change color. However, while Beukes's story ends with the words "you can't dehumanize something that isn't human," Olukotun suggests that perhaps we can learn to honor the agency of both human and nonhuman alike (Beukes 182). Afrofuturists would agree since for so long in the New World, particularly the United States, enslaved Africans were treated like animals.

Although Olukotun was not initially aware of the Nigerian space program's viability, I would like to think that he is open to including other mammals in the expansion of how "person" is defined as well. I read "Wale" as echoing "whale." We need to save ourselves by breaking down science fictional categories of difference and welcoming everyone's talents. Saving the whales, who have more in common with us than environmentally important abalone, is beneficial to humanity too.

All life on Earth is interdependent.

Works Cited

"Abimbola Alale: The Woman Taking Nigeria to Space." *BBC News*, 19 Dec. 2016, http://www.bbc.com/news/av/world-africa-38367073/abimbola-alale-the-woman-taking-nigeria-to-space. Accessed 24 Oct. 2017.

Aguirre, Abby. "Octavia Butler's Prescient Vision of a Zealot Elected to 'Make America Great Again.'" *New Yorker*, 26 Jul. 2017, http://www.newyorker.com/books/

second-read/octavia-butlers-prescient-vision-of-a-zealot-elected-to-make-america-great-again. Accessed 24 Oct. 2017.

Beukes, Lauren. "Unaccounted." *Slipping: Stories, Essays & Other Writing*. Tachyon, 2016, pp. 173–82.

Cummings, Mike. "Novelist Credits Yale for Inspiring 'Sense of Wonder.'" *YaleNews*, 18 Jul. 2017, https://news.yale.edu/2017/07/18/novelist-credits-yale-inspiring-sense-wonder. Accessed 24 Oct. 2017.

Dery, Mark. "Black to the Future: Interviews with Samuel R. Delany, Greg Tate, and Tricia Rose." *South Atlantic Quarterly*, vol. 92, no. 4, 1993, pp. 735–78.

Falla, Ric, and John Mosig. *Australian Fish Farmer: A Practical Guide to Aquaculture*. Landlinks Press. 2004.

Henning, Paul, creator. *The Beverly Hillbillies*. Filmway Television/CBS, 1962–1971.

Kessler, Carol F. *Daring to Dream: Utopian Stories by United States Women, 1836–1919*. Pandora Press, 1984.

Krugman, Paul. "When the President is Un-American." *New York Times*, 14 Aug. 2017, https://www.nytimes.com/2017/08/14/opinion/when-the-president-is-un-american.html. Accessed 9 Jan. 2020.

Monks, Kieron. "Nigeria Plans to Send an Astronaut to Space by 2030." *CNN*, 6 Apr. 2016, http://www.cnn.com/2016/04/06/africa/nigeria-nasrda-space-astronaut/index.html. Accessed 24 Oct. 2017.

@Nnedi Okorafor, PhD. "This is why I call Akata Witch and Akata Warrior #AfricanJujuism. Some of the African traditions that many think r fantasy r real & it's woven in seamlessly with that which is made up & because these traditions are known by so so few, this isn't well understood." *Twitter*, 17 Nov. 2018, 8:39 a.m., https://twitter.com/Nnedi/status/1063834093660454912. Accessed. 8 Feb. 2019.

Olukotun, Deji Bryce. "It's Not an Email Scam, People, Nigeria Really Is Sending an Astronaut into Space" *Quartz Africa*, 27 Mar. 2016, https://qz.com/648441/its-not-an-email-scam—people-nigeria-really-is-sending-an-astronaut-into-space. Accessed 24 Oct. 2017.

———. "Meeting My Protagonist." *Slate*, 19 Sept. 2014, http://www.slate.com/articles/technology/future_tense/2014/09/nigerians_in_space_my_sci_fi_novel_turned_out_to_be_closer_to_the_truth.html. Accessed 24 Oct. 2017.

———. *Nigerians In Space*. Unnamed Press, 2014.

Padnani, Amisha. "U. R. Rao, Who Guided India Into Space, Dies at 85." *New York Times*, 13 Aug. 2017, pp. 1, 8.

Paper, Brittle. "Book Review: *Nigerians In Space*." *Voices of Africa*, 3 Jun. 2014, http://voicesofafrica.co.za/book-review-nigerians-in-space/. Accessed 24 Oct. 2017.

CHAPTER 12

Faster than Before

Science Fiction in Amos Tutuola's *The Palm-Wine Drinkard*

Nedine Moonsamy

> Then I remembered one of my juju which had escaped me and I performed it to stop us, but instead of that, we started to move faster than before.
> —AMOS TUTUOLA, THE PALM-WINE DRINKARD

With this single line, Amos Tutuola gives readers the sense of a protagonist whose affable brand of heroic action yields the most inadvertent results. Similarly, when Tutuola published the book including this line, he unleashed an unassuming narrative whose reach he could never anticipate and whose effects he could never contain. Penned by a Nigerian clerk who took to writing to alleviate boredom, *The Palm-Wine Drinkard* (1952) caused a stir in various literary circles, and to this day, Tutuola's debut novel is celebrated as an exemplar of innovative African fantasy.[1] Deploying Samuel R. Delany, Jr.'s linguistic exegesis of genre, however, I opine that *The Palm-Wine Drinkard* can more suitably be classified as a pioneering work of African science fiction (SF). Tutuola takes great pains to domesticate the fantastic by embed-

---

1. *Editors' note*: As we explain in the introduction to this collection, all of the authors featured in *Literary Afrofuturism* are bound together by a mutual interest in the aesthetic and political issues defining Afrofuturism in the twenty-first century. In many cases, they also focus their critical attention on texts published in this era, but in others, they explore earlier works of art that anticipate such issues (see, for example, the chapters by De Witt Douglas Kilgore and Mark Bould). Amos Tutuola is a particularly significant author in this respect, as he is often included in contemporary lists of Afrofuturist artists, but one whose work, as Moonsamy argues here, also reveals key differences between the kinds of speculative fiction written by African and Afrodiasporic authors.

ding it in an empirical reality; linking the reader's sense of wonder to his or her context as opposed to some fantastic elsewhere.

Contrary to current claims that African SF should be read on its own geographical and cultural terms, I contend that *The Palm-Wine Drinkard* is one at home in the global lexicon of SF. Furthermore, while authors and critics increasingly include Tutuola in the specific history of Afrofuturist SF, I argue that the domestic aspects of Tutuola's technique point to salient differences between Afrofuturism and African SF.[2] While Afrofuturist artists often use SF tropes to explore narratives of displacement and diasporic nomadism, Tutuola's text possesses a certain ease of amalgamation—and even ownership—of the otherworldly, thus reinforcing the sense that *The Palm-Wine Drinkard* is always already at home within the genre of SF.

The novel opens with an introduction to the Drinkard, who passes his days consuming palm-wine in the company of his friends. The bonhomie ends abruptly when his beloved tapster dies after falling from a tree; no longer able to access palm-wine, the Drinkard soon loses favor with his friends. He then resolves to bring back the tapster from "Deads' Town," but what ensues is a clumsy and rambunctious journey that does not end tidily. The Drinkard passes through many strange towns, meets a smorgasbord of bizarre creatures, and even marries during the course of his quest. It is only years later that he finally reunites with his tapster—only to learn that a dead person cannot leave Deads' Town. Bereft, the Drinkard returns to his village and, having matured over the course of his journey, he is no longer a nonchalant drunkard. Instead, he is a fully engaged citizen whose newfound sense of civic responsibility is demonstrated when he helps to bring an end to a famine.

Given the nature of the protagonist's tumultuous quest and character maturation, *The Palm-Wine Drinkard* can be read as a coming-of-age narrative with allegorical underpinnings. Tutuola wrote his novel during the precarious inception of Nigeria as a postcolonial state that still had to contend with the disruptive influences of Western modernity. The contradictions of his historical moment can be seen in *The Palm-Wine Drinkard*. While Tutuola sought to preserve local folktales by appropriating them for his narrative

---

2. As early as 1994, Mark Dery—following Greg Tate—included Amos Tutuola in his list of artists who could be considered as pioneering Afrofuturists; more recently, SF author Nisi Shawl and black media studies scholar Reynaldo Anderson have explored Tutuola as one of many African speculative writers who challenge us to redefine Afrofuturism itself. For further reading, see Mark Dery, *Flame Wars* (1994); Seth Ferranti's "Exploring the Future of Astro-Blackness" (2017); and Nisi Shawl's "Beyond Boundaries" (2019).

(Lindfors 252), many Western critics hailed *The Palm-Wine Drinkard* for its highly inventive, avant-garde technique (Hart 179). Furthermore, the fact that Tutuola's book was the very first West African novel written in English to receive international publication (with Faber and Faber UK) made it notorious amongst Nigerian scholars who felt either affronted or confused by Tutuola's use of English (Lindfors 251).

Tutuola's use of the English language provoked controversy amongst critics, because while he does technically write in English, he does not adhere to "standard written English." Western defenders suggested that Tutuola was exploring the possibility of a regional or vernacular English. Yet Nigerian respondents argued that no such English existed in their country, even in a purely spoken or pidgin form. Undertaking a thorough linguistic analysis of the novel, A. Afolayan suggests that "Tutuola's English largely represents the differences between the two languages, Yoruba and English" (206). Ultimately, Afolayan uncovers a complex dual deployment of Yoruba deep grammar and English surface grammar in Tutuola's work. He thus tentatively concludes that Tutuola writes in "Yoruba English," because his language evokes but belongs to neither of these camps exclusively. Arriving at similar conclusions, Marc Caplan asserts that *The Palm-Wine Drinkard* can be understood as an otherworldly entity because the "existential location between languages" produces "the narrative's strangeness" (32). This state of profound linguistic deterritorialization is significant; the novel clearly evoked anxiety amongst early readers, thus intimating at that which is unsettling, unknown—and even alien.

Whatever else they might say about Tutuola's text, critics agree that his use of language is sublime. The *Palm-Wine Drinkard* bears the ability to transport the reader into the unknown, which, according to Samuel R. Delany, Jr., is exactly the manner in which SF deploys language. In "About 5,750 Words," Delany provides an insightful explanation of how SF is able to "generate the infantile wonder" of the reader through language (8). Unlike other forms of writing, he argues, SF engenders an expansive set of possibilities in relation to our current reality. It transports us into a world we marvel at and leaves us in awe of the potential of the world to come. Most salient to my argument here is Delany's meticulous examination of *how* these effects are produced in and through language in a SF novel. Tracing generic particularities, Delany suggests that "a distinct level of subjunctivity informs all the words in an SF story at a level that is different from that which informs naturalistic fiction, fantasy, or reportage" (10). "Around the meaning of any word," he argues, "is a certain margin in which to correct the image of the object we arrive at (in old grammatical terms, to modify)," and in the case of SF, the field of linguistic interpretation is particularity elastic (4). Using the example of a "winged dog," Delany states that "as naturalistic fiction it is meaningless. As fantasy it is merely a visual correction. At the subjunctive level of SF, however, one must momentarily consider, as one makes that visual correction, an entire track of evolution" (12). Whereas naturalistic fiction cannot accommodate modifications of this kind because they operate on a subjunctive level of what "could have happened" (Delany 11), SF inspires the right kind of wonder to consider a world and technology that would allow for such a creature to exist. Hence the approach to language when reading SF is distinct. It is one where the imagination opens up a conceptual space for "events that have not happened" by interpreting word modifications as inventive rather than fanciful in nature (Delany 11).

Yet when it comes to making generic distinctions about *The Palm-Wine Drinkard*, many critics[3] have lodged it conclusively in the subjunctive domain of fantasy where, according to Delany, we are subjected to events that "could not have happened" (11). While many theorists read the text as an easy exemplification of African fable and folklore, I argue that Tutuola was actually inventing a variety of linguistic strategies to convey science fictional ideas and create science fictional effects in a literary environment where they did not exist yet, working incredibly hard to imbue his narrative with a level of plausibility more appropriate to SF subjunctivity.

The first technique that Tutuola utilizes to achieve this aim is to build a series of empirical correlatives that connect his narrative to our own modern, mundane world. For example, the Drinkard explains that he and his wife attained immortality because they "had 'sold our death' to somebody at the door for the sum of £70: 18: 6d and 'lent our fear' to somebody at the door as well on interest of £3: 10: 0d per month, so we did not care about death and we did not fear again" (66). In Tutuola's narrative, existential states like death and anxiety literally can be worn superficially, like clothing. Indeed, like everything else in our consumerist culture, they can be traded or rented for a fee. The reference to an exact amount in British pounds further connects this seemingly bizarre, even estranging, turn of events to the reader's reality; it marries our familiarity with economic exchange with the wondrous potential that we may one day discard existential inconveniences with a trader's ease.

The same empirical correlatives also serve to make sense of all of the imaginary creatures in Tutuola's novel. For example, in the forest the Drinkard meets

---

3. See Harold Collins, Carolyn Hart, and Saradashree Choudhury.

> a terrible animal. . . . I could not approach him as he was *as big as an elephant*. His fingernails were long to *about two feet*, his head was bigger than his body ten times. He had a large mouth which was full of teeth, these teeth were *about one foot long* and *as thick as a cow's horn*, his body was almost covered with black long hair *like a horse's tail hair*. He was very dirty. There were five horns on his head and curved and levelled to the head, his four feet were *as big as a log of wood*. (46; italics mine)

Later, Tutuola's narrator describes a creature whose head *"resembled a big pot of about ten feet in diameter,* there were two large eyes on his forehead *which were as big as bowls.* . . . Both feet were very long and *thick as a pillar of a house"* (106–7; italics mine). As noted by Harold Collins, Tutuola is a fan of the simile,[4] making his descriptions lengthy. This, however, is evidence itself of the strain involved in weaving the fanciful into the reader's reality. He modifies each phrase through meticulous and slow expansion, invoking the close observation and attention to standard units of measurement so often associated with science precisely because the "subjunctive level of SF expands the freedom of the choice of words that can follow another group of words meaningfully, but it [also] limits the way we employ the corrective process as we move between them" (Delany 11). Here then, we see Tutuola is invested in a balancing act; counterpoising the empirical and the imaginary in order to stretch the limits of the naturalistic mode and to reign in the borderlessness of the fantastic mode.

Delany further explains:

> The subjunctive level of SF says that we must make our correction process in accord with what we know of the physically explainable universe. And the physically explainable has a much wider range than the personally observable. The particular verbal freedom of SF, coupled with the corrective process that allows the whole range of the physically explainable universe, can produce the most violent leaps of imagery. (12)

This insight is germane in understanding Tutuola who, for every fantastic suggestion, provides an empirical equivalent that alters the limits of our experience. As we see in the two examples above, every aspect of the marvelous is domesticated through a form of measurement or comparison to an

---

4. Collins argues that "these Westernizing similes [have] a rather curious effect, as though Tutuola were leading his compatriots out of their acculturating, Westernizing world, with its ready acceptance of Western technology, back into the old mythical world" (83).

object that belongs to our world. The subjunctivity of the fantastic is thus sufficiently calibrated in order to allow these innovative creatures to gain some form of empirical credibility that is more fitting to SF.

A second notable feature of *The Palm-Wine Drinkard* that corresponds with Delany's definition of SF is that of making the figurative literal. In particular, the verbification of both nouns and adjectives serves to modify our understanding of how objects work in Tutuola's universe. Delany argues that a writer of SF proves his mettle "by the way he can maneuver existing tensions between words and associated images" (14), meaning that SF must disrupt our trained patterns of linguistic interpretation. Tutuola achieves this by cheekily foregrounding what is alien within the idiomatic. The most compelling example in this regard is that of the man who is introduced as "a beautiful 'complete' gentleman," who is "dressed with the finest and most costly clothes" (15). Mesmerized, an unwitting young lady follows this "complete gentleman" into the forest, only to face the literal potential lurking in the phrase that Tutuola uses to describe this character when the narrator states that "all the parts of his body were completed"—and the man proceeds to detach one body part at a time and "began to return the hired parts of his body to the owners and he was paying them the rentage money" (15, 16). The figurative notion of the "complete gentleman" is thus modified to describe a commodified and mechanical assemblage of human body parts into a seemingly singular and fine figure. After being reduced to just a skull, this particular character identifies himself as a "half-bodied incomplete gentleman" (17), which confirms that the modification of "complete" from the figurative to the literal is a deliberate narrative strategy to convey the technological wonder of a creature that is much like Frankenstein's monster. It is only in hindsight, then, that Tutuola's strategy of placing the word "complete" in inverted commas makes sense: he emphasizes the very word that will subsequently undergo modification later in the narrative, thereby preparing readers for this change.

Tutuola employs a similar strategy later in the same episode, when he relates that "the complete gentleman in the market was reduced to a 'SKULL' and this lady remained with only 'skull.' When the lady saw that she remained with only Skull, she began to say that her father had been telling her to marry a man, but she did not listen to or believe him" (18). Upon witnessing the disassembly of the complete gentleman, the lady—to her dismay—is left with just a skull. The word "skull" is rendered in three different typographical states in this example, providing a sense that Tutuola sought to transform and expand the signification of the word itself. In the first instance, "SKULL" is an early intimation for the reader to shift to

SF subjunctivity as it relies on personification in order to fashion a proper noun for a character called "SKULL." This produces incredible irony as the conventional symbol of death becomes its very animated opposite. Tutuola also signals to readers that this creature possesses all the classic qualities of a skull—wit and agility—which we gather from the emphasis on the word "Skull," but performs them in a verb-like fashion (18). For example, when the lady tries to bolt, "Skull chased her and within a few yards, he caught her, because he was clever and smart as he was only Skull and he could jump a mile to the second before coming down" (18). Quickness is not merely a mental faculty as Skull is physically agile too. Finally, by the time the reader meets the third rendering of the word "Skull" in this last previous quotation, Tutuola seems to be satisfied that he has suitably conveyed all the elasticity he invests in the word "skull,"' since none of his subsequent uses of the word are subject to typographical modifications of this kind.

Delany suggests that the SF writer "utilizes the information generated by any verbal juxtapositioning" (13). Arguably then, the typographical idiosyncrasies of *The Palm-Wine Drinkard* compensate for the fact that Tutuola himself did not have in mind, and hence could not rely on readers accessing, the generic expectations of SF. It is the cumulative development of linguistic tension and contrasts that serve as a generative engine for the more abstract imaginative and conceptual leaps of SF and, by extension, we can read Tutuola's curious application of language as that which breaks ground for the as-yet-unknown ideological terrain of African SF. It is thus somewhat antithetical—though perhaps not entirely surprising—that Sunday Anozie claims Tutuola "is not an African writer of science-fiction" because he "poses the scientific imagination against the imagination fastened upon traditional folklore" (240, 241). Despite noting "the interpenetration of the symbols which come from European technocracy and the images which have African cosmo-mythic significance," Anozie nevertheless sees an irreconcilable juxtaposition of tradition and modernity in the novel (242–43). As he explains,

> One does not expect to find such diverse phenomena of Western technological culture side by side with primitive African magic in the same folkloristic world. This coexistence has socio-psychological importance. For example, it shows us, first, how much Tutuola is aware of the problems of acculturation and colonial alienation, physical and well as psychic, in Africa. (244)

In Anozie's analysis, technology comes to represent the "threat" of the colonial enterprise and the possibilities of a neocolonial state that merely refashions its values.[5] The lack of synthesis between these two worlds is indicative of the pressures and angst experienced by local cultures and African subjects. Because Tutuola does not embrace technology fully but rather seems to include it in a partial and uneven fashion in an otherwise indigenous tale, Anozie reads these insertions as indicative of psychic disturbance. For him, *The Palm-Wine Drinkard* is thus a fantastic caveat that speaks forebodingly about the encroachments of modernity on a fading African past—everything that is averse to the alleged futurism of SF narrative.

Yet while Anozie struggles to read the conflicting currents of the precolonial and the technological under the banner of SF, the discourse of Afrofuturism makes room for just these kinds of interpretation. Due to the fact that "Afrofuturism is an extension of the historical recovery projects that black Atlantic intellectuals have engaged in for well over 200 years" (Yaszek 47), "the oscillation between industrial Africa and scientific Africa" (Eshun 294) is a common theme. In responding to the various traumas of the Black Atlantic slave trade that have not only erased the past but also repressed the corresponding webs of futurity that may have extended out of them, Afrofuturists apply themselves to the creation of a virtual archive that represents feelings of profound loss and alienation. Both Lisa Yaszek and Kodwo Eshun argue that SF tropes and technology are thus used to account for "the everyday implications of forcibly imposed dislocation and the constitution of Black Atlantic subjectivities" in order to highlight the erasure of the past *and* the future because of the violence of Western modernity and technology (Eshun 299).

In the hands of the correct artists, then, SF tropes and representations of technology can indeed aid in the expression of trauma, alienation, and estrangement that Anozie finds in *The Palm-Wine Drinkard*. States of literal displacement and alien realities are indicative of identities subjected to, rather than subjects of, a projected technological future. Yet my contention is that Anozie's assessment of technological alienation in *The Palm-Wine Drinkard* is ultimately overdetermined. The nuance that warrants some attention here is that the appraisal of SF in the African context speaks to a need to *domesticate* the genre rather than deploying it as a vehicle for representations of estrangement and nonbelonging, as is the case with much Afrofuturist art. Indeed, while Afrofuturist stories often focus on the fantastic journeys of diasporic nomads who "live the estrangement that SF writ-

---

5. For example, the assembled body of the complete gentleman is often read as an "illusion that conceals terror, entrapment, imprisonment, and death" (Caplan 68), which tends to make a monstrous rather than wondrous prospect out of his technology.

ers envision" (Eshun 298) from both technoscientific reality and the stories we tell about it, the turn in African SF involves seeing subjects as always already at home in the genre.

If we look at the Drinkard's encounter with the Faithful-Mother in the white tree, this incident is full of technological features that aid in telling a rather affectionate and utopian tale. The example of Faithful-Mother is poignant because she is by far the wealthiest and the most technologically adept character in the book and, contrary to Anozie's suggestion that the appearance of either are symbolic of cultural alienation or psychological angst, she is also the most beneficent creature they encounter. Upon approaching the white tree, the Drinkard and his wife "noticed that somebody peeped out and was focusing us as if a photographer was focusing somebody" (65). This makes them extremely anxious, but after they enter the tree and meet Faithful-Mother, all their fears are allayed. Faithful-Mother is a Good Samaritan, and she escorts them "to the largest dancing hall" where they "saw that over 300 people were all dancing together. The hall was decorated with about one million pounds (£) and there were many images and our own too were in the centre of the hall" (67–68). Life inside the white tree is a series of bountiful modern parties, replete with disco lights and endless amounts of food, which are funded by Faithful-Mother's British pounds. Faithful-Mother also helps the Drinkard and his wife make sense of the new technologies transforming their world. When the couple encounter photographs that were taken of them before they entered the town, they do not understand how photography works and are frightened by images that "resembled us too much" (68). However, Faithful-Mother quickly explains that she displays such photos "for remembrance and to know those she was helping from their difficulties and punishments" (68). The prospect of photography as a malicious form of technology that produces psychological distress is subverted in favor of its benevolent uses. In this incident, there is little doubt that photography can add value to society. Moreover, despite the self-indulgent nature of the place, life in the white tree is not entirely hedonistic—it is nourishing and healing too. The Drinkard and his wife arrived badly injured and traumatized after passing though the Unreturnable-Heaven's town, and Faithful-Mother provides them with free, modern hospitalization. Soon, the Drinkard notes that they "had forgotten all our past torments," implying that the couple had reached a utopian plateau that they never wish to leave (69). Arguably then, what Anozie describes as a "problematic" synthesis between modernity and tradition is something else entirely, and readers need a different method for assessing this early African SF text (240).

According to Harry Garuba, we are prone to reading modernity as a unidirectional force that squeezes out, contests, and eventually annihilates local cultures. However, he argues that it is just as possible to discern the influence of animism—which he reads as central to the African imaginary—on modernity as it is to see the opposite. Garuba claims that

> "magical elements of thought" are not displaced but, on the contrary, continually assimilate new developments in science, technology, and the organization of the world within a basically "magical" worldview. Rather than "disenchantment," a persistent re-enchantment thus occurs, and the rational and scientific are appropriated and transformed into the mystical and magical. (267)

As part of a subconscious collective culture, animism imbues matter and objects with various spiritual and psychological properties; it colors the world with a nonempirical sense of time, place, and being. Whereas Afrofuturism finds its creative impulse in the melancholic quest for lost homes and identities, the "re-enchantment" that Garuba proposes is fundamental to African modes of existence.

For many modern thinkers, this "enchanted" mode of thinking has ebbed since the arrival of modernity because the rational discourses of science and technology are seen as being in direct conflict with animistic belief systems. Yet in a refreshing turn, Garuba insists that tradition does not survive *despite* technology. Instead, he argues that animism enfolds nonlocal technologies into local cultures. The exerting force for ideological and sociopolitical mutation is thus animistic enchantment, not empiricism. It is animism that imbues technology and science with the otherworldly and makes allowance for its incorporation into African societies.

Tutuola makes a parallel argument in *The Palm-Wine Drinkard*, after the Drinkard has his tender reunion with his dead tapster. They establish that the tapster cannot return with him because he cannot leave Deads' Town, but the tapster gives the Drinkard "an 'EGG'" as a token of abiding friendship (103). Now accustomed to Tutuola's technique, the reader should be well-equipped to understand that the egg—rendered in capital letters and placed in inverted commas—will function different from our expectations. Using a form of exposition that is common to SF, the Drinkard tells us that "the use of the egg was to give me anything that I wanted in this world and if I wanted to use it, I must put it in a big bowl of water, then I would mention the name of anything that I wanted" (103). The Drinkard takes this wishing egg home with him, and during a severe famine, is quick to use the egg to produce food for his entire community. Much to everyone's delight, the egg produces vast quantities of food upon demand and only stops producing food once the careless citizens knock it over and break it—much like one would a machine. Again, in this episode, the metaphoric is made literal as the connotations of the egg—fertility and nourishment—apply, but in a hyperbolized and mechanized fashion. Acts of reproduction shift from organic to mechanic, and this is not treated as an encroachment on an otherwise agrarian society, but as a source of good that helps accelerate food production in a time of crisis. It is worth noting that it is only the greed of the people that compromises the use of this "egg technology" in the Drinkard's community.

In this instance, the magical egg is used to explain the place and nature of mechanical production in this society. Tutuola reenchants industrialized food production with animistic logic in order to integrate it into the social fabric, not to illustrate the "problems of synthesis," as Anozie's more Manichean reading of the novel would imply (240). As per the aims of animist materialism, it follows that Tutuola "destabilises the hierarchy of science over magic and the secularist narrative of modernity by reabsorbing historical time into the matrices of myth and magic" (Garuba 270). Similarly, Tutuola uses animism to undermine this infantilizing logic, insisting on a refashioned Western modernity that might assist in the telling and retelling of African realities.

Not surprisingly, more recent studies on African SF approach cultural syncretism on more complimentary terms. For example, Nnedi Okorafor's notion of "Organic fantasy," Ian MacDonald's identification of "jujutech,"[6] and Marleen Barr's notion of "anti-science fiction"[7] all point toward instances where Western technology fuses with African myth, fable, and fantasy to produce a hybrid mode of storytelling. Okorafor and MacDonald are

---

6. MacDonald examines a number of African novels that are indicative of a style he calls *"jujutech"* where the "dichotomies of orature and literature, of fabulism and empiricism, present and past, and present and future which otherwise approach one another from agonistic extremes," meet in complex representations of African spaces and realities (196).

7. For Barr, black SF often seeks to acknowledge how science and technology have been culpable in the production of racist discourse. In response, Barr notes that black writers do not adhere to the generic bifurcation of fantasy and SF. Hence, "magical" modes of knowing come to supplement and even override rationality and technology and allows for the critique of the excesses of science. In this manner, black SF can be considered anti-SF because "writers alter genre conventions to change how we read and define SF itself" (Barr xv).

particularly clear in their appreciation of African SF as rooted in local style. In "Organic Fantasy," Okorafor explores her own style and technique as typical of African literature and cites examples from previous authors, like Ben Okri, to illustrate how fantasy has always been a trenchant part of African literature and perception. Hence, she asserts that the style she employs is not new or invented but rather an inherited and organic mode of experience and storytelling in Africa.[8] MacDonald also explores earlier African fiction where "Western technology fuses with religion and African-coded fabulism" (186) and he cites Tutuola as a prescient example of African SF in its current form. Overall, these critics seek to carve out a niche for a more self-determined conception of what has increasingly gained traction as African SF.

Arguably, my analysis of *The Palm-Wine Drinkard* can be read in relative terms; Tutuola does indeed amalgamate aspects of Western technology and indigenous tropes. Yet more central to my engagement is also Delany's formal unpacking of generic characteristics that belies the kind of exceptionalism that has crept into our understanding of African SF. In wanting to argue for the status of African SF as a unique—or even resistant—manifestation of SF, the global application of generic features is hastily maligned as a form of ideological imposition. Consequently, there is a tendency to demote the notion of a "world literature," where it is possible to read African novels as participating in popular genres, like SF.

Contrary to this stance, I have shown that *The Palm-Wine Drinkard* stretches language in ways that Delany insists are universally crucial to SF. By domesticating the fantastic through a series of empirical correlatives, Tutuola delivers the subjunctive level that is appropriate to SF and thus inspires wonder at the possibilities of a world to come. Arguably, the success of this project can be discerned in Collins's speculation that "modern science and technology—and their own ingenuity—will one day provide the Nigerians with marvels almost as incredible as those in Tutuola's novels" (118).

In his bardic appraisal of the novel, Taban Lo Liyong asks, "When the machine is taking up more and more of man's former dominion, isn't it refreshing to find a man who is man enough to stand up against the machines? For what is language but a machine? And learning grammar makes us more and more slavish to it" (121). Lo Liyong's evaluation of language as a form of technology is useful, if not prescient, for while many assumed that Tutuola's shortcoming was that of not using language effec-

---

8. Okorafor's entire canon testifies to the manner in which indigenous form can accommodate representations of aliens and technology.

tively, we see that the evaluation criteria for the absorption of this machine is neither that of success nor failure. Instead, Tutuola has reenchanted language through his idiosyncratic command and by rising up against the machine in order to reassemble its parts, he built the lexicon of SF a home in African storytelling.

Works Cited

Afolayan, A. "Language and Sources in Amos Tutuola." *Critical Perspectives on Amos Tutuola,* edited by Bernth Lindfors, Three Continents, 1975, pp. 193–208.

Anozie, Sunday O. "Amos Tutuola: Literature and Folklore, or the Problem of Synthesis." *Critical Perspectives on Amos Tutuola,* edited by Bernth Lindfors, Three Continents, 1975, pp. 237–53.

Barr, Marleen S. *Afro-Future Females: Black Writers Chart Science Fiction's Newest New—Wave Trajectory.* The Ohio State UP, 2008.

Caplan, Marc. *How Strange the Change: Language, Temporality and Narrative Form in Peripheral Modernisms.* Stanford UP, 2011.

Choudhury, Saradashree. "Folklore and Society in Transition: A Study of *The Palm-Wine Drinkard* and *The Famished Road.*" *African Journal of History and Culture,* vol. 6, no. 1, 2014, pp. 3–11.

Collins, Harold R. *Amos Tutuola.* Twayne Publishers, 1969.

Eshun, Kodwo. "Further Considerations of Afrofuturism." *CR: The New Centennial Review,* vol. 3, no. 2, 2003, pp. 287–302.

Delany, Samuel R., Jr. "About 5,750 Words." *The Jewel-Hinged Jaw: Notes on the Language of Science Fiction.* 1977. Wesleyan UP, 2009, pp 1–15.

Dery, Mark. *Flame Wars: The Discourse of Cyberculture.* Duke UP, 1994.

Ferranti, Seth. "Exploring the Future of Astro-Blackness." *Vice,* October 18, 2017, https://www.vice.com/en_ca/article/d3yaaq/exploring-the-future-of-astro-blackness.

Garuba, Harry. "Explorations in Animist Materialism: Notes on Reading/Writing African Literature, Culture and Society." *Public Culture,* vol. 15, no. 2, 2003, pp. 261–85.

Hart, Carolyn. "In Search of African Literary Aesthetics: Production and Reception of the Texts of Amos Tutuola and Yvonne Vera." *African Cultural Studies,* vol. 21, no. 2, 2009, pp. 177–95.

Lindfors, Bernth. "Amos Tutuola: Debts and Assets." *Critical Perspectives on Amos Tutuola,* edited by Lindfors, Heinemann, 1980, pp. 224–55.

Lo Liyong, Taban. "Tutuola, Son of Zinjanthropus." *Critical Perspectives on Amos Tutuola,* edited by Bernth Lindfors, Three Continents, 1975, pp. 115–22.

MacDonald, Ian P. 2014. "Alter-Africas: Science Fiction and the Post-Colonial Black African Novel." Dissertation, Columbia University, 2014.

Okorafor, Nnedi. "Organic Fantasy." *African Identities,* vol. 7, no. 2, 2009, pp. 275–86.

Shawl, Nisi. "Beyond Boundaries: My Life in the Bush of Ghosts by Amos Tutuola." Tor.com, March 14, 2019, https://www.tor.com/2019/03/14/beyond-boundaries-my-life-in-the-bush-of-ghosts-by-amos-tutuola/.

Tutuola, Amos. *The Palm-Wine Drinkard.* 1952. Faber and Faber, 2014.

Yaszek, Lisa. "Afrofuturism, Science Fiction, and the History of the Future." *Socialism and Democracy,* vol. 20, no. 3, 2006, pp. 41–60.

CODA

Wokeness and Afrofuturism

Isiah Lavender III and Lisa Yaszek

We began this collection with the alarm Richard Wright sounded eighty years ago in his searing American classic, *Native Son*. We wanted readers to wake up and stay woke (to borrow the popular black cliché connoting political awareness of racial and social justice) just like Wright asked of his own audience. We wanted to make conscious the utility of Afrofuturism as a critical term in the battle to stake claims for people of color—and people of all colors—in the future imaginary. More than mere intellectual sparring, this seemingly abstract aesthetic battle is of the utmost importance in an historical moment when people of color are rising and find themselves (once again) facing a resurgence of white supremacist anger.

The word "Afrofuturism" was only coined in 1993, but it refers to cultural works from the nineteenth century to the present. The mainstream of science fiction and futuristic speculation, at least in an Anglo-American context, has largely been centered on white people; Afrofuturist creators seek to envision futures that contain black people and that allow for black cultural expression outside the white supremacist parameters that define consensus reality. Indeed, just as white science fiction writers have long imagined alternative pasts and strange new futures, so too Afrofuturists have reimagined the past and envisioned marvelous new futures—although in this case, with a specific political goal: to turn both against the oppressions of the actual present.

With important scholarly works that concentrate on technology, sound, and image like Reynaldo Anderson and Charles E. Jones's *Afrofuturism 2.0: The Rise of Astro-Blackness* (2016); Paul Youngquist's *A Pure Solar World: Sun Ra and the Birth of Afrofuturism* (2016); and Erik Steinskog's *Afrofuturism and Black Sound Studies: Culture, Technology, and Things to Come* (2017), we thought it important to concentrate on the genre we know best in this collection—literature. We also like to think that we have achieved our goal in showcasing the best new scholarship on Afrofuturism as a twenty-first-century aesthetic and critical practice. While Afrofuturism has always been a multimedia aesthetic movement, the authors in this volume complement and extend such scholarship by demonstrating the historical and contemporary centrality of print-based storytelling to Afrofuturism. At the same time, their use of diverse critical perspectives enables them to ask hard questions about who and what counts as Afrofuturism—questions that have become increasingly important to artists and scholars alike as stories about science, technology, race, and futurity become increasingly central to the public imagination.

We are tremendously thrilled to present an author roundtable with well-known and emerging writers so our audience can learn their opinions about overly loose uses of the term and about the relation of its African American focus to the African diaspora and literary production within Africa itself. Afrofuturism is increasingly misapplied to any and all works of black speculative fiction, regardless of where their authors come from or what issues they address. Without doubt "Africanfuturism," as Nnedi Okorafor calls it, exists in its own right, and we very much look forward to a new generation of artists and scholars who will explore it in depth. Like pioneering Afrofuturist author and editor Sheree R. Thomas, we are very excited by what's over the horizon. For example, Nigerian American Tochi Onyebuchi's debut *Beasts Made of Night* (2017) is a dark fantasy that explores guilt and justice through the sin eater Taj in the imaginary walled city of Kos (for those who want more, he completes the tale in *Crown of Thunder* [2018]). The same author's *War Girls* (2019) features cyborgized Nigerian sisters Onyii and Ify fighting to get back to each other in a 2172 war-torn Nigeria marked by global climate change, nuclear disaster, and battle mechs. Zambian writer Namwali Serpell's debut novel *The Old Drift* (2019) features generational conflicts, Afronauts, and microdrones composed of wings made with "solar tape" that are sold "to the powers that be" (508). Certainly, we are pleased to include a range of different voices in this collection and hope others recognize the contribution this kind of work makes to science fiction scholarship, which needs to be as diverse as science fiction itself! We have sought to craft a strong editorial framework for this book that will make it accessible to the widest range of audiences possible, whatever their disciplinary background or level of scholarly expertise, as we amplify the study of Afrofuturism across time and space. While it is true that Africa is a vast continent with a diverse range of speculative traditions, the study of these traditions is still very new, and we are delighted that we were able to recruit some up-and-coming African science fiction writers and scholars alike for this project.

Our main regret with this collection is that we simply did not have the space to imagine what lies beyond Afrofuturism. The term has been around for a quarter century now, and we are keenly interested in the question of what might coexist with or go beyond Afrofuturism. But as students of genre history know well, every two to three decades there is a sea change as the science fiction community redefines the thematic and stylistic concerns of "good" science fiction, and, in doing so, paves the way for new modes of speculative storytelling. So, it's only natural to ask: is Afrofuturism a "colored wave" within science fiction history, analogous to aesthetic movement such as the New Wave or cyberpunk, or might its multigenre status provide some kind of energy that transcends (and transforms) science fiction history as we know it? We believe it is the latter and so we say: welcome to the COLORED AGE of science fiction and fantasy! Welcome to the emancipatory landscapes of social justice and alternative futurisms! Get woke and stay woke!

Works Cited

Anderson, Reynaldo, and Charles E. Jones, editors. *Afrofuturism 2.0 The Rise of Astro—Blackness.* Lexington Books, 2016.

Onyebuchi, Tochi. *Beasts Made of Night.* Razorbill, 2017.

———. *Crown of Thunder.* Razorbill, 2018.

———. *War Girls.* Razorbill, 2019.

Serpell, Namwali. *The Old Drift.* Hogarth, 2019.

Steinskog, Erik. *Afrofuturism and Black Sound Studies: Culture, Technology, and Things to Come.* Palgrave Macmillan, 2017.

Youngquist, Paul. *A Pure Solar World: Sun Ra and the Birth of Afrofuturism.* U of Texas P, 2016.

CONTRIBUTORS

Marleen S. Barr is known for her pioneering work in feminist science fiction and teaches English at the City University of New York. She has won the Science Fiction Research Association Pilgrim Award for lifetime achievement in science fiction criticism. Barr is the author of *Alien to Femininity: Speculative Fiction and Feminist Theory* (1987), *Feminist Fabulation: Space/Postmodern Fiction* (1992), *Lost in Space: Probing Feminist Science Fiction and Beyond* (1993), *Genre Fission: A New Discourse Practice for Cultural Studies* (2000), and *Afro-Future Females: Black Writers Chart Science Fiction's Newest New-Wave Trajectory* (2008). Barr has edited many anthologies and coedited the science fiction issue of *PMLA*. She has published the novels *Oy Pioneer!* (2003) and *Oy Feminist Planets: A Fake Memoir* (2015). Her *When Trump Changed: The Feminist Science Fiction Justice League Quashes the Orange Outrage Pussy Grabber* (2018) is the first single-authored Trump short story collection.

Mark Bould is Reader in Film and Literature at the University of West England, Bristol. He is the recipient of the International Association for the Fantastic in the Arts Distinguished Scholarship Award (2019) and the Science Fiction Research Association's Pilgrim Lifetime Achievement Award for Critical Contributions to the Study of Science Fiction and Fantasy (2016). He coedits the *Studies in Global Science Fiction* monograph series and is the founding (but now retired) editor of *Science Fiction Film and Television*. His most recent books are *M. John Harrison: Critical Essays* (2019), *Solaris* (2014), *SF Now* (2014), and *Africa SF* (2013). He is currently completing *The Anthropocene Unconscious* (2020).

Gerry Canavan is Associate Professor in the English Department at Marquette University, specializing in twentieth and twenty-first-century literature. An editor at *Extrapolation* and *Science Fiction Film and Television*, he has also coedited *Green Planets: Ecology and Science Fiction* (2014), *The Cambridge Companion to American Science Fiction* (2015), and *The Cambridge History of Science Fiction* (2019). His first monograph, *Octavia E. Butler*, appeared in 2016 in the Modern Masters of Science Fiction series at University of Illinois Press.

Lisa Dowdall is a writer and academic based in Sydney, Australia. She has a PhD in Creative Practice/English Literature from the University of New South Wales. Her research focuses on speculative fiction, postcolonial studies, ecoliterature, and women's writing. Her essays have previously been published in *Paradoxa* and *Science Fiction Studies*.

Rebecca J. Holden is a fan and scholar of feminist and African American science fiction. She earned her PhD in English from the University of Wisconsin-Madison in 1999 and is currently a Senior Lecturer in the Professional Writing Program at the University of Maryland, College Park. Holden has published essays and reviews on various science fiction writers and books in *Foundation*, *Science Fiction Studies*, *Oxford Bibliographies in American Literature*, *LA Review of Books*, *Women of Other Worlds: Excursions through Science Fiction and Feminism*, and *Luminescent Threads: Connections to Octavia Butler*. Holden has served as a reviewer for *Extrapolation*, *African American Review*, and the Masters of Science Fiction series from the University of Illinois Press. With Nisi Shawl, Holden coedited and contributed to *Strange Matings: Science Fiction, Feminism, African American Voices, and Octavia E. Butler* (2013). She also edited a collection of essays on WisCon, a feminist science fiction convention, titled *Regenerating WisCon* (2014). In 2014, Holden cochaired the annual SFRA (Science Fiction Research Association) conference.

De Witt Douglas Kilgore is Associate Professor of English and American Studies at Indiana University. He is the author of *Astrofuturism: Science, Race and Visions of Utopia in Space* (2003). His recent work includes an essay on *Planet of the Apes* (1968) for *Oxford Bibliographies in Cinema and Media Studies* (2019) and "A Cinema of Consolation: Visualizing the War on Terror in

Post-9/11 Cinematic Science Fiction Invasion Fantasy," in *The In/visibility of America's 21st Century Wars* (2017). His current book project is *Galactic Club: Seeking a Postracial Universe in Science/Fiction*, an inquiry into the intellectual and narrative traffic between the astronomical search for extraterrestrial intelligence (SETI) and science fiction in literature and film.

Isiah Lavender III is the Sterling-Goodman Professor of English at the University of Georgia, where he researches and teaches courses in African American literature and science fiction. His books include *Race in American Science Fiction* (2011), *Black and Brown Planets: The Politics of Race in Science Fiction* (2014), *Dis-Orienting Planets: Racial Representations of Asia in Science Fiction* (2017), and *Afrofuturism Rising: The Literary Prehistory of a Movement* (2019). Most recently, he has been named a coeditor of the oldest science fiction journal, *Extrapolation*.

Nedine Moonsamy is Senior Lecturer in the English Literature department at the University of Pretoria. She is currently writing a monograph on contemporary South African fiction and otherwise conducts research on science fiction in Africa. Her debut novel, *The Not Famous Five*, is published by Modjaji Books (2019).

Stacey Robinson, Assistant Professor of graphic design at the University of Illinois, is an Arthur Schomburg fellow who completed his Masters of Fine Art at the University at Buffalo. His multimedia work discusses ideas of "Black Utopias" as decolonized spaces of peace by considering self-sustaining affluent black communities, black protest movements, and the art that document(ed) them. As part of the collaborative team called "Black Kirby" with artist John Jennings, he creates graphic novels, gallery exhibitions, and lectures that deconstruct the work of comic book creator Jack Kirby to reimagine resistance spaces inspired by black diasporic cultures. His exhibition *Binary ConScience* (2017) explores ideas of W. E. B. Du Bois's "double consciousness" as a black cultural adaptation and a means of colonial survival. Meanwhile, his exhibition *Branding the AfroFuture* (2017–18) looks at designing and constructing black futures through various cultural, collage aesthetics. His graphic novel, *I Am Alfonso Jones* (2017, with writer Tony Medina) is available from Lee & Low books.

Sheree R. Thomas is a Memphis-based short fiction writer, poet, and editor whose work appears in *Sycorax's Daughters, Do Not Go Quietly, Memphis Noir, Stories for Chip, So Long Been Dreaming, Ghost Fishing, The Ringing Ear,*

Apex Magazine, Fiyah, Fireside, Strange Horizons, Transition, Callaloo, and the *New York Times.* She edited the *Dark Matter* speculative fiction volumes that won two World Fantasy Awards. Her short story collection, *Sleeping Under the Tree of Life* (2016), was longlisted for the 2016 James Tiptree, Jr. Award and honored with a *Publishers Weekly* Starred Review. Another collection, *Shotgun Lullabies* (2011), was described as a "revelatory work like Jean Toomer's *Cane.*" She is Associate Editor of *Obsidian: Literature & Arts in the African Diaspora* and Founding Editor of *Mojo.* Look for *Trouble the Waters* and her story collection *Nine Bar Blues* (both forthcoming in 2020).

Elizabeth A. Wheeler is Associate Professor of English and Founder-Director of the Disability Studies Minor at the University of Oregon. The University of Michigan Press recently published her book *HandiLand: The Crippest Place on Earth* (2019). *HandiLand* examines young adult and children's literature and the emergence of young people with disabilities into public spaces since the worldwide disability rights laws of the 1990s and 2000s. Wheeler's work on literature for young readers, disability, race, and environmental justice has also appeared in the anthologies *Constructing the (M)other* (2019) and *Disability Studies and the Environmental Humanities* (2018) and the journals *Children's Literature Quarterly* and *ISLE.* She also coedited a 2018 special issue of *The Journal of Literary and Cultural Disability Studies* on literature for young people. In 2018 she received the LILAC Award for community outreach to people with disabilities. In 2018–19 she held the Ottilie-Wildermuth guest professorship at the University of Tübingen, Germany.

Jerome Winter, PhD, is a full-time lecturer at the University of California, Riverside. His book, *Science Fiction, New Space Opera, and Neoliberal Globalism* (2017), was published by the University of Wales Press as part of their New Dimensions in Science Fiction series. His scholarship has appeared in *The Oxford Handbook of Science Fiction, Foundation, Extrapolation, Journal of Fantastic and the Arts,* the *Los Angeles Review of Books,* the *SFRA Review,* and *Science Fiction Studies.*

Gina Wisker is Professor of Contemporary Literature and Higher Education at the University of Brighton. Her principal research interests include contemporary women's Gothic and postcolonial writing. She has published: *Contemporary Women's Gothic Fiction* (2016), *Margaret Atwood, an Introduction to Critical Views of Her Fiction* (2012), *Key Concepts in Postcolonial Writing* (2007), and *Horror* (2005). Her books on postgraduate study and supervision include *The Postgraduate Research Handbook* (2001, 2008), *The Good Supervisor*

(2005, 2012), and *Getting Published* (2015). Wisker edits the online dark fantasy journal *Dissections* and the poetry magazine *Spokes,* and is a member of the World Horror Association. She also serves as a board member of *Femspec* and the Katherine Mansfield Association, and is past chair of the Contemporary Women's Writing Association. She is currently writing a book about contemporary women's ghost stories.

Lisa Yaszek is Regents Professor of Science Fiction Studies in the School of Literature, Media, and Communication at Georgia Tech. Her works include *The Self-Wired: Technology and Subjectivity in Contemporary American Narrative* (2002/2014), *Galactic Suburbia: Recovering Women's Science Fiction* (2008), *The Future is Female!: 25 Classic Science Fiction Stories by Women* (2018), and *Beyond Afrofuturism* (coedited with Isiah Lavender III, 2020). Her ideas about science fiction as the premiere story form of modernity have been featured in venues including the *Washington Post*, the AMC miniseries *James Cameron's Story of Science Fiction,* and the Wired.com podcast *Geeks Guide to the Galaxy*. A past president of the Science Fiction Research Association, Yaszek currently serves as an editor for the Library of America and as a juror for the John W. Campbell and Eugie Foster Science Fiction Awards.

INDEX

47 (Mosley), 12, 51, 89–90, 96–99

abalone, 203, 211, 214. *See also* animals
abolitionists/abolition, 67–71, 74, 124, 124n15. *See also* emancipation of slaves; manumission
"About 5,750 Words" (Delany), 218
Abyssinia/Abyssinian peoples and culture, 63–67. *See also* Ethiopia
activism, 38, 90, 145
Adinkra (West African writing system), 34
Adulthood Rites (Butler), 154, 154n2
affordable housing, lack of, 138. *See also* Fair Housing Act; poverty; and segregation
Africa, 9, 31–35, 50, 89–204, 208–9, 214, 232–33: imperial control of, 78; progress, 201, 213; representations of, 6, 14–15, 59–71; return to, 123; stereotypes about, 176–77, 191–92, 198–200
African American authors, 1–6, 3n2, 6n4, 8–9, 11–15, 23–42, 31n2, 42, 44–48, 50–51, 53, 59–72, 63–64n7, 75, 81, 88, 96, 109–27, 110n1, 115n7, 118n8, 128–45, 149–67, 154n2, 156n3, 171–88, 182n1, 182n9, 190–92, 196–98, 200, 203–16, 217n2, 218–22, 122n13, 227, 232
African American literature, culture, and history, 3–6, 3n2, 6n4, 8–9, 11–15, 23–28, 31–33, 31n2, 36–42, 44–48, 50–51, 53, 59–72, 63–64n7, 79–84, 88, 91, 96, 109–27, 110n1, 115n7, 118n8, 122n13, 128–45, 153–54, 154n2, 156n3, 171–88, 182n1, 182n9, 190, 203–217, 232
African authors, 6, 6n5, 8, 11–12, 14–15, 23–36, 28n1, 75, 77, 77n1, 189, 216–28, 216n1, 217n2, 220n4
African bioregion, 191–202
African colonists, 62–67, 63–64n7
African-derived knowledge, 63, 71
African dominance, 59–71
African global nomadism, 15, 204
African history, culture, and traditions, 6–7, 11–15, 27–55, 62–71, 208, 227, 232. *See also* black cultural traditions
African literature, 8, 11–13, 24–25, 28–29, 32–36, 75, 109–27, 110n10, 118n8,

241

189, 208, 227, 232–33: written in English, 216–30
African Immortals series (Due), 50–51
African Methodist Episcopalian church, 31. *See also* Christianity
African science fiction, 24, 30, 52, 74–75, 77, 77n1, 84, 203–28, 216–28, 217n2, 226n6, 231–33: differences from Afrofuturism, 75, 217
"African Science Fiction 101" (Bould), 77n1
"African SF" (Bould), 77n1
African speculative fiction. *See* African science fiction
African Speculative Fiction Society, 30, 52, 52n4
Africanfuturism, 6, 206, 206n1, 232
Africentric, 6, 24, 27–28, 28n1, 32, 59–71: fusion politics, 67–71; science fiction, 61n4. *See also* Afrocentric/Afrocentricity
afroaquanauts, 13, 128–48
Afrocentric/Afrocentricity, 6, 13, 24, 26–27, 66. *See also* Africentric
Afrocentricity: The Theory of Social Change (Asante), 31n6
Afrodiaspora/Afrodiasporic artists and art, 3–6, 8, 11–12, 14–15, 25, 27–32, 35, 42–43, 47, 51–53, 59–60, 62, 65, 78, 81–82, 88–89, 88n2, 91, 100, 102, 113, 153–54, 159, 174, 191, 216n1, 217, 223, 232
Afrodiasporic histories, 81, 153, 159
Afro-Future Females: Black Writers Chart Science Fiction's Newest New-Wave Trajectory (Barr), 8
Afrofuturism: alternative terms, 6–7, 7n6; as allegory, 158; centrality of print fiction, 8, 10; contemporary aesthetics, 10, 159; definitions of, 1–11, 25–30, 39–40, 87–88, 87n1, 231–33; environmental, 189–202; listserv community, 39–40, 88; literary history of, 10, 39–40; negative, 128–45; positive, 129–45; progressive political agenda, 68; relationship to Africa, 10
Afrofuturism 2.0: The Rise of Astro-Blackness (Anderson and Jones), 10
Afrofuturism and Black Sound Studies: Culture, Technology, and Things to Come (Steinskog), 232

Afrofuturism: The World of Black Sci-Fi and Fantasy Culture (Womack), 10
afronauts, 130, 232
AfroSF series (Hartmann), 9, 24–25, 33
AfroSF: Science Fiction by African Writers (Hartmann), 24–25
AfroSFv2 (Hartman), 25
"AfroVision" (Robinson), 20
After the Flare (Olukotun), 6n4
Agboola, Olufemi, 205, 209, 212
Age of Ruin, The (Faucette), 110, 117–21
agency, 12, 37–55, 69, 80–85, 89, 91–103, 162, 164, 206, 214
agrarian societies, 67, 89–90, 96–99, 226
Alchemists of Kush, The (Faust), 24
Alexander, Michelle, 140
alien invasion, 110, 157
alienation, 3, 64, 84, 204, 208, 222–24: technological, 223
aliens, 4–5, 39, 45–47, 52, 96–14, 112–25, 118n8, 129–30, 135, 154n2, 157, 159, 163, 166, 178, 192, 196–201, 214, 227n8: humanoid, 196–98; migrants as, 206
allohistory. *See* alternate history
alternate history, 11–12, 27, 43, 59–71, 68n11, 68n12, 69n13, 75
alternative stories, 79–85
American Civil War, 12–13, 62, 67–72, 68n12, 68n13, 69n15, 92n4, 122n13, 123–25, 124n15: Northern victory in, 70; Southern victory in, 68. *See also* American South; Reconstruction
American hegemony, 172, 185, 205–6
American history, 59–72
American imperialist power, 172, 185
American South, 5, 12–13, 44–45, 47, 50–51, 59–72, 68n11–13, 69n15, 82n4, 92n4, 114, 122n13, 123–25, 124n15, 128–45, 153, 203, 208
Americans. *See* United States, the
Americas, colonization of, 63–67, 209
Anansi storytelling, 74
ancestors, 41, 46–48, 76, 95, 99, 101
Ancient Astronomers of Timbuktu, The (Hawkes), 32
Ancient Egyptian: medicine, 197–98; mythology 196–98
Anderson, Reynaldo, 5, 7, 7n6, 10, 15, 80, 217n2, 232

INDEX • 243

Andersonville prisoner of war camp, 123
androids, 2, 91
animals, 199–200, 203, 211, 213–14: as Earthlings, 198; medical experimentation on, 213–14. *See also* abalone; dogs; extinction of species; swordfish
animism, 225–26
Antebellum Era, 2, 63, 89–90, 96–99, 123, 153. *See also* American Civil War
Anthropocene era, 5, 30, 33, 47, 92n4, 129, 131–33, 151–66, 232
anti-apartheid, 213
anti-blackness, 44, 46. *See also* blackness
anti-racism, 32, 60, 67, 183
"anti-science fiction" (Barr), 226, 226n7
apartheid, 214
APB: Artists against Police Brutality (Campbell, Rodriguez, and Jennings), 23
Arabic-derived knowledge, 63
aristocracy, 62–67 177, 185: feudal, 66
Armstrong, Neil, 142, 190, 210
artificial wombs, 116–17
Asante, Molefi Kete, 27, 31n6
aspirations, cultural suppression of, 41–45, 162, 205, 223
assimilation of cultures and peoples, 119, 119n10, 153–59, 182
astro-blackness, 5–6, 6n7, 88
Astrofuturism: Science, Race, and Visions of Utopia in Space (Kilgore), 8, 236–37
astronauts, 130, 189–90, 203, 209, 211, 232: female, 213; Nigerian, 213. *See also* afronauts
Attebery, Brian, 197
"Aye Gomorrah" (Delany), 111
Azanian Bridges (Wood), 25, 33

Babel-17 (Delany), 111
Baltimore, Maryland, 13, 128, 131–34, 137–42, 145. *See also* Sandtown
Bannekerade, 174–75
Banneker, Benjamin, 174
Baraka, Amiri, 1
Barnes, Steven, 12–13, 59–62, 68–71, 63–64n7, 91, 110, 125
Barr, Marleen S., 8–9, 14–15, 203–15, 226, 226n7, 235
Beloved (Morrison), 31n1, 156n3

Binti (Okorafor), 52, 88, 150
Binti series (Okorafor), 52
biological matter, 159–65
biopower, 164
Black Arts Movement, 48–49, 113
black Atlantic authors, 1–6, 3n2, 6n4, 6n5, 8–9, 11–15, 23–40, 28n1, 43–44, 46, 50–52, 59–62, 65, 68–71, 63–64n7, 73–86, 78n1, 82n4, 91, 109–27, 110n1, 115n7, 118n8, 129, 149–67, 154n2, 182, 182n1, 182n9, 190–92, 196–98, 200, 203–16, 217n2, 218–22, 227
black history and culture, 7, 12, 39–41, 45, 40, 81, 153, 159: recovery of, 3–4, 89, 223; stories centered on, 88
black fantasy, 5, 10, 117–21, 216. *See also* fantasy genre
"black genius" figure, 157, 171–80
Black Lives Matter movement, 142
black middle class, 31, 111. *See also* class hierarchy
black nationalism, 121
Black Panther (Coates), 171–88, 182n9
Black Panther (Coogler), 2, 41, 52, 171–75, 180n7, 182n8
"Black Power SF" (Bould), 112n4, 122
black quantum futurism, 7, 7n6
black revenge trope, 113, 122–23
black science fiction, 1–6, 6n4, 6n5, 7n6, 8–15, 23–28, 28n1, 30–33, 36–40, 44, 50–51, 59–60n1, 73–74, 77, 77n1, 84, 87–89, 109–25, 110n1, 115n7, 118n8, 128–45, 149–66, 154n2, 182, 182n1, 182n9, 190, 203–16, 217n2, 218–22, 226n7, 227, 231–33: history of, 3n2
Black Science Fiction (Faucette), 110, 112, 125
black spiritual traditions, 48–49. *See also* African Methodist Episcopalian church; Candomblé; Christianity; Church of God in Christ; Hoodoo; Santeria; Vodou
black supremacy, 60, 60–61n2
"Black to the Future" (Dery), 3, 39, 190, 206
black upper class, 48–49, 62–67. *See also* class hierarchy
Black Wall Street Massacre. *See* Tulsa Race Riot
black women writers/artists, 1–5, 3n2, 8–9, 10–14, 23–28, 31–33, 31n2, 36–55,

65, 73–88, 78n1, 82n4, 91, 96, 110, 110n1, 114, 115n7, 122, 122n13, 125, 128–45, 149–67, 154n2, 156n3, 182, 182n1, 182n9, 190–92, 196–98, 200, 207, 217n2
black-on-black racism, 49. *See also* classism; colorism
blackness, 4, 27, 30–32, 41, 53, 62–67, 84, 97–98, 111–27, 140, 159, 186, 206. *See also* anti-blackness; astro-blackness; literary blackness
blacks, absence of in science fiction and fantasy fiction, 40, 73, 77, 80, 91, 212, 232
Blake, or the Huts of America (Delany), 4–5, 27, 197
Bloodchildren: Stories by the Octavia E. Butler (Shawl), 25
blues, 39, 44–45, 50
Bould, Mark, 3n2, 12–13, 77n1, 109–27, 110n1, 112n4, 122n14, 172n1, 177, 216n1, 235–36
Broken Earth trilogy (Jemisin), 2, 13, 24, 149–66
Brother from Another Planet, The (Sayles), 25, 27, 39
Brown, Adrienne Marie, 3n1, 68, 68n10
Brown Girl in the Ring (Hopkinson), 24, 40
Buckell, Tobias S., 8
Burning: Massacre, Destruction, and the Tulsa Race Riot of 1921, The (Madigan), 31n4
Butler, Octavia, 5, 9, 11, 13, 28, 38–40, 44, 50–51, 88, 110, 110n1, 114, 115n7, 122, 125, 153–54, 154n2, 182, 182n1, 182n9, 190, 207

Campbell, Bill, 11, 23, 25, 29, 33, 35
Canadian writers, 5, 24, 40
Canavan, Gerry, 14, 171–88, 172n1, 182n8, 182n9, 191n2, 236
Candomblé, 42, 100
capitalism, 33, 60, 68, 70, 79, 119n10, 122, 137–39, 142, 164: disaster, 119n10; global, 119, 119n10
Caribbean writers, 8, 25–26, 74, 79–84
Caribbean Canadian writers, 8, 11–12, 24–26, 32–33, 36–37, 40, 43–44, 46,
51–52, 65, 73–88, 78n1, 82n4, 91, 125, 190
Carrington, André, 10
"Case for Reparations, The" (Coates), 124n15
castration anxiety, 120–21
Chaos, The (Hopkinson), 24
"Chicago 1927" (Gomez), 50
Christianity, 31, 42, 63
chronic illness, 132, 143–44: politics of, 128
"City Born Great, The" (Jemisin), 150
civil rights, denial of, 135
Civil Rights Act of 1968, 116
Civil War. *See* American Civil War
class hierarchy, 4, 6, 13, 48–51, 67, 101, 111: prohibition of, 124
climate change, 30, 33, 47, 92n4, 129, 131–33, 165–66, 232
Coates, Ta-Neshi, 124n15, 171–86
code switching, 133
cognitive impairments, lead-derived, 139–42
Cold War, the, 180, 185
Collins, Harold, 219n3, 220, 220n4, 227
colonial narratives, 189–202
colonial taxonomies, 149–66
colonialism, 6, 14, 30, 32, 34, 49, 62–67, 75–86, 111, 111n3, 119–20, 120n12, 123, 150, 156–66, 171–72, 93, 100–101, 174, 175n2, 176–77, 180, 183–84, 189–202, 222, 237: justifications for, 150; threats to, 222–23. *See also* Americas, colonization of
colonization 151–59: internalization of, 73–74
colorism, 46, 100
"Come Alive by Saying No" (Bould), 112n4, 122n14
comic books, 2, 10, 14, 28, 52, 114, 119n9, 171–86, 176n4, 177–86, 182n8–9, 211, 237. *See also* graphic novels
Confederacy, the/Confederate States of America, 62, 67–71, 68n11–12, 69n13. *See also* American Civil War
conjurers, 41–46. *See also* magic
consensus reality, 231
Coogler, Ryan, 2–3, 41, 52, 171–75, 180n7, 182n8

countermemory, 111, 117. *See also* memory
Coyote Kings of the Space-Age Bachelor Pad, The (Faust), 23–34
"Creating Races" (Jemisin), 153n1
criminal justice system, 139–41
Crown of Infinity (Faucette), 110, 112–18, 121, 125
cultural erasure, 4, 28, 44, 79, 190, 223
cultural literacy, 204
cyberpunk, 233
cyborgs, 159, 163, 232

Dahomey warrior women, 45–46
dark fantasy, 232. *See also* fantasy genre
Dark Matter: A Century of Speculative Fiction from the African Diaspora (Thomas), 3n2, 8, 11, 25, 29, 40, 50, 125, 238
Dark Matter: Reading the Bones (Thomas), 8, 40, 238
Davis, Milton, 6, 32
Dawn (Butler), 154n2
decolonization, 78, 183
dehumanization, 81–82, 88, 99, 150, 154, 156–59: resisting, 198
Delany, Martin R., 3n2, 4, 27, 197
Delany, Samuel R., 1–3, 11, 13, 23, 25–28, 38–39, 110–12, 110n1, 122, 125, 129, 190, 216, 218–22, 227
Dery, Mark, 3–4, 8–9, 11, 14, 25–26, 28–29, 39, 60, 88, 88n2, 110, 159, 190, 206, 217n2
diabetes, 132
diasporas, 156–59. *See also* Afrodiaspora
difference, 76, 114, 120, 151, 159, 166, 176, 192, 205–6, 211, 214: biological, 157; ecological, 192; racial, 181, 208–9
differential environmental risk, 128–45
digital divide, 4
digital humanities, 5, 9–10
disabilities, people of color with, 128–45
disability, medical model, 132
disability services, lack of, 139–42
Disco Hustle (Faucette), 110
diversity, 1–10, 30, 35, 38, 51, 74, 84, 91–92, 102–3, 166, 190, 194–95, 211, 231: in the science fiction/fantasy community, 149–51, 231
"Diversity in Technology" initiative, 2
Dogon civilization and culture, 32, 65
double-consciousness, 91: historic, 63; reverse, 88
Douglas, Aaron, 28
Dowdall, Lisa, 13–14, 149–67, 236
Dred Scott v. Sanford, 64n9
Dreamblood Duology, The (Jemisin), 196–98
drug laws, 139–42
drug trade, 46, 139
DuBois, W. E. B., 3n2, 4, 8–9, 27, 88, 110, 237
Due, Tananarive, 50–51, 91
dying Earth fiction, 5, 118, 121–25, 128–67
dystopia, 13, 65, 76, 90, 128–48, 186: science fiction story trope, 76–77
dystopic science fiction, 38, 89–90, 128–45

Earth Will Be Avenged, The (Faucette), 125
ecocriticism, 190–202: Western, 199
economic exploitation, 30, 137–39
ecoterrorism, 199–200
Edisonade, 174–75
education: colonial, 192–96; unequal access to, 42, 111, 141–43
egalitarianism, racial, 65–66, 70–71
Egypt/Egyptian people and culture, 5–6, 28, 31, 43, 59, 63–67 196–201
Egyptology, 196–98, 197n4
Einstein Intersection, The (Delany), 111
electoral politics, 138–39
emancipation of slaves, 67–76, 69n13. *See also* abolitionists/abolition
emergency management laws, 134–35
empathy, 88, 91, 102
energy, 160–62, 211: harnessing of, 162; production of, 160
environment, 10, 13–14, 43, 128–32, 134–48, 152–53, 161–62, 189–202, 191n2, 214. *See also* natural world
environmental apocalypse/disaster/degradation, 13–14, 49, 79, 128–45, 149–66, 189, 191, 196, 200
environmental conquest, 189–202

environmental humanities, 160
environmental illness, 128–45
environmental justice, 129–45, 191n1, 194, 199, 238
environmental racism, 13, 125–48
environmental regeneration, 196, 199
environmental science fiction, 128–45, 149–67, 189–202, 191n2: Northern authors of, 189
environmentalism, 90, 95, 189–202
epic fantasy, 118, 192–200
epidemics, 128–45
Eshun, Kodwo, 3–4, 111, 117, 159, 223–24
Ethiopia/Ethiopian people and culture, 31–32, 50
ethnic stereotypes, 116. *See also* racial stereotypes; racism
eugenics, 114–17
European colonialism and imperialist power, 34, 59, 63, 172, 182, 185
evacuation, 132–33
Everfair (Shawl), 24, 27, 31–33
excessive policing of blacks, 139–42
Exxon Valdez oil spill, 200, 200n5

Fair Housing Act, 116
Famine, 225–26
Famished Road, The (Okri), 75
fantastic, the, 14–15, 26, 40, 44, 57, 62, 73–74, 79–85, 99, 102, 119, 119n10, 189–200, 203–4, 210–12: domestication of, 216–28
fantastic moonlight trope, 15, 203–4, 211–12
fantasy genre, 3, 5, 7, 10, 24, 26–28, 30, 40, 45, 60n1, 61n5, 66, 70, 75, 84, 88–89, 118–19, 150, 191–201, 216, 218–20, 226–27, 226n7, 232–33: genre conventions, 226–27, 226n7. *See also* black fantasy; dark fantasy; epic fantasy; high fantasy; quest fantasy; speculative fantasy; sword and sorcery fantasy; and sword and soul fantasy
Farnham's Freehold (Heinlein), 60, 60–61n2, 63–64n7, 65
Faucette, John M., 12–13, 109–27, 110n1, 118n8

Faust, Minister, 6, 6n5, 11, 23–24, 27–28, 28n1, 31–33, 36
female protagonists, 46, 52, 79–84, 88, 99–102, 128–45, 194–98, 203–4, 209, 211–12
feminism, 38–53, 80, 117, 137–38. *See also* womanism/womanist aesthetic
feminist science fiction, 5, 9, 11, 13, 28, 38–40, 44, 48, 50–51, 53, 88, 110, 110n1, 114, 115n7, 117, 121–22, 125, 151–66, 154n2, 182, 182n1, 182n9, 190, 207
Ferguson, Missouri, 153
feudalism, 62–67, 70, 118
Fifth Season, The (Jemisin), 149, 151–57, 163–66
Filter House (Shawl), 24
Fledgling (Butler), 51
Flint, Michigan, 13, 128, 131, 134–36, 143–45: bankruptcy of, 134–35. *See also* racism: environmental
Flint River, 135–36, 144. *See also* water pollution
flooding, 128–29, 143
folk culture and knowledge, 37–53, 41–46
folklore/folktales, 25, 40–46, 51, 73, 77–78, 91, 95–99, 219, 222: African, 78, 217–29, 226–27; African American, 95–99, 96n6; Caribbean, 25, 51, 78; European, 73
forced breeding, 114, 116–17, 152–54
From the Notebooks of Doctor Brain (Faust), 24
future: African-inspired, 192–201, 226n6; alternative, 12, 59, 67–71, 68n11, 68n12, 75–77, 84; alternatives to white-centered, 1–10, 36, 51, 60, 91–103, 174, 231; black-led, 60–65, 60–61n2, 69–70; capitalist, 68; dystopian, 6, 28n1, 60, 70, 128–48; erasure of, 223; feminist, 38, 48; liberated, 82, 85; multiracial/multicultural, 1–10, 30, 38, 51, 74, 84, 91–92, 102–3, 166, 190, 194, 231; projected technological, 3, 28, 30, 51, 60, 80, 99, 174, 223; "race-less" or postracial, 36, 89, 159; survivable, 128–45; utopian, 65, 70, 76–77; white-centered future, 1, 36, 60–61, 91, 174

Gamergate, 1–2, 2n1

gang warfare, 121
Garner, Eric, 130, 136n3
Garner, Margaret, 31, 31n2, 156n3
gender, 13, 37–55, 120–21
gender roles, 30, 65, 94, 116–17. *See also* sexism; women, subordination of
genetic engineering, 114–17, 153, 157
genetic mutations, 92, 112–21, 152–54
genocide, 32, 70, 113–25, 152, 156–59, 186
geology, 13, 149–65, 203, 205
geontology, 13, 149–65
Get Out (Peele), 40
"Ghost Writer, The" (Faucette), 109
ghosts, 96–99, 109. *See also* haints
Gilda Stories, The (Gomez), 49–50
global African nomad, 208
goddesses, 43–44, 47
Gomez, Jewelle, 44, 49–50
Gothic, the, 5, 12, 75–77, 84–85. *See also* postcolonial gothic
government neglect of people of color, 128–45
graphic novels, 28, 35, 237. *See also* comic books
Gray, Freddie, 130–31, 134, 138–42, 145
Grayson, Sandra M., 8–9
Greenwood Massacre. *See* Tulsa Race Riot
Gumbs, Alexis Pauline, 37, 48
Gunn, Bill, 48–49

haints, 45, 52
Hairston, Andrea, 37, 44–47, 53
Haiti/Hattian, 41–43, 43n3, 51, 70
Hamilton, Virginia, 95
Harlem Renaissance, 81, 81n3
Harris, Wilson, 8, 76
Hartmann, Ivor W., 9, 24
Hausa people, 207–8
healers, 41–46, 97–98, 158, 197–98. *See also* rootwork
Heinlein, Robert A., 60, 60–61n2, 63–64n7, 65, 90
herbalists, 41–43, 96
high fantasy, 192–94, 192, 194. *See also* fantasy genre

High John the Conqueror folktale, 42, 96–99
Hiroshima, Japan, American nuclear bombing of, 125
histories of marginalized peoples, recovery of, 80–85, 91, 95, 99, 194–95
history, 59–71: as cyclical, 80–84; definitions of, 89; dominant narratives of, 4, 7, 10, 12, 48, 61, 74–75; erased, suppressed, or misrepresented, 4, 7, 10, 12, 48, 61–62, 68, 80–85, 92–93, 92n4, 190; as narrative, 75, 92–95; non-European perspectives of, 80; of those who are unrepresented in dominant narratives, 74–75, 78; white Eurocentric, 92
Holden, Rebecca J., 12, 25, 87–108, 238
Holloway House, 110–11
"Holy Fucking Shit I Won a Hugo" (Jemisin), 150
Hoodoo, 42, 44–45
Hopkins, Pauline, 3n2, 110
Hopkinson, Nalo, 8, 11–12, 24–26, 32–33, 36–37, 40, 43–44, 46, 51–52, 65, 73–88, 78n1, 82n4, 91, 125, 190
housing discrimination, 135. *See also* affordable housing, lack of; Fair Housing Act; segregation
Hugo awards, 2, 13, 24, 149–50: ceremonies, 2, 149–50; diversity of nominees, 150
human, definitions of, 39, 51, 83, 88, 152, 156, 159–60, 165, 204, 214: as a technology of exclusion, 159
human exceptionalism, 121: white-as-default, 122
human interdependence, 204, 207: raced and gendered, 207
Hurricane Katrina, 129, 131, 133
Hurston, Zora Neal, 38, 40–42, 45, 96
hyphenated Americans, 206, 210

Identity, 15, 28, 38, 114, 117, 120, 160–61, 163, 204: African American, 112–13; black, 1, 7; cultural, 44, 206; essentialist notions of, 159; ethnic, 156; group, 197; hybrid, 79–85; international visions of, 209; national, 62, 204, 209; posthuman, 159; racial, 4, 111–27; speculative, 159

Igbo people, 30, 34, 81, 82n4
Imago (Butler), 154n2
Imarisha, Walidah, 68, 68n10
Imhotep-hop, 6, 28, 28n1
immigrants. *See* migrants/immigrants
imperialism, 6, 76, 78, 128, 162, 174, 182, 185, 193: alternatives to, 182; undermining the legacy of, 78. *See also* American imperialist power; European colonialism and imperialist power
incest, 52. *See also* rape; sexual abuse/violence
Indigenous African: beast fables, 198; ecological practices and ecologies, 191–202; medicine, 197–98, 197n4, 200
indigenous culture, 37–53
indigenous peoples, 70, 189–202: exploitation of, 190–202
industrial decline, 134–37
industrialized food production, 226
intellectual disabilities, 131, 134, 139, 141–42. *See also* special education
Invisible Man (Ellison), 3n2
invisibility, 44, 46, 48, 93–94
Islam, 59: history and culture, 62–67
Islamic-derived knowledge, 63
"It's Not an E-mail Scam" (Olukotun), 213

Jackson, Sandra, 9–10
Jamaica, 11, 24, 35, 51–52
Jamaican Canadian writers, 11
jazz, 48, 50, 196: jazz age, 50
Jazz (Morrison), 81, 81n3
Jemisin, N. K., 1–3, 11, 13–14, 24–27, 31, 36, 88, 149–67, 191–92, 196–98, 200
Jennings, John, 5, 23, 237
Jim Crow laws/era, 67, 111, 117, 134, 139
Johnson, Alaya Dawn, 12, 50, 87–92, 99–102
Jones, Charles E., 10, 88, 232
jujutech, 7, 226, 226n6
juvenile justice system, 141–43

Kenyan Canadian authors, 6, 6n5, 11, 23–24, 27–28, 28n1, 31–33, 36

Kilgore, De Witt Douglas, 8, 11–12, 59–72, 172n1, 216n1, 236–37
Killing Moon, The (Jemisin), 14, 196–98
Kincaid, Jamaica, 8
Kindred (Butler), 5, 51, 114
King, Martin Luther Jr., 116
Koontown Killing Kaper (Campbell), 23

Lagoon (Okorafor), 198–201
language, use of in science fiction, 218–19
language as technology, 227–28
"The Last Shall Be First" (Robinson), 168
Lavender, Isiah III, 1–36, 3n1, 63, 131, 231–34
Laymon, Kiese, 51
Le Guin, Ursula K., 30
lead exposure lawsuits, 138
lead poisoning, 128–45: effects on children, 134
libraries, 193–95
life, definitions of, 159–66
Lion's Blood (Barnes), 12, 59–72, 63–64n7
literacy, 34, 192–96: access to, 42, 47, 141–42
Long Division (Laymon), 51
"Looking for the Invisible" (Thomas), 40
Lost Cause revisionary history of the American Civil War, 62, 68. *See also* American Civil War
low-income neighborhoods, 128, 131, 134–38, 143–45
lynching, 31, 31n4, 45

M. Archive (Gumbs), 48
magic, 38, 42–47, 51, 75, 79–85, 92, 98, 119n10, 156–66, 192, 196, 222–26, 226n7: African, 222; Afro-Caribbean, 25, 51; for healing, 196–98; as resistance, 158–66. *See also* the fantastic; Obeah; rootwork
"Making the Impossible Possible" (Hopkinson), 87
Malcolm X, 32, 32n7
Mama Day (Naylor), 42, 46–47
Mandela, Nelson, 213
manumission, 66, 97–98
Marooned on the Levels (Faucette), 110

Mars, 70, 189–90, 212
Marvel Comics, 2, 14, 52, 114, 171–86
mass incarceration, 96, 129–41: for drug offenses, 139–40
mass suicide, 81–84
matriarchy, 99–102
McGee, Vonetta, 51
mechanical reproduction, 226
medical care, lack of access to, 131
medical experimentation on blacks, 120n12, 132
medical racism, 88, 132
memory, 41–48, 69, 69n15, 110–11, 117, 164, 204
Mendlesohn, Farah, 194
menopause, 79
menstruation, 121
mer people, 12, 43, 73–86
metaphysics, 5, 88, 159
middle class, 67, 111. *See also* class hierarchy
Middle Passage, the, 12, 73, 79–84, 123. *See also* slavery, African chattel; slavery, transatlantic slave trade
middle-aged, 79–84
Midnight Robber (Hopkinson), 24, 51–52
migrants/immigrants, 9, 59, 191, 206–7, 210, 214
Mindscape (Hairston), 53
modernity, 3, 7, 28, 217, 222–26, 224: technoscience/technocultural, 7, 30, 119n10; Western, 192, 217, 223, 226
Moonsamy, Nedine, 15, 216–30, 216n1, 237
More Brilliant Than the Sun (Eshun), 117
Morrison, Toni, 3, 31n2, 42, 44, 81, 156n3
Moses, Man of the Mountain (Hurston), 41–42
Mosley, Walter, 12, 51, 89, 91, 96–99, 117
Mothership: Tales from Afrofuturism and Beyond (Campbell and Hall), 23, 29
MOVE bombing, 31, 31n3
Mules and Men (Hurston), 41
Mundane Afrofuturism, 5
music, 2, 26–27, 30, 33, 39, 44–45, 48, 50, 80, 128, 196
musicians, 2–3, 26, 28, 39–40, 41n2, 48, 50–51, 91

My Booty Novel (Campbell), 23
My Soul to Keep (Due), 50
My Soul to Take (Due), 50
myth. *See* folklore/folktales

Nagasaki, Japan, American nuclear bombing of, 125
Nama, Adilifu, 9, 177n5
NASA, 189, 203, 205, 209
National Space Research and Development Agency (Nigeria), 205, 213
nationality, 208–14
Native Son (Wright), 1, 231
natural disasters, 92, 128–45, 151
natural resources, exploitation of, 79, 93–94, 162, 177, 184
natural world, 128–45, 149–67, 211, 226: African-inspired visions of, 190–91; human connection to, 151–66; Orientalized descriptions of, 192, 194. *See also* environment, the
Nelson, Alondra, 4–5, 8, 11, 39, 88
neoslave narrative, 122, 122n13
New Moon's Arms, The (Hopkinson), 12, 24, 73–85, 82n4
New Wave science fiction, 121, 232
Nevèrÿon series (Delany), 122
Nigeria as postcolonial state, 217
Nigeria/Nigerian people and culture, 15, 28, 30–31, 34, 65, 82n4, 198–200, 203–18, 227, 232
Nigerian American authors, 6, 6n4, 12, 14–15, 26, 28, 37, 52, 65, 88–89, 91–95, 97, 150, 191–92, 198–201, 203–15, 206n1, 226–27, 227n8, 232
Nigerian authors, 75, 189, 227
Nigerian space program, 203–14
Nigerians in Space (Olukotun), 6n4, 14–15, 203–15
"Night Market" (Onwualu), 189
"Noir Town" (Peele), 40
nonhuman community, 204, 211. *See also* aliens; animals
"Not the Affirmative Action You Meant, Not the History You're Making" (Jemisin), 150
nuclear disasters, 232
nuclear weapons, 180

Obama, Barack, 144
Obeah, 42
Obelisk Gate, The (Jemisin), 24, 88, 149–50, 156–62
Ojetade, Balogun, 6
Okorafor, Nnedi, 6, 12, 14, 26, 28, 37, 52, 65, 88–89, 91–95, 97, 150, 191–92, 198–201, 206n1, 226–27, 227n8, 232
Okri, Ben, 75, 227
Olukotun, Deji Bryce, 6, 6n4, 14–15, 203–15
Onwualu, Chinelo, 11, 24, 29–30, 34, 36, 189–90
"Organic Fantasy" (Orkrafor), 95, 226–27
Orientalism, 192–98: deconstruction of, 200; ecological, 194–95, 200; literary, 192–94
Orleans (Smith), 13, 128–45
others/othering, 73–77, 87–88, 91–92, 130, 157: intimacy with, 165; new forms of, 158; woman as, 77

Palm-Wine Drinkard, The (Tutuola), 15, 75, 216–28
Parable of the Sower series (Butler), 51
Parable of the Trickster (Butler), 51
paranormal elements. See the fantastic; supernatural elements
passing, racial, 115, 115n7. See also skin color
patriarchy/patriarchal oppression, 53, 94, 100, 116–17, 195, 197: capitalist, 137–38. See also sexism; women, subordination of
Patternist series (Butler), 122, 182n9
Peacemakers, The series (Faucette), 124–25
Peele, Jordan, 40–41, 41n2
People Could Fly: American Black Folktales, The (Hamilton), 95
"People vs. T'Challa, The" (Coates), 175, 176n3, 184–85
personhood, 204, 214. See also human, definitions of
petty crime, arrests for, 139. See also mass incarceration; school-to-prison pipeline
pharmaceutical industry: alternatives to, 196, 200
Pickens, Therí A., 140

planetary romance, 76–77, 117–25
plantocracy, 66–71
police brutality, 130–31, 134, 136n3, 138–42, 153, 145: black women as victims of, 130, 140; and sexual violence, 137
postapocalyptic fiction, 92–102, 110, 118–21, 128–45, 151–66
postcolonial gothic, 12, 75–77, 84–85
postcolonial literature, 12, 73–86, 77n1. See also postcolonial gothic; postcolonial science fiction
postcolonial science fiction, 73–86, 77n1
postcolonialism, 14, 74–78, 77n1, 84–85, 164, 174, 183, 189–202, 217, 236, 238
posthuman, 114–17, 159–61
postindustrial economy, 134–37, 143–45
postracial, 36, 60–61n2
poverty, 46, 49, 88, 93, 98, 101, 128–45, 165, 200
power, alternative models of, 80–85, 97–103, 163–64, 171–86; dominant narratives of, 68
predatory lending industry, 138–39. See also capitalism
"Princess Steel, The" (DuBois), 3n2, 9
prison. See mass incarceration
prosthetic community, 128, 139, 141
pulp science fiction, 113–27
Puppygate, block-voting controversies of 2015 and 2016, 1–2, 2n1, 13–14, 149–51, 165

quarantine, 128–45
quest fantasy, 15, 118–21, 194, 217

Rabid Puppies. See Sad/Rabid Puppies
race, conventional notions of, 159. See also racism
race as a technology of control, 159, 206. See also racism
RaceFail '09 flame war, 1, 2n1
racial profiling, 130, 139, 141. See also police brutality
racial stereotypes, 116, 176, 176n4, 204–5, 207, 211. See also ethnic stereotypes; racism
racial taxonomies, 60–71, 149–66: based on pseudoscience, 120, 150, 153, 156–59, 213

racialization of black bodies, 206. *See also* racism
racially segregated housing, 116, 131, 134, 139. *See also* segregation
racism, 1–2, 1n2, 6, 13, 30–31, 31n4, 35–36, 39, 48, 53, 60–67, 60–61n2, 76, 91, 93–94, 96, 110–11, 116, 129–41, 149–50, 154, 159, 176, 176n4, 183, 204–7, 211, 226: immigration-generated, 206; as learned, 208, 213; medical, 132. *See also* anti-blackness; anti-racism; black-on-black racism; colorism; environmental racism; ethnic stereotypes; medical racism; racial stereotypes; racist discourse; scientific racism
"Racism in Science Fiction" (Delany), 1
racism in the science fiction/fantasy community, 1–2, 2n1, 13–14, 149–51, 165
"Radical Imagination" (Robinson), 56
rape, 32, 117, 137, 154. *See also* sexual abuse/violence
Reconstruction, 67. *See also* American Civil War; American South
"Red Thread, The" (Samatar), 47
Redwood and Wildfire (Hairston), 44–45
refugees, 48. *See also* migrants
religion, 5, 32, 42–46, 52, 63, 88, 92, 197, 227
reverse colonization narrative, 180, 182–83, 183n10
revolutions, 186, 193–96
Rieder, John, 111, 196n3
"Road to Black Science Fiction, The" (Faucette), 111, 121, 124–25
Robinson, Stacey, 10, 20, 56, 106, 168, 237
rootwork, 37, 41–42. *See also* healers; magic
Rosarium Publishing, 23, 33
Rose, Tricia, 3, 39, 110
rule of law, 180–87

Sad/Rabid Puppies, 1–2, 2n1, 13–14, 149–51, 165
Salaam, Kiini Iburra, 8, 37, 48
Salt Roads, The (Hopkinson), 24, 43, 46
Samatar, Sofia, 11, 14, 37, 47–48, 191–96, 200
Sanctified Church, The (Hurston), 41–42

Sandtown (Baltimore, Maryland), 13, 128, 131, 134, 137–38, 145. *See also* cognitive impairment, lead derived; lead exposure lawsuits; lead poisoning; racism, environmental
"Sanfoka of the Mind" (Robinson), 106
Santeria, 42
Saunders, Charles R., 7, 32, 110
Sayles, John, 25, 27, 39
Schalk, Sami, 8–9
school-to-prison pipeline, 142
Schuyler, George S., 3n2, 29, 110, 115, 115n7
science and technology, 92–103, 171–80: American, 177; definitions of, 89; ethical use of, 90, 102; European, 177, 222; global development of, 212; history of, 92; misuse and dangers of, 90–95, 102; philosophy of, 5; rational discourses of, 225–26, 226n7; Western, 191, 196
science fiction/speculative fiction genre, 1–15, 3n2, 5n3, 6n4, 7n6, 24–30, 32, 38–53, 59–71, 59–60n1, 61n4, 73–85, 77n1, 87–93, 87n1, 88n2, 98–99, 102, 109–12, 112n4–5, 117–31, 133, 137, 149–67, 189–229, 216n1, 217n2, 226n7, 231–33: definitions of, 68, 77, 214; genre conventions, 73, 77n1, 214, 226–27, 226n7; golden age of, 30; history of, 75, 151, 231–33. *See also* African science fiction; black science fiction; dystopic science fiction; environmental science fiction; feminist science fiction; New Wave science fiction; planetary romance; postcolonial science fiction; pulp science fiction; young adult fiction
scientific racism, 132
scientists of color, 174, 203–14
seers, 41–46
segregation, 116, 128–45
seismic activity, 153–59
selective breeding, 153–59
self-harm, 137–38, 140
selkies, 48
semiotics, 48
"Seven Possible Futures for a Black Feminist Artist" (Gumbs), 48
sexism, 6, 13–14, 20, 44, 46, 48, 53, 65, 77, 94, 100, 116–17, 120–21, 137–38, 149–

50, 165, 195, 197, 205, 207. *See also* patriarchy/patriarchal oppression; others, woman as; women, subordination of; women's bodies, revulsion toward
sexual abuse/violence, 32, 52, 117, 137, 117, 154. *See also* rape
sexuality, 46, 51, 79–80
Shadow Speaker, The (Okorafor), 12, 89, 92–95
Shadowed Sun, The (Jemisin), 14, 196–98
Shawl, Nisi, 3n2, 4–5, 8, 11, 23–28, 31–33, 36–37, 217n2, 236
Shrinking the Heroes (Faust), 24
Siege of Earth (Faucette), 110m 121–25
Sister Mine (Hopkinson), 24
skin color, 98, 115, 115n7, 153n1, 157, 206, 208, 211: absence of, 122
slave rebellions, 67–71, 82n4
slavery, 2, 5, 42, 59–76, 63n7, 152–57, 180: African chattel, 3, 5, 12, 28–29, 43, 47, 49–51, 60–88, 63n7, 67n13, 82n4, 89–92, 92n4, 94–101, 114–19, 123–24, 152–56, 159, 164, 180, 180n7, 214, 223; and erasure, 28–29, 62; escape from, 81–83, 95–101, 110, 122–23, 156; escape through death, 31, 31n2, 82–83, 82n4, 156, 156n3; history of, 67, 79–85, 95–99, 114n6, 117; of humans by alien species, 119, 122; justifications for, 150; reparations for, 124n15; trauma of, 3, 62, 94–98, 223; US economic dependence on, 124n15; women's experiences of, 137. *See also* Middle Passage; slave rebellions; transatlantic slave trade
Smith, Sherri L., 13, 128–45
So Long Been Dreaming (Hopkinson), 73–74, 84
social justice, 2, 13, 50, 52, 129–45, 149, 152, 159, 191n1, 184, 231–33
social media, 4, 7, 29
social safety net, lack of, 141–43
Song of Solomon (Morrison), 42
South Africa/South Africans, 11, 25, 33, 35–36, 75, 119, 203–4, 207–11, 213–14, 237
space exploration/travel, 4, 15, 51–52, 70, 93, 97, 112–18, 121–25, 205–209, 212–13: American, 203, 205, 209, 212; Chinese, 212; imperial politics of, 209, 212; Indian, 212; Nigerian, 203–14

space stations, 70
special education, 142. *See also* intellectual disabilities
species, 13, 112–13, 112n5, 115, 119, 121, 123, 125, 129, 151, 154n2, 156, 161–63, 165–66, 199
speciesism, 113–25, 150–59. *See also* aliens; animals
speculative art, 1, 4–5, 9–11, 25, 87n1
Speculative Blackness: The Future of Race in Science Fiction (Carrington), 10
speculative fantasy, 70. *See also* fantasy genre
speculative fiction. *See* science fiction/speculative fiction
speculative histories, 75
speculative philosophy, 5, 88
spirituality, 42–46
"Stars Are Ours, The" (Jemisin), 151
state surveillance, 131–39
state violence, 31, 31n3–4, 128–45: resistance to, 131–45. *See also* police brutality
steamfunk, 6
steampunk, 6, 27, 36
Steinskog, Eric, 232
Stone Chameleon, The (Wood), 25
Stone Sky, The (Jemisin), 24, 149–50, 156–57, 161
Stories for Chip: A Tribute to Samuel R. Delany (Campbell and Shawl), 23, 25, 237
Stranger in Olondria, A (Samatar), 14, 47, 192–96
Summer Prince, The (Johnson), 12, 88–89, 99–102
Sunshine Patriots (Campbell), 23
supernatural elements, 41, 50, 74, 84–85, 89, 198. *See also* the fantastic
sword and sorcery fantasy, 117–21: black, 110, 117–21
sword and soul fantasy, 7
Syms, Martine, 5–7

Tate, Greg, 3, 39, 110, 206, 217n2
technologies of survival, 130, 132, 143
technoscience, 12, 14, 177, 190, 204, 224: white dominated, 14, 60
telepathy, 49–50, 114, 117, 120

Tell My Horse (Hurston), 41
Their Eyes Were Watching God (Hurston), 38
Thomas, Sheree E., 3n2, 8, 10–11, 29, 37–58, 87, 125, 232, 237–38
"Time Considered as a Helix of Semi-precious Stones" (Delany), 111
"Time to Pick a Side" (Jemisin), 165
time travel, 2, 4, 51–53, 113
"Too Many Yesterdays, Not Enough Tomorrows" (Jemisin), 1
toxic economy, 137–39, 142. *See also* capitalism
toxic landscape, 128–45. *See also* environmental apocalypse/disaster/degradation; environmental justice; environmental racism
transatlantic slave trade, 74, 78–79, 223: Wakandan complicity in, 180n7. *See also* Middle Passage
"transgressive disfigurement" (Barber), 130, 137–38
transmogrification, 81–84, 196, 199
transnational corporate polluters, 200: advertising campaigns of, 200. *See also* capitalism; environmental apocalypse/disaster/degradation; environmental racism
Tubman, Harriett, 68–71
Tulsa Race Riot, 31, 31n4. *See also* state violence; white supremacy
Tuskegee Institute, 111
Tuskegee Syphilis Study, 132
Tutuola, Amos, 15, 75, 216–28, 216n1, 217n2, 220n4

United States, the, 59–71, 203–4, 209
Universal Negro Improvement Association, 31
utopia/utopian, 12, 59, 61, 67–71, 74, 76, 77n1, 85, 100–101, 166, 182, 191, 197, 200, 205, 224, 237: science fiction trope, 76–77

vampires, 48–51, 76
Van Veen, Tobias C., 158–59, 166
vigilantism, 31, 31n4, 45, 180–87
Vodou, 42, 43n3

war, 92–103, 185, 194, 232: interplanetary, 112–17, 121–25: nuclear, 92, 99–100, 118–25. *See also* American Civil War
War & Mir series (Faust), 24
Ward, Cynthia, 25
warrior women, 41, 45–46, 93–94
Warriors of Terra, The (Faucette), 110, 121–25
"Water Must Fall" (Wood), 33
water pollution, 128, 131, 134–37, 143–45. *See also* cognitive impairments, lead derived; environmental racism; Flint River; lead exposure lawsuits; lead poisoning
Western imperial hegemony, 34, 59, 63, 172, 182, 185 205–6: competitors to, 171–86; escape from, 172
Western medicine, 192: alternatives to, 196–98, 197n4, 200
Wheeler, Elizabeth A., 13, 128–48, 238
Whispers from the Cotton Tree Root (Hopkinson), 8
white hegemony, 60–63, 61n5, 69n13, 71, 74, 89–92, 96–99, 118n8, 122, 128–45, 149–51, 174, 182–87: subversion of, 60, 175, 182–87
white male resentment of authors of color, 1–2, 2n1, 13–14, 149–51, 165
white privilege, 191, 206
white science fiction authors, 1, 11, 14, 25, 28–29, 32–36, 60–61, 60–61n2, 63–64n7, 65, 91, 112, 112n5, 149–51, 153, 165–66, 189–90, 231
white supremacy, 1–2, 2n1, 14, 31, 31n4, 45, 62, 67–71, 68n11, 69n13, 149–51, 174–75, 184, 231: challenges to, 1, 67–71; threat of, 175, 177, 183n10, 184
whiteness, 60–63, 61n5, 71, 186: alternatives to, 182; as marker of violence and corruption, 63, 186; monstrosity of, 120, 182
Wild Seed (Butler), 115n7
Will Do Magic for Small Change (Hairston), 45–46
Winged Histories, The (Samatar), 14, 192–96
Winter, Jerome, 114, 89–202, 238
WisCon Chronicles 5: Writing and Racial Identity, The (Shawl), 25
Wisker, Gina, 73–86
Womack, Ytasha L., 4, 10, 85, 159, 198

womanism/womanist aesthetic, 38–53. *See also* feminism
women, subordination of, 30, 53, 65, 94, 100, 116–17, 137–38, 195, 197. *See also* sexism; patriarchy/patriarchal oppression
women's bodies, revulsion toward, 120–21. *See also* sexism; patriarchy/patriarchal oppression
Wood, Nick, 11, 25, 28–29, 32–36
Wright, Richard, 1, 110, 231
Writing the Other: A Practical Approach (Shawl and Ward), 25

Xenogenesis trilogy (Butler), 154, 154n2

Yaszek, Lisa, 1–36, 3n2, 133, 157, 174–75, 223, 231–34
Yoruba civilization and culture, 15, 31, 52, 65, 208, 218
young adult Afrofuturism, 87–104, 128–45, 149–66
young adult fiction, 12–13, 51, 87–108, 89n3, 128, 131, 139, 141, 238
Young, Helen, 71
Youngquist, Paul, 232

Zambian writers, 25, 232
Zimbabwe/Zimbabweans, 203–4, 208–9, 212
zombies, 76, 82

NEW SUNS: RACE, GENDER, AND SEXUALITY IN THE SPECULATIVE
Susana M. Morris and Kinitra D. Brooks, Series Editors

Scholarly examinations of speculative fiction have been a burgeoning academic field for more than twenty-five years, but there has been a distinct lack of attention to how attending to nonhegemonic positionalities transforms our understanding of the speculative. New Suns: Race, Gender, and Sexuality in the Speculative addresses this oversight and promotes scholarship at the intersections of race, gender, sexuality, and the speculative, engaging interdisciplinary fields of research across literary, film, and cultural studies that examine multiple pasts, presents, and futures. Of particular interest are studies that offer new avenues into thinking about popular genre fictions and fan communities, including but not limited to the study of Afrofuturism, comics, ethnogothicism, ethnosurrealism, fantasy, film, futurity studies, gaming, horror, literature, science fiction, and visual studies. New Suns particularly encourages submissions that are written in a clear, accessible style that will be read both by scholars in the field as well as by nonspecialists.

Literary Afrofuturism in the Twenty-First Century
    EDITED BY ISIAH LAVENDER III AND LISA YASZEK

Jordan Peele's Get Out: *Political Horror*
    EDITED BY DAWN KEETLEY

Unstable Masks: Whiteness and American Superhero Comics
    EDITED BY SEAN GUYNES AND MARTIN LUND

Afrofuturism Rising: The Literary Prehistory of a Movement
    ISIAH LAVENDER III

The Paradox of Blackness in African American Vampire Fiction
    JERRY RAFIKI JENKINS

www.ingramcontent.com/pod-product-compliance
Lightning Source LLC
Chambersburg PA
CBHW020645230426
43665CB00008B/325